Enrichment

MATH & READING

Grades 5 & 6

SO-ALE-736

Dear Young Learner,

Welcome to your new *Enrichment Book.* Inside, you'll find challenging games, puzzles, and contests, exciting ideas for stories to write, funny jokes and riddles, and even a few surprises. And best of all, you'll have the chance to share all the fun with your family or friends.

While you are having fun, you will also be learning some important math and reading skills, skills you will be able to use in school and for the rest of your life.

We know this book will be one of your favorite ways to learn-- and to have fun!

Sincerely,

Your Learning Partners at
American Education Publishing

Table of Contents
Math Grade 5

Pages

Pages

Table of Contents
Math Grade 6

Pages

Measurement and Geometry

Statistics, Probability and Problem Solving

Reading Grade 5

Pages

Forms of Writing

Reading Grade 6

Forms of Writing

Enrichment
Math Grade 5

AMERICAN
EDUCATION
PUBLISHING

The Case Of The Missing Sign

LESSON
1

Put in an addition sign to make each sentence true.

1. 4 8 6 5 9 3 = 1,079

2. 7 9 5 6 2 0 1 = 6,996

3. 9 4 3 2 9 = 9,441

4. 3 2 6 8 7 8 = 3,346

5. 8 2 6 7 3 2 1 = 8,147

6. 2 0 4 7 5 1 7 7 = 7,224

7. 3 4 2 8 6 5 9 0 = 10,018

8. 3 7 6 8 9 4 2 = 68,979

9. 8 4 9 2 6 4 8 5 = 85,411

10. 3 2 8 6 5 3 2 1 6 = 56,502

11. 1 0 4 7 3 9 5 2 0 = 40,567

12. 2 6 4 3 9 3 8 6 4 3 = 65,082

Palindromes

A **palindrome** reads the same forward as backward.
The word *radar* is a palindrome.
The number 3,443 is a palindrome.

You can start with any number and make a palindrome.
Follow these steps.

Step 1: Pick a number.

Step 2: Reverse the number.

Step 3: Add the numbers.

Step 4: Repeat steps 2 and 3 until
you get a palindrome.

$$\begin{array}{r} 58 \\ + \ 85 \\ \hline 143 \end{array}$$

$$\begin{array}{r} + \ 341 \\ \hline 484 \end{array}$$

Work with a member of your family.
Take turns thinking of a number and making it into a palindrome.
Show the work to make three palindromes.

Think of words you know that are palindromes.
Write as many as you can.

Using Addition

LESSON
2

The Greatest

Subtract. The answer is a world record.

1.
$$\begin{array}{r} 4,124 \\ -\ 3,954 \end{array}$$
The greatest number of chin-ups without stopping.

2.
$$\begin{array}{r} 8,650 \\ -\ 4,793 \end{array}$$
The greatest number of push-ups without stopping.

3.
$$\begin{array}{r} 23,036 \\ -\ 10,540 \end{array}$$
The greatest number of rope jumps in one hour.

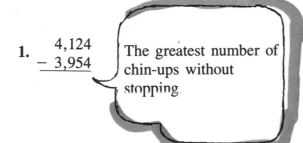

4.
$$\begin{array}{r} 57,904 \\ -\ 49,563 \end{array}$$
The greatest number of somersaults without stopping.

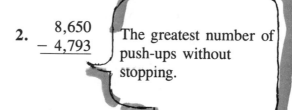

5.
$$\begin{array}{r} 40,607 \\ -\ 19,009 \end{array}$$
The greatest number of leg raises without stopping.

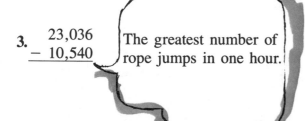

6.
$$\begin{array}{r} 91,835 \\ -\ 56,584 \end{array}$$
The greatest number of two-arm push-ups without stopping.

7.
$$\begin{array}{r} 82,513 \\ -\ 37,486 \end{array}$$
The greatest number of jumping jacks without stopping.

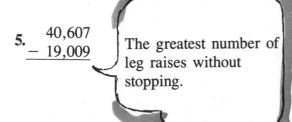

8.
$$\begin{array}{r} 79,714 \\ -\ 6,968 \end{array}$$
The greatest number of sit-ups without stopping.

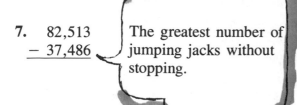

The Big Difference

Play this game with a friend.

You will need:

■ Two sets of number cards, one set for each player.

Number Cards

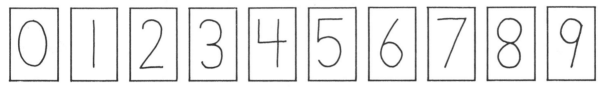

■ Subtraction boxes for each player.

Subtraction Boxes

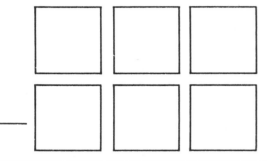

On each round:

■ Each player mixes up a set of number cards, places them face down in a pile, and draws 6 cards.

■ Each player writes one of the six numbers in each box and subtracts.

■ The player with the greater difference scores one point.

After five rounds, the player with the greatest score is the winner.

Line Up

Here are four number lines.

Line B has the
numbers from
10,001 through 20,001.

```
A  +——————————————————+
   1                  10,000
B  +——————————————————+
   10,001             20,000
C  +——————————————————+
   20,001             30,000
D  +——————————————————+
   30,001             40,000
```

Which line has the point for the product?

1. ___ 676
        × 8

2. ___ 259
        × 4

3. ___ 900
        × 6

4. ___ 813
        × 2

5. ___ 1,523
        × 9

6. ___ 5,781
        × 5

7. ___ 1,802
        × 7

8. ___ 9,145
        × 9

9. ___ 4,098
        × 8

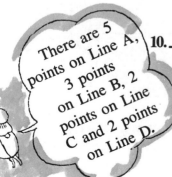

There are 5
points on Line A,
3 points
on Line B, 2
points on Line
C and 2 points
on Line D.

10. ___ 7,764
         × 4

11. ___ 2,966
         × 2

12. ___ 3,073
         × 5

Product Line

This is a game for you and a friend.

To play:

■ Take turns.

■ Pick one number from Sign A and one number from Sign B.

■ Multiply the numbers.

■ Mark the product on the gameboard with your **X** or **O.**

The first players with four **X**s or **O**s in a row, column, or diagonal is the winner.

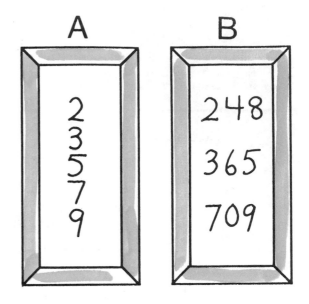

A

2
3
5
7
9

B

248

365

709

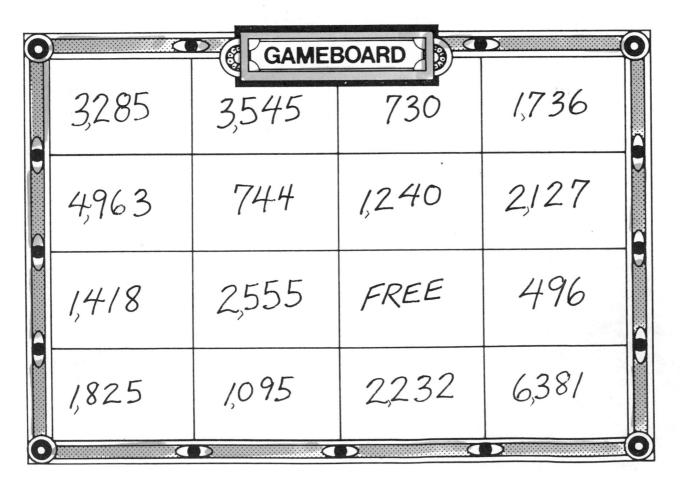

GAMEBOARD

3,285	3,545	730	1,736
4,963	744	1,240	2,127
1,418	2,555	FREE	496
1,825	1,095	2,232	6,381

Cross-Number Puzzle

Multiply.
Write the product in the cross-number puzzle.

ACROSS

1. 825 × 150
5. 581 × 36
7. 26 × 3
8. 11 × 9
10. 689 × 30
11. 15 × 4
12. 283 × 144
13. 27 × 9
14. 56 × 14

DOWN

2. 400 × 500
3. 882 × 807
4. 127 × 7
6. 850 × 80
9. 291 × 324
10. 167 × 16

Beehive

This is a game for two teams.
One team is the **X** team.
The other team is the **O** team.

Rules:

- Take turns.
- Pick a number from each sign.
- Multiply the numbers.
- If the answer is on the gameboard,
  mark your **X** or **O** on the answer.

103
210
502
705
901

20
40
60
70
80

The winner is the first team to make a path connecting its two sides of the gameboard.

Gameboard

Team X

Team O

8,240
12,600
20,080
14,100
30,120
14,700
36,040
72,080
2,060
7,210
10,040
18,020
42,300
54,060
49,350
4,200
63,070
28,200
56,400
35,140
16,800
6,180
4,120
40,160
8,400

Team O

Team X

Multiplying by 2- and 3-Digit Numbers

Charge It

IN WHAT YEAR WERE PLASTIC CREDIT CARDS FIRST ISSUED
IN THE UNITED STATES?

THE YEAR WAS _____   _____   _____   _____ .

1.

4)156   2)184

The only digit that is in both
answers is _____ .
Write this digit in the
hundreds place of the year.

2.

3)420   9)639

The only digit that is in both
answers is _____ .
Write this digit in the
ones place of the year.

3.

5)715   8)1,728

The only digit that is in both
answers is _____ .
Write this digit in the
thousands place of the year.

4.

6)630   7)2,275

The only digit that is in both
answers is _____ .
Write this digit in the
tens place of the year.

Dividing by a 1-Digit Number

Average Facts

This is an activity for you and three friends.

For each person, record the:
- number of letters in the entire name (first, middle and last).
- height in inches.
- age in months.
- number of heart beats in one minute.

Find the averages by dividing the totals by 4.

Name	Number of Letters in Name	Height (in inches)	Age (in months)	Number of Heart Beats (per minute)
1.				
2.				
3.				
4.				
Total				
Average				

Whose height is closest to the average height? _____

Whose number of heart beats is closest to the average number of heart beats? _____

Dividing by a 1-Digit Number

Quotient Match

Estimate the quotient to match the football with the helmet.
Write the correct football letter under each helmet.

1.
$31\overline{)93}$

2.
$22\overline{)880}$

3.
$70\overline{)910}$

4.
$11\overline{)792}$

_____   _____   _____   _____

5.
$58\overline{)1,798}$

6.
$15\overline{)1,305}$

7.
$93\overline{)2,046}$

8.
$79\overline{)4,582}$

_____   _____   _____   _____

K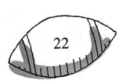
58

T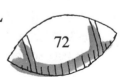
3

C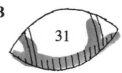
22

L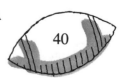
72

A
87

I
13

B
31

A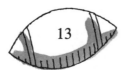
40

Dividing by a 2-Digit Number

Estimating Quotients

This is a game for two players.
Take turns.

On each turn.
■ Pick a division example.
■ Estimate the quotient.
■ Use paper and pencil or a calculator to check your estimate.
■ Cross out the example.
■ Find your score.

When all of the division examples are crossed out,
add to find your total score.

The winner is the player with the greater score.

82)8,118	43)1,677	18)864	80)6,480	62)868
56)3,584	49)4459	98)7,056	11)561	32)800

If your quotient is between
10 and 30 score 4 points
30 and 50 score 3 points
50 and 70 score 5 points
70 and 90 score 2 points
90 and 100 score 6 points

Round	Player 1	Player 2
1		
2		
3		
4		
5		
Total		

Dividing by a 2-Digit Number

Number Search

Read the word name.
Find the number on the number board.
Look **down**, **across**, and **diagonally**.
Numbers may overlap.
Circle the number.

1. Three hundred sixty-four thousand, two hundred eighty-three

2. Eighty-seven million, two hundred eighty-four thousand, two hundred thirty-seven

3. Two million, four hundred thousand, seven hundred eighty-seven

4. Five million, four hundred twenty-six thousand, three hundred ninety-five

5. Four million, eight hundred seven thousand, forty-eight

6. Ten thousand, four hundred seventy-two

7. Seven million, three hundred eighty-seven thousand, seven hundred

8. Eight hundred seventy-two million, nine hundred fifty-one thousand, four hundred twenty-six

9. Forty-eight thousand, ninety-seven

10. Sixty-nine million, thirty-eight thousand, seven hundred ninety-five

Number Board

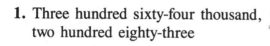

4	8	7	2	9	5	1	4	2	6
8	7	3	4	2	0	0	8	3	9
7	2	3	8	8	1	4	0	6	0
2	6	9	8	1	0	2	0	4	3
8	4	8	7	7	4	9	5	2	8
4	2	4	0	0	7	8	7	8	7
2	0	8	4	6	2	0	3	3	9
3	4	6	1	5	3	2	0	9	5
7	9	0	5	4	2	6	3	9	5

Pick And Score

Play this game with a member of your family.

Make a set of these cards for each player.

Rules:
- Take turns.
- Mix up the set of 9 cards.
- Turn the cards over in order to make a 9-digit number.
- Write the number on the line below.
- Score the number.

NUMBER	SCORE
Player 1:	
Player 2:	

Score 1 point for each of the following that is true.

- ■ The number is greater than six hundred million.
- The digit in the ten millions place is greater than 3.
- The digit in the ones place is less than 5.
- The digit in the one millions place is an odd number.
- The digit in the hundred thousands place is an even number.
- The digit in the ten thousands place is 2.

The winner is the player with the greater score.

World Capitals

Try to match each country with its capital.

Draw a line to match each mixed number with its improper fraction.
The matching improper fraction gives the capital for the country.
Score 1 point for each correct match on your list.

1. India $1\frac{2}{3}$ $\frac{11}{6}$ Oslo

2. France $2\frac{1}{5}$ $\frac{27}{8}$ Madrid

3. Spain $3\frac{3}{8}$ $\frac{5}{3}$ New Delhi

4. Norway $1\frac{5}{6}$ $\frac{11}{5}$ Paris

5. Argentina $1\frac{6}{7}$ $\frac{11}{4}$ Tokyo

6. Japan $2\frac{3}{4}$ $\frac{13}{7}$ Buenos Aires

7. Hungary $3\frac{1}{3}$ $\frac{15}{7}$ Canberra

8. Greece $4\frac{1}{6}$ $\frac{10}{3}$ Budapest

9. Italy $1\frac{4}{5}$ $\frac{23}{8}$ Peking

10. Australia $2\frac{1}{7}$ $\frac{9}{5}$ Rome

11. China $2\frac{7}{8}$ $\frac{25}{6}$ Athens

How many points did you score? _____

Using Mixed Numbers and Improper Fractions

25

Concentrate

This is a game for you and a friend.
Make these 10 improper fraction cards.

Improper Fractions

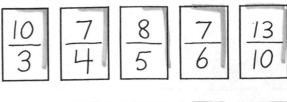

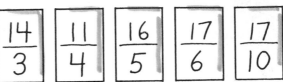

Mixed Numbers

Make these 10 mixed number cards.

To Play:

■ Mix up the 20 cards and lay them
face down in four rows with five
cards in each row.
■ Take turns.
■ Turn over two cards.
If the improper fraction matches the mixed number,
keep the cards.
If the cards do not match, turn them over.

**After each player has had four turns, the player
with the greater number of cards is the winner.**

Using Mixed Numbers and Improper Fractions

Boxing Fractions

LESSON
9

Put one number in each box
to make a true sentence.

Use all of the numbers.

1. Use 1, 1, 2, 3.

$$\frac{\Box}{\Box} + \frac{\Box}{\Box} = \frac{5}{6}$$

2. Use 1, 2, 3, 4.

$$\frac{\Box}{\Box} + \frac{\Box}{\Box} = \frac{5}{4}$$

3. Use 1, 1, 3, 5.

$$\frac{\Box}{\Box} + \frac{\Box}{\Box} = \frac{8}{15}$$

4. Use 1, 3, 5, 10.

$$\frac{\Box}{\Box} + \frac{\Box}{\Box} = \frac{7}{10}$$

5. Use 2, 3, 3, 4.

$$\frac{\Box}{\Box} \quad \frac{\Box}{\Box} = \frac{17}{12}$$

6. Use 1, 3, 9, 10.

$$\frac{\Box}{\Box} \quad \frac{\Box}{\Box} = \frac{23}{20}$$

7. Use 1, 6, 7, 8.

$$\frac{\Box}{\Box} \quad \frac{\Box}{\Box} = \frac{25}{24}$$

8. Use 2, 5, 6, 9.

$$\frac{\Box}{\Box} \quad \frac{\Box}{\Box} = \frac{19}{18}$$

Fraction Toss

Play this game with a friend.

Rules:

- Take turns.
- Toss two coins onto the playing board.
- Add the numbers.
- Score the sum.

After five rounds, the player with the greater number of points is the winner.

Scoring

- 2 points if the sum is 1 or more.

- 1 point if the sum is less than 1.

Playing Board

$\frac{1}{3}$	$\frac{1}{5}$	$\frac{7}{10}$	$\frac{1}{8}$
$\frac{3}{4}$	$\frac{5}{6}$	$\frac{2}{3}$	$\frac{3}{5}$
$\frac{8}{9}$	$\frac{7}{8}$	$\frac{11}{12}$	$\frac{1}{6}$
$\frac{3}{8}$	$\frac{1}{4}$	$\frac{2}{5}$	$\frac{5}{8}$

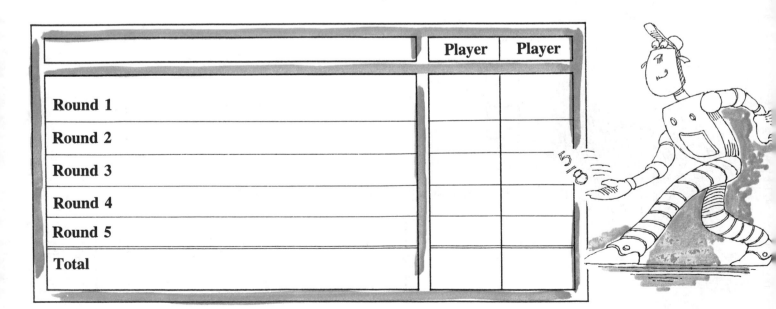

	Player	Player
Round 1		
Round 2		
Round 3		
Round 4		
Round 5		
Total		

Adding Fractions with Unlike Denominators

Fraction Squares

Subtract **across** and **down**.
Reduce the answers to lowest terms.
Write the answers in the squares.

1.

$\frac{7}{8}$	$-$	$\frac{3}{8}$	$=$	
$-$		$-$		$-$
$\frac{1}{4}$	$-$	$\frac{1}{8}$	$=$	
$=$		$=$		$=$
	$-$		$=$	

2.

$\frac{9}{10}$	$-$	$\frac{2}{5}$	$=$	
$-$		$-$		$-$
$\frac{3}{10}$	$-$	$\frac{1}{5}$	$=$	
$=$		$=$		$=$
	$-$		$=$	

3.

$\frac{2}{3}$	$-$	$\frac{1}{5}$	$=$	
$-$		$-$		$-$
$\frac{2}{5}$	$-$	$\frac{1}{15}$	$=$	
$=$		$=$		$=$
	$-$		$=$	

4.

$\frac{3}{4}$	$-$	$\frac{1}{3}$	$=$	
$-$		$-$		$-$
$\frac{1}{2}$	$-$	$\frac{1}{6}$	$=$	
$=$		$=$		$=$
	$-$		$=$	

Fraction Subtracto

Find someone to play this game with you.
Make these cards.
Mix up the cards and place them face down.

$\boxed{0}$ $\boxed{\frac{1}{12}}$ $\boxed{\frac{1}{6}}$ $\boxed{\frac{1}{4}}$ $\boxed{\frac{1}{3}}$ $\boxed{\frac{5}{12}}$

Rules:
- Take turns.
- Pick a card. Write the number in one of the squares below.
- Score one point for making a true statement.
- After all the cards have been used, the player with the greater number of points is the winner.

$\boxed{\frac{1}{2}}$ $\boxed{\frac{7}{12}}$ $\boxed{\frac{2}{3}}$ $\boxed{\frac{5}{6}}$ $\boxed{\frac{11}{12}}$ $\boxed{1}$

$\square > \frac{1}{3}$ $\qquad$ $\square < \frac{5}{6}$

$\square < \frac{1}{2}$ $\qquad$ $\square > \frac{1}{2}$

$\square - \frac{1}{6} > \frac{1}{4}$ $\qquad$ $\square - \frac{1}{4} < \frac{5}{12}$

$1 - \square < \frac{1}{2}$ $\qquad$ $1 - \square > \frac{1}{2}$

$\square - \square < \frac{7}{12}$ $\qquad$ $\square - \square > \frac{1}{6}$

The winner is _____ .

Subtracting Fractions with Unlike Denominators

Number Facts

Fill in the blanks.

1. The number of countries in South America is equal to $\frac{1}{3}$ of 39, or _____ .

2. The number of strings on a violin is equal to $\frac{2}{7}$ of 14, or _____ .

3. The number of U.S. Presidents before Lincoln is equal to $\frac{3}{4}$ of 20, or _____ .

4. The number of provinces in Canada is equal to $\frac{5}{8}$ of 16, or _____ .

5. The number of U.S. Senators is equal to $\frac{1}{10}$ of 1,000, or _____ .

6. The number of stories in the Empire State Building is equal to $\frac{2}{3}$ of 153, or _____ .

7. The number of cards in a regular deck is equal to $\frac{1}{2}$ of 104, or _____ .

8. The number of pencils in a gross is equal to $\frac{3}{5}$ of 240, or _____ .

9. The number of home runs hit by Hank Aaron is equal to $\frac{5}{6}$ of 906, or _____ .

10. The number of calories in a peanut butter and jelly sandwich is equal to $\frac{11}{12}$ of 300, or _____ .

Toss A Fraction

This is a game for two players.
Get a coin.
Make these cards.

| 84 | 36 | 18 | 30 | 54 | 72 |

| 24 | 48 | 66 | 12 | 78 | 60 |

Rules
- Take turns.
- Pick a card and toss the coin.
- If the coin lands heads up, find one-half of the number on the card.
- If the coin lands tails up, find one-third of the number on the card.
- Write the answer on the score card.

The player with the greatest total score after six rounds is the winner.

Score Card

Round	Player 1	Player 2
1		
2		
3		
4		
5		
6		
Total		

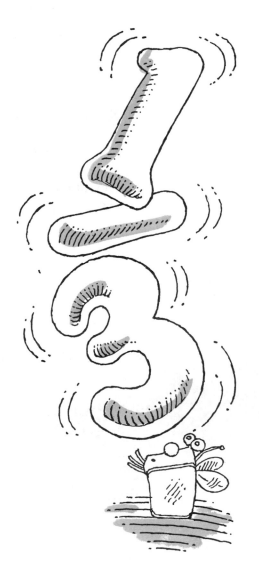

Multiplying a Fraction and a Whole Number

Up And To The Right

Follow the arrow directions.
Multiply up. Multiply across.
Complete the square.

1.

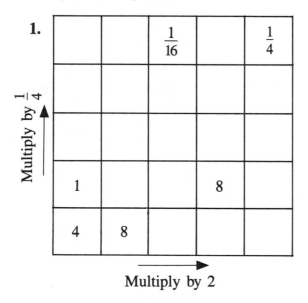

Multiply by $\frac{1}{4}$

Multiply by 2

2.

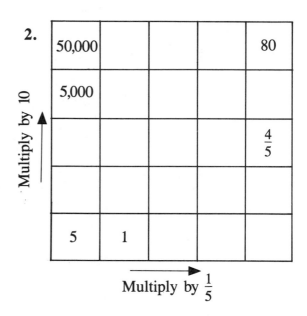

Multiply by 10

Multiply by $\frac{1}{5}$

3.

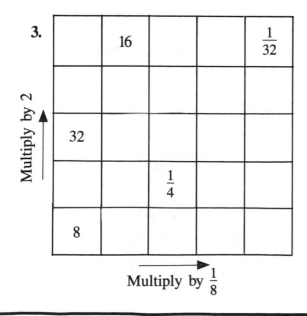

Multiply by 2

Multiply by $\frac{1}{8}$

4.

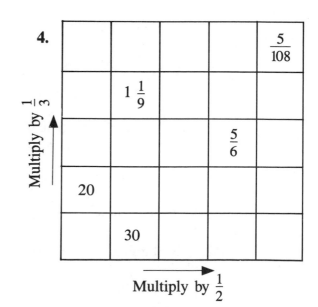

Multiply by $\frac{1}{3}$

Multiply by $\frac{1}{2}$

Trivial Facts

This is a game for you and your family.
First, each player tries to answer the questions.
Then multiply to check the answers.
The product gives the answer to the question.
Ring the correct answer.
The winner is the one with the most correct answers.
There can be more than one winner.

1. $\frac{2}{3} \times \frac{4}{5} =$ How many letters are in the longest name of a state in the United States?

$\frac{6}{8}$ There are 10 letters.

$\frac{6}{15}$ There are 11 letters.

$\frac{22}{15}$ There are 12 letters.

$\frac{8}{15}$ There are 13 letters.

2. $\frac{1}{2} \times \frac{4}{5} =$ How many small squares are on a scrabble board?

$\frac{5}{7}$ There are 64 small squares.

$\frac{5}{10}$ There are 100 small squares.

$\frac{2}{5}$ There are 225 small squares.

$\frac{1}{2}$ There are 400 small squares.

3. $\frac{3}{10} \times \frac{5}{6} =$ How many letters are in the Greek alphabet?

$\frac{1}{2}$ There are 32 letters.

$\frac{15}{16}$ There are 28 letters.

$\frac{8}{60}$ There are 26 letters.

$\frac{1}{4}$ There are 24 letters.

4. $1\frac{3}{4} \times \frac{8}{9} =$ How many stars are in the Big Dipper?

$1\frac{5}{9}$ There are 7 stars.

$\frac{8}{9}$ There are 10 stars.

$1\frac{2}{13}$ There are 12 stars.

$1\frac{23}{36}$ There are 16 stars.

5. $2\frac{1}{8} \times 2 =$ How old was Christopher Columbus when he first arrived in the New World?

$4\frac{1}{8}$ Columbus was 24 years old.

$4\frac{1}{4}$ Columbus was 41 years old.

$2\frac{1}{16}$ Columbus was 53 years old.

$2\frac{1}{4}$ Columbus was 62 years old.

Multiplying Fractions and Mixed Numbers

Taking Chances

You have this bag of blocks.
With your eyes closed, you pick a block.
What is the probability that you will pick:

1. 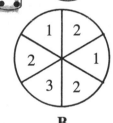 ? _____

2. ? _____

3. ? _____

4. or ? _____

5. or 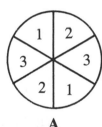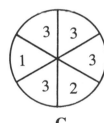 ? _____

1 | 2	1 | 2	3 | 3
3 | 3	2 | 1	1 | 3
2 | 1	3 | 2	3 | 2
A	**B**	**C**

Identify the spinner.

6. The probability of spinning a 2 is $\frac{2}{6}$. _____

7. The probability of spinning a 32 is $\frac{1}{6}$. _____

8. There is an equal probabilty of spinning a 1 or a 2. _____

Which spinner would you choose?

9. You win if you spin a 3. _____

10. You win if you spin a 2. _____

11. You win if you spin a 2 or a 3. _____

12. You win if you spin a 1 or a 2. _____

Number Please?

Work with someone in your family.

- Choose 50 telephone numbers from your telephone book.
- Add the first and last digits of each number.
- Make a tally mark for each sum in Table 1.
- Find the total number for each sum.

1. Which sum occurred most often?

_____

2. What is the probability that given any telephone number, the sum of the first and last digits will be the sum you gave in Exercise 1?

_____

Check out the probability with another 50 telephone numbers. Record your data in Table 2.

3. Did the same sum occur most often?

_____

TABLE 1			TABLE 2		
Sum	Tally	Total	Sum	Tally	Total
2			2		
3			3		
4			4		
5			5		
6			6		
7			7		
8			8		
9			9		
10			10		
11			11		
12			12		
13			13		
14			14		
15			15		
16			16		
17			17		
18			18		

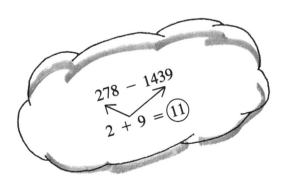

LESSON
14

Riddle Fever

WHY SHOULDN'T YOU TELL A SECRET TO A PIG?

Write the decimal equivalent.

Then write the letter of the fraction on the line above its decimal equivalent.

I $\frac{1}{2}$ = ____   C $\frac{6}{10}$ = ____   L $\frac{85}{100}$ = ____   T $\frac{1}{5}$ = ____

A $\frac{1}{4}$ = ____   Q $\frac{3}{4}$ = ____   E $\frac{9}{50}$ = ____   A $\frac{1}{10}$ = ____

I $\frac{3}{10}$ = ____   B $\frac{16}{20}$ = ____   E $\frac{7}{10}$ = ____   S $\frac{4}{25}$ = ____

W $\frac{1}{25}$ = ____   L $\frac{23}{50}$ = ____   U $\frac{2}{100}$ = ____   E $\frac{3}{20}$ = ____

U $\frac{2}{5}$ = ____   L $\frac{18}{20}$ = ____   S $\frac{6}{25}$ = ____

YOU SHOULDN'T TELL A SECRET TO A PIG

$\overline{0.8}$ $\overline{0.18}$ $\overline{0.6}$ $\overline{0.1}$ $\overline{0.4}$ $\overline{0.16}$ $\overline{0.15}$ $\overline{0.5}$ $\overline{0.2}$

$\overline{0.04}$ $\overline{0.3}$ $\overline{0.9}$ $\overline{0.46}$ $\overline{0.24}$ $\overline{0.75}$ $\overline{0.02}$ $\overline{0.7}$ $\overline{0.25}$ $\overline{0.85}$

Changing Fractions to Decimals

Decimal Tic-Tac-Toe

Play this game with a friend.

How to Play

☐ Take turns.
☐ Pick a number from the sign.
☐ Mark the decimal equivalent on the gameboard
   with your **X** or **O**.
☐ Cross off the number on the sign.

The first player with four **X**s or
Os in a row, column, or
diagonal is the winner.

$\frac{1}{2}$	$\frac{1}{5}$	$\frac{2}{5}$	$\frac{3}{5}$
$\frac{4}{5}$	$\frac{3}{10}$	$\frac{7}{10}$	$\frac{9}{10}$
$\frac{1}{4}$	$\frac{3}{4}$	$\frac{7}{20}$	$\frac{11}{20}$
$\frac{1}{50}$	$\frac{12}{25}$	$\frac{3}{50}$	$\frac{81}{100}$

GAMEBOARD

0.8	0.25	0.7	0.06
0.02	0.5	0.35	0.75
0.48	0.81	0.6	0.2
0.4	0.9	0.55	0.3

Decimal Detective

Use the clues to find the number in the cloud.
Draw a ring around the number.

1.

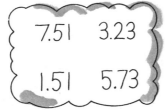

7.51   3.23

1.51   5.73

Each digit is an odd number.
The digit in the tenths place is
the greatest digit.
The digit in the hundredths place is 3.

2.

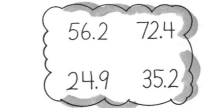

56.2   72.4

24.9   35.2

- The number is greater than 26.3
- The digit in the tens place is 3 more
  than the digit in the tenths place.
- The digit in the ones place is not 6.

3.

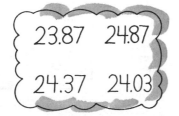

23.87   24.87

24.37   24.03

Rounded to the nearest whole number,
the number is 24.
The digit in the hundredths place is 7.
The digit in the tenths place is 3.

4.

2.86   5.83

6.86

1.84   4.36

- The digit in the tenths place is 8.
- Each digit is different.
- The sum of the digits is 16.
- The digit in the hundredths place is 6.

5.

2.124   8.224

6.482

4.824   4.826

Each digit is even.
The digit in the hundredths place is 2.
The digit in the thousandths place is 4.
The digit in the tenths place is 8.

6.

3.472   3.089

3.55

3.21   3.275

- Each digit is different.
- The number is greater than 3.1.
- The digit in the hundredths place is 7.
- The digit in the thousandths place
  is odd.

Close To The Target

This is a game for you and a friend.
Make these cards.
Mix up the cards and place them face down.

Rules:

- Take turns turning over a card.
- Both players write the digit shown on the card in one of their 10 boxes.
- When the boxes are filled, players put in a decimal point in each of their three numbers.
- Compare each player's number to the target number. Ring the one that is closer.

The player with the most ringed numbers is the winner.

Player 1	Target Number	Player 2
□ □ □	10	□ □ □
□ □ □	3	□ □ □
□ □ □ □	6	□ □ □ □

The winner is _____ .

The Way To Go

Write the decimal numbers on the lines from least to greatest.
Write the letter of each decimal number under the number.
The letters will spell the name of a vehicle.

1. X   0.231   _____   _____   _____   _____

    I   0.406

    A   0.057

    T   0.009

2. T   0.007   _____   _____   _____   _____   _____

    N   0.6

    R   0.01

    I   0.299

    A   0.082

3. L   0.018   _____   _____   _____   _____   _____   _____   _____

    R   0.005

    N   0.107

    P   0.016

    E   0.871

    A   0.097

    I   0.004

    A   0.001

Comparing and Ordering Decimals

Invention Time Line

Work with someone in your family to find out when each of the items listed below was invented.

- Work together.
- Use a pencil.
- Write the name of the invention next to its date.

To check your answers, arrange the decimal numbers in order from least to greatest. The order of the decimals gives the order in which the items were invented.

0.02	Carpet Sweeper
0.003	Match
0.01	Lawn Mower
0.029	Ballpoint Pen
0.012	Safety Pin
0.42	Long Playing Record
0.412	Automatic Toaster
0.209	Zipper
0.294	Air Conditioning

Invention	Date
	1827
	1831
	1849
	1876
	1888
	1891
	1911
	1918
	1947

Decimal Towers

Complete the decimal towers.
- Start at the bottom.
- Add two numbers that are side by side.
- Write the answer in the block above.

1.

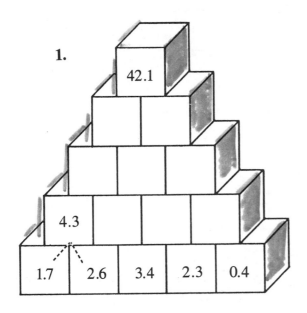

42.1

4.3

1.7   2.6   3.4   2.3   0.4

2.

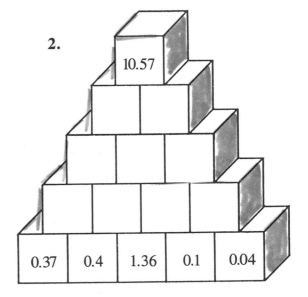

10.57

0.37   0.4   1.36   0.1   0.04

3.

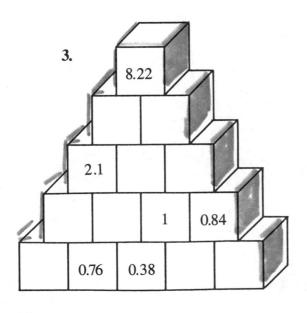

8.22

2.1

1   0.84

0.76   0.38

4.

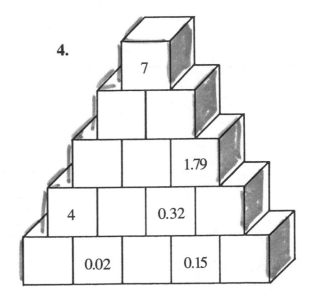

7

1.79

4   0.32

0.02   0.15

Decimal Duel

Play this game with a friend.

Rules:
- Take turns.
- Pick two numbers from the number board.
- Find the sum of the two numbers.
- Cross out the two numbers on the number board.
- Find the sum on the number line. Write the score for the sum.

When all of the numbers are crossed out, the player with the greater total score is the winner.

Number Board

25.4	36.4	43.27	50.2
6.32	52.1	0.46	3.26
4.86	24.6	1.39	11.7
3.4	12.06	21.52	23.3
9.63	34.3	0.28	13.9
17.1	49.5	5.97	0.98

Player 1	Player 2

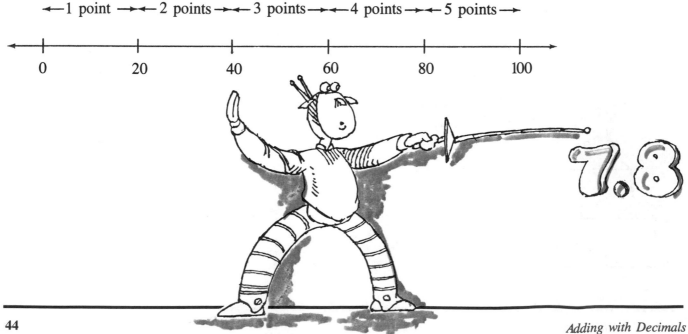

←—1 point —→←— 2 points —→←— 3 points —→←— 4 points —→←— 5 points —→

0   20   40   60   80   100

Adding with Decimals

Missing Points

A decimal point in each example is missing.
Estimate to write the decimal point in the correct place in the answer.
Complete the examples in each row.
Then find the total number of decimal places to the right of the decimal
points in the answers.
Is the total the same as the check number for the row?

1.	2.6	2.	20.6	3.	5.5	4.	50.3	5.	6.28
	× 7		× 0.5		× 3.2		× 7.5		× 0.5
	182		103		176		37725		314

Check Number: 7

6.	7.6	7.	80.5	8.	24.5	9.	36.7	10.	1.3
	× 22		× 0.36		× 5.8		× 3.8		× 0.9
	1672		2898		1421		13946		117

Check Number: 8

11.	0.05	12.	3.48	13.	5.24	14.	2.56	15.	30.7
	× 36		× 0.5		× 6.5		× 10		× 14
	18		174		3406		256		4298

Check Number: 7

16.	340	17.	54.6	18.	98.5	19.	149.6	20.	25.25
	× 0.89		× 34.2		× 0.6		× 0.03		× 3.02
	3026		186732		591		4488		76255

Check Number: 10

Decimals In A Line

Here is a game for two players, player **X** and player **O**.

Rules:
- Take turns.
- Pick two numbers from the sign.
- Multiply the numbers.
- Mark the answer on the gameboard with your **X** or **O**.

The first player with four **X**s or **O**s in a row, column, or diagonal is the winner.

6	3.2
1.6	10.5
0.32	20.1

GAMEBOARD

32.16	5.12	120.6	6.4312
1.024	3.36	16.8	FREE
0.512	3.36	19.2	211.05
33.6	64.32	63	9.6

The winner is _____ .

Match Up

Match the divisors with the dividends
so that all the quotients are the same.
Write the divisor on the line.
Divide to check the quotient.

Divisors

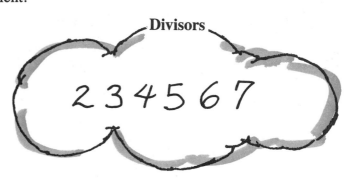

2 3 4 5 6 7

The quotient is 1.2.

1. ___ $\overline{)3.6}$ 2. ___ $\overline{)2.4}$ 3. ___ $\overline{)6.0}$

4. ___ $\overline{)7.2}$ 5. ___ $\overline{)4.8}$ 6. ___ $\overline{)8.4}$

Divisors

2 3 5 6 8 9

The quotient is 2.41.

7. ___ $\overline{)4.82}$ 8. ___ $\overline{)21.69}$ 9. ___ $\overline{)12.05}$

10. ___ $\overline{)14.46}$ 11. ___ $\overline{)19.28}$ 12. ___ $\overline{)7.23}$

Fast Ball

NOLAN RYAN HOLDS THE RECORD AS THE FASTEST PITCHER. HOW FAST WAS HIS RECORD-SETTING PITCH?

To answer this question, work with a friend.

- Take turns.
- Divide.
- Cross off the answers on the mitt.
- The number that is left is the speed of the ball.

11.17
9.69   203.1
8.12   15.43
100.9   122.1
68.4   7.08

1. $3\overline{)609.3}$

2. $2\overline{)30.86}$

3. $5\overline{)610.5}$

4. $4\overline{)273.6}$

5. $6\overline{)58.14}$

6. $2\overline{)278.8}$

7. $7\overline{)49.56}$

8. $9\overline{)73.08}$

9. $8\overline{)89.36}$

THE PITCH WAS MEASURED AT A SPEED OF _____ MILES PER HOUR.

Dividing Decimals by Whole Numbers

Measure Up

This crayon is 6 centimeters long and weighs 12 grams.

Measure the length of each of these crayons.

Estimate the weight.

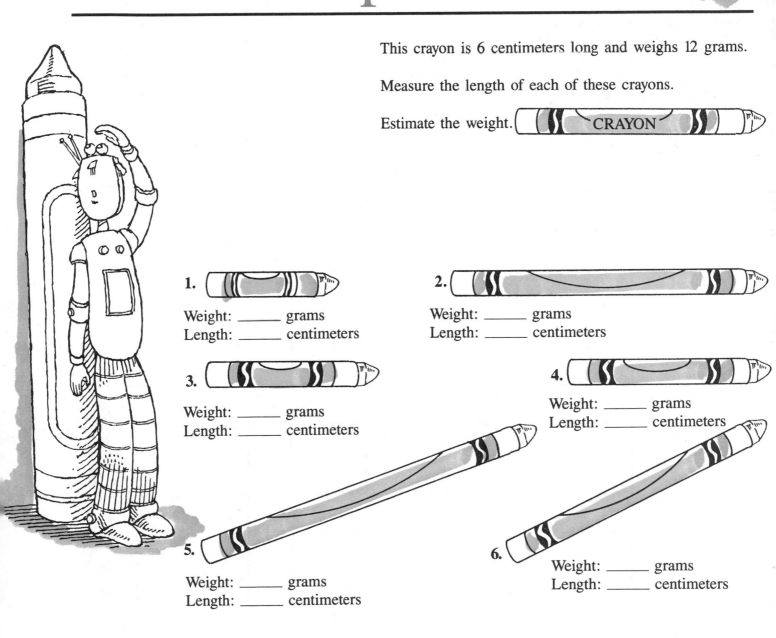

1.
Weight: _____ grams
Length: _____ centimeters

2.
Weight: _____ grams
Length: _____ centimeters

3.
Weight: _____ grams
Length: _____ centimeters

4.
Weight: _____ grams
Length: _____ centimeters

5.
Weight: _____ grams
Length: _____ centimeters

6.
Weight: _____ grams
Length: _____ centimeters

7.
Weight: _____ grams
Length: _____ centimeters

Metric Maze

Follow the line.

Work with a friend.

Find the path from START to FINISH.

Measure the length of the path to the nearest centimeter.

START

FINISH

The length of path is _____ cm.

Using Metric Units

Measurement Comparisons

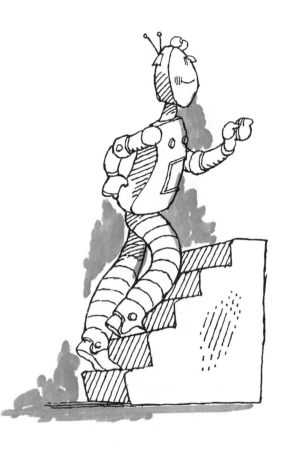

Compare the measures.

Write **>** , **<** , or **=** in each ◯ .

1. 6 yd ◯ 18 ft   2. 40 in. ◯ 1 yd

3. 3 lb ◯ 33 oz   4. 4 pt ◯ 9 c

5. 2000 lb ◯ / 1T   6. 23 in. ◯ 2 ft

7. 2 c ◯ 1 pt   8. 8 qt ◯ 15 pt

9. 2 yd ◯ 60 in.   10. 3 qt ◯ 9 gal

11. 3 lb ◯ 60 oz   12. 16 oz ◯ 1 lb

13. 5 gal ◯ 18 qt   14. 10 ft ◯ 3 yd

15. 4 ft ◯ 48 in.   16. 5 pt ◯ 2 qt

Climb up one stair for
each **>**. Climb down one
stair for each **<**. Do not
move for each **=**. If your
answers are correct, you
should end up at the top of
the staircase.

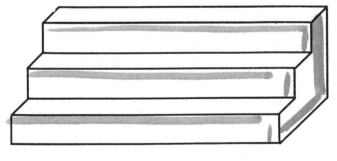

START

Body Measures

Do this activity with someone in your family.
Estimate first.
Write your estimate. Then measure.

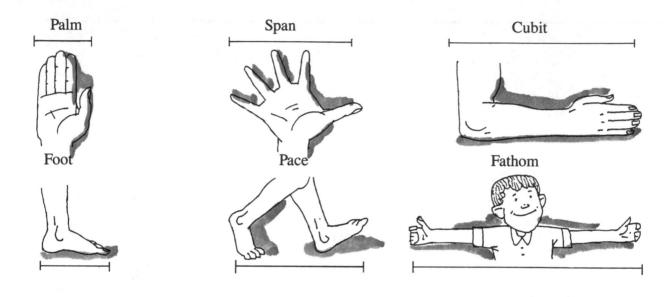

What To Measure	Estimate	Measurement
length of your arm in palms		
length of your leg in feet		
length of a room in paces		
length of a chair in cubits		
length of a car in fathoms		
length of a table in spans		

Using Nonstandard Units

Hidden Figures

Find the number of triangles and quadrilaterals in each figure.

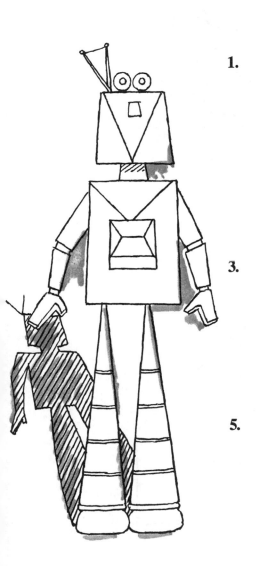

1.

_____ triangles

_____ quadrilaterals

2.

_____ triangles

_____ quadrilaterals

3.

_____ triangles

_____ quadrilaterals

4.

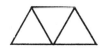

_____ triangles

_____ quadrilaterals

5.

_____ triangles

_____ quadrilaterals

6.

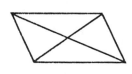

_____ triangles

_____ quadrilaterals

Did you find a total of 24 triangles and 12 quadrilaterals?

Geo-Puzzle

Ask someone in your family to do this activity with you.
Trace the figure below twice.
Cut along the lines.
Give each person a set of seven pieces.

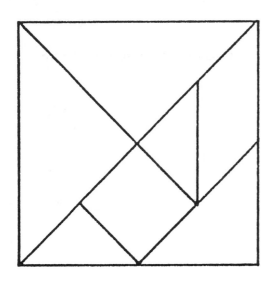

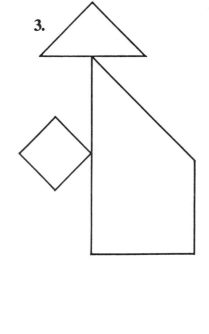

Try to make these pictures using the seven pieces.

1.

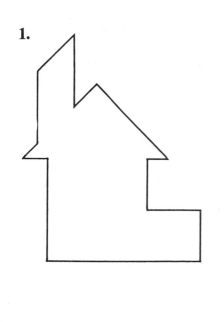

2.

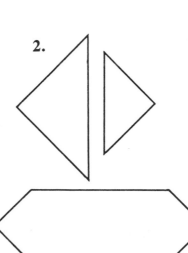

3.

Using Polygons

Picture Puzzle

Use the perimeter and area
clues to identify each person's photograph.
Write the name of the person under the photograph.

 4cm

4cm

4cm

1. _____

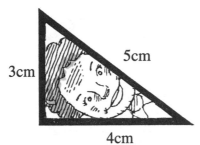 3cm

5cm

4cm

2. _____

 3cm

3cm

3. _____

3cm

4cm

4. _____

 2cm

5cm

5. _____

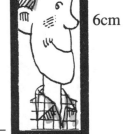 6cm

2cm

6. _____

CLICK

Elliot
Perimeter = 16 cm
Area = 12 sq cm

Rosa
Perimeter = 14 cm
Area = 12 sq cm

Jack
Perimeter = 12 cm
Area = 9 sq cm

Ben
Perimeter = 16 cm
Area = 16 sq cm

Sara
Perimeter = 12 cm
Area = 6 sq cm

Mele
Perimeter = 14 cm
Area = 10 sq cm

Finding Perimeter and Area Using Metric Units

Size It

Do this activity with someone in your family.

- Find pictures in books or magazines.
- Use a centimeter ruler to measure the length and width.
- Find the perimeter.
- Find the area.

1. Find a picture of a building.
   Length of picture _____ cm
   Width of picture _____ cm
   Perimeter _____ cm
   Area _____ sq cm

2. Find a picture of a person.
   Length of picture _____ cm
   Width of picture _____ cm
   Perimeter _____ cm
   Area _____ sq cm

3. Find a picture of a car.
   Length of picture _____ cm
   Width of picture _____ cm
   Perimeter _____ cm
   Area _____ sq cm

4. Find a picture of a flower.
   Length of picture _____ cm
   Width of picture _____ cm
   Perimeter _____ cm
   Area _____ sq cm

Finding Perimeter and Area Using Metric Units

The Birthday Presents

A
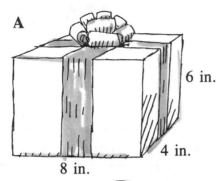
6 in.
4 in.
8 in.

B
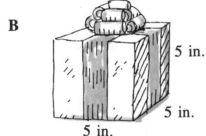
5 in.
5 in.
5 in.

C

2 in.
4 in.
10 in.

D
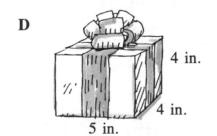
4 in.
4 in.
5 in.

E
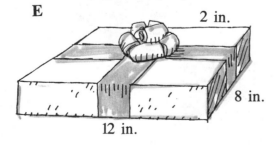
2 in.
8 in.
12 in.

Identify each person's birthday present.
Fill in the blank with the letter of the box.

1. Eric
   "The volume of the box is 125 cubic inches.
   My present is in Box _____ ."

2. Pam
   "The volume of the box is 80 cubic inches.
   The height and width of the box are the same.
   My present is in Box _____ ."

3. Sue
   "The volume of the box is 192 cubic inches.
   The length of the box is twice the width.
   My present is in Box _____ ."

4. Jerry
   "The volume of the box is 80 cubic inches.
   The height of the box is half the width.
   My present is in Box _____ ."

5. Allison
   "The volume of the box is 192 cubic inches.
   The length of the box is one foot.
   My present is in Box _____ ."

Box It

This is an activity for you and your family.

■ Find 4 boxes. Each box must be rectangular in shape.

■ In the table below, write the names of the types of boxes in order by size.
   Make Box 1 be the box you think has the greatest volume.
   Make Box 4 be the box you think has the smallest volume.

■ Measure the length, width and height of each box to the nearest inch.
   Record these measurements.

■ Find the volume of each box.

■ Ring the box with the greatest volume.

	Name	Length	Width	Height	Volume (cubic inches)
Box 1					
Box 2					
Box 3					
Box 4					

Were you a good estimator?

Which box has the greatest volume? _____

Which box has the smallest volume? _____

Finding Volume Using Customary Units

Building Figures

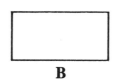

A   B   C

These shapes are used as faces to build the
three-dimensional figures shown below.
How many of each face are needed?
Don't forget about the faces you cannot see.
Always use the fewest number of faces possible.

1.
___A

___B

___C

2.
___A

___B

___C

3.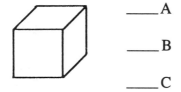
___A

___B

___C

4.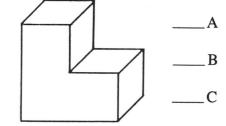
___A

___B

___C

5.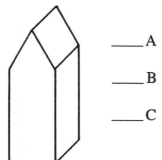
___A

___B

___C

6.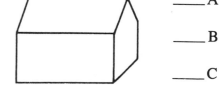
___A

___B

___C

Check your totals:

A - 19
B - 20
C - 6

Space Figures

Here are pictures of four space figures.

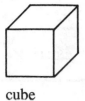

cube

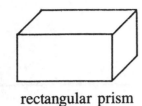

rectangular prism

sphere

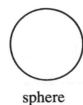

cone

Ask an adult to help you with this activity.

- Get a magazine and a pair of scissors.
- Cut out pictures of objects suggested by each space figure.
- Tape the pictures below.
- Write the name of each figure below the picture.

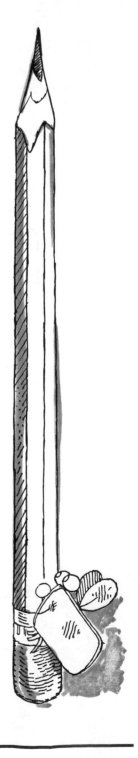

Finding Three-Dimensional Figures

Drawing Conclusions

1. Barbara is taller than Nicole. Nicole is taller than Kimberly. Who is taller, Barbara or Kimberly?

   _____

2. My birthday is the day after tomorrow. Yesterday was Wednesday. On what day of the week is my birthday?

   _____

3. Matt, Jon, and Mario ran a race. Matt did not finish last. Mario finished first. Who finished last?

   _____

4. There are three children in a family. They are 5, 7, and 10 years old. Mike is the oldest. Kim is not younger than Edward. How old is Edward?

   _____

5. Samantha bought a ball, a bat, and a mitt. The prices were $11.50, $4.50 and $6.50. The mitt cost $5 more than the bat. What was the cost of the ball?

   _____

6. Mr. Phearson planted a row each of carrots, squash, and peppers. The peppers were planted to the right of the squash. The carrots were planted to the left of the squash. Which vegetable was planted just left of the peppers?

   _____

7. The movie was shown at 11:00 AM, 1:00 PM, 3:00 PM, 5:00 PM, and 7:00 PM. Mrs. Kelly went to see the movie before 3:00 PM. She did not see a morning show. At what time did Mrs. Kelly see the movie?

   _____

8. Tricia, Dan, Mia, and Pedro all work for the same company. Pedro has worked there the longest. Mia has worked there longer than Tricia and Dan. Dan has worked there longer than Tricia. Who has worked there the shortest amount of time?

   _____

Picaria

Picaria is a game that was brought to the United States by Spanish settlers. It is a game for two players.

You need six game pieces, three for each player.
You could use three coins and three beans.

Rules:

■ Players take turns placing a game piece in a circle on the Picaria Board.

■ When all six pieces have been placed, players take turns moving their pieces.

■ On each turn a player moves one piece along a straight line to a circle without a piece.

The first player with three game pieces in a line is the winner.

Picaria Board

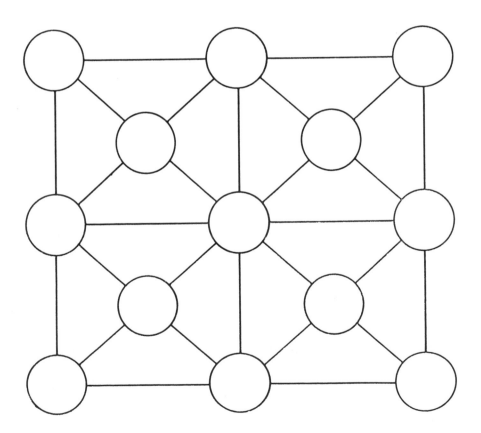

Using Thinking Skills

Don't Lose Balance

■ Choose weights to put on the scales to make the scales balance.

■ Write the numbers in the boxes.

■ You may use a weight more than once.

■ All of the measures are in ounces.

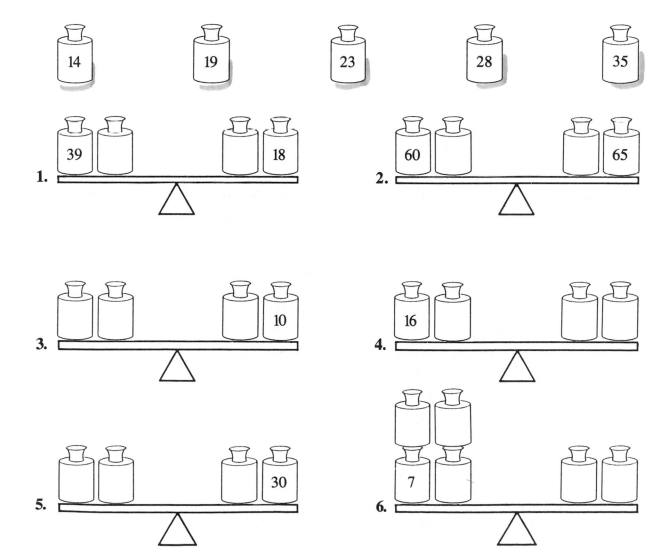

Star Sum

This is an activity for you and someone in your family.
Work together.

■ Use the numbers 1, 2, 3, 4, 8, 10 and 11.

■ Put one number in each circle so that the four numbers in each line add to 28.

HINT
Put numbers on pieces of paper. Move the papers around and test the sums.

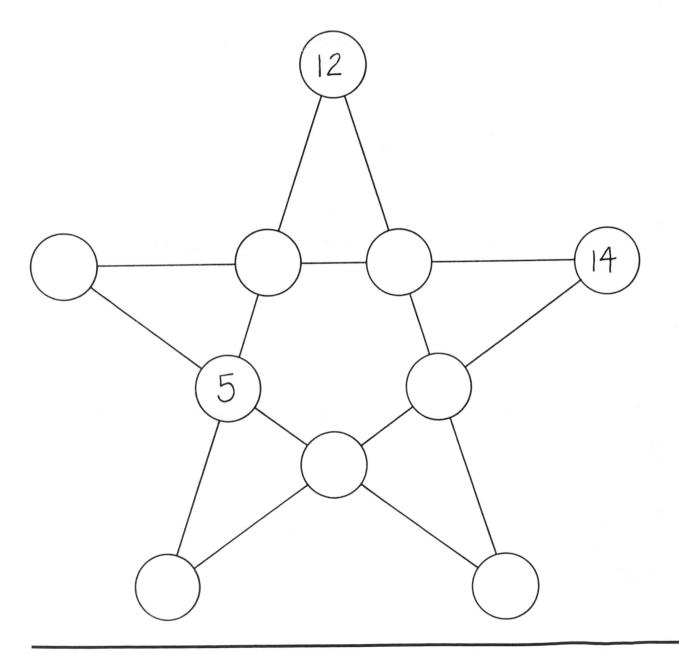

Guessing and Checking

Budget Time

Marcie earned $36 last month. The circle graph shows how Marcie spent her money.

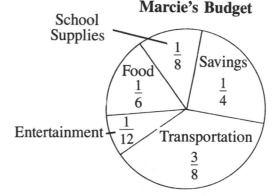

Marcie's Budget

School Supplies — $\frac{1}{8}$

Food $\frac{1}{6}$

Savings $\frac{1}{4}$

Entertainment — $\frac{1}{12}$

Transportation $\frac{3}{8}$

1. In which category did Marcie spend the least amount of money?

_____

2. In which category did Marcie spend the most amount of money?

_____

3. Name 2 categories in which Marcie spent half of her money.

_____

4. Name 3 categories in which Marcie spent half of her money.

_____

5. How much money did Marcie spend for food?

_____

6. How much money did Marcie save?

_____

7. How much more did Marcie spend for transportation than entertainment?

_____

8. Altogether, how much money did Marcie spend for school supplies and food?

_____

9. If Marcie spent the same amount of money for transportation each month, how much would she spend in one year?

_____

Day By Day

Have someone in your family
help you think about how you
spend your day.

Make a list of activities
that you do.

Write down the number
of hours you spend doing each activity.

Activity	Number of Hours

Here is a circle graph that is
divided in 24 sections.
Each section stands for 1 hour.
Label the sections for the activities.

My Day

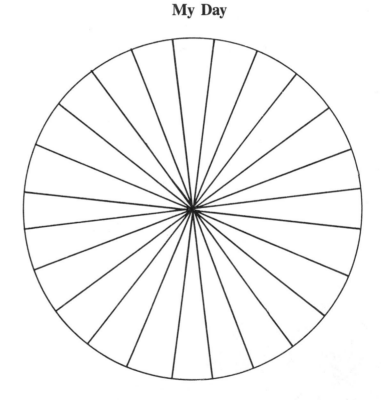

In which activity do you spend the most time each day? _____

Making a Circle Graph

Penny's Payroll

The Penny Power Company has its employees sign in and sign out at work. The company then computes how much to pay the employees based on the number of hours worked.

For work of more than 8 hours per day, a bonus of $3 per hour is paid for the overtime.

Complete the table. It might be helpful to use a calculator.

Employee	Time In	Time Out	Total Number of Hours	Hourly Wage	Total Wage
1. A. Barrons	7:00AM		8	$5.35	$42.80
2. B. Cartright	7:30AM	1:30PM	6	$4.50	
3. C. Davenport	7:00AM	4:00PM	9		$60.60
4. D. Elio	8:00AM	12:00PM		$7.50	$30.00
5. E. Franzio	8:30AM	3:00PM	$6 \frac{1}{2}$	$6.80	
6. F. Galt		2:30PM	$7 \frac{1}{2}$	$8.30	$62.25
7. G. Hertz	7:30AM	3:30PM	8		$54.00
8. H. Lee	8:00AM	6:00PM		$4.25	$48.50

Likely Letters

This is an activity for you and your family.

WHAT LETTER OCCURS MOST OFTEN IN BOOKS?

Write your guess here. _____

Now test your guess.

- Open any book.
- Pick out five sentences.
- Tally each letter below.

Letter	Number of Times	Letter	Number of Times	Letter	Number of Times
A		J		S	
B		K		T	
C		L		U	
D		M		V	
E		N		W	
F		O		X	
G		P		Y	
H		Q		Z	
I		R			

1. Which letter occurred most often? _____

2. Which vowel occurred most often? _____

3. Which consonant occurred most often? _____

　　　Try again.
- Use a different book.
- Pick out five sentences.
- Make another tally.

4. Did the same letter occur most often? _____

Using Information in a Table

Tree Diagrams

The Kendall Card Company makes cards in three shapes: circle, triangle, and rectangle.

The cards may be blue or yellow in color.

How many different cards can the Kendall Card Company make?

You can use a tree diagram to find out.

For each shape there are 2 colors.

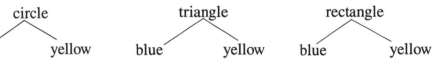

The Bixby Block Company makes blocks in two shapes: sphere and cylinder.
The block may be red or brown in color.
The blocks may be large or small in size.

1. Complete the tree diagram to identify the different blocks that can be made.

One block is a large red sphere.

(shape)

(color)

(size)

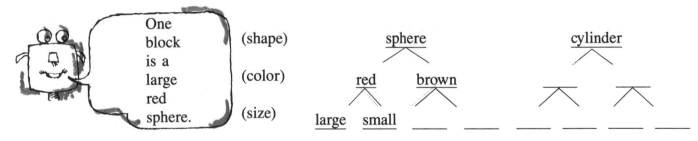

2. How many different blocks can the Bixby Block Company make? _____

3. How many of the blocks are red? _____

4. How many of the blocks are spheres? _____

5. How many of the blocks are large? _____

6. How many of the blocks are small and brown? _____

7. How many of the blocks are large cylinders? _____

8. How many of the blocks are red spheres? _____

Menu Matters

Plan some meals with your family.   _____ _____ _____
Start with lunch.
   Identify three soups.
   Identify three sandwiches.   _____ _____ _____

1. Use a tree diagram to find how
   many different lunches you can make.

(soup)

(sandwich) ___ ___ ___ ___ ___ ___ ___ ___ ___

2. How many different lunches can you make? _____

Now plan some dinners.

   Identify three main dishes.   _____ _____ _____
   Identify two salads.
   Identify two desserts.   _____ _____

3. Use a tree diagram to find how many different dinners you can make.

(main dish)

(salad)

(dessert) ___ ___ ___ ___ ___ ___ ___ ___ ___ ___ ___ ___

4. How many different dinners can you make? _____

Treasure Map

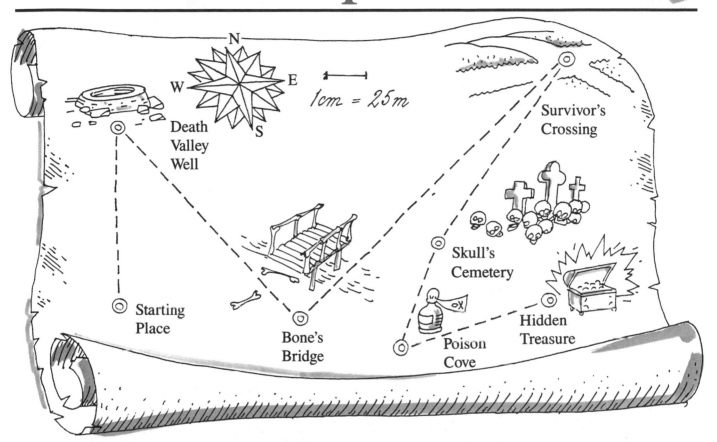

Use a centimeter ruler and the map to answer each question.
Stay on the roads.

1. What is the actual distance from Bone's Bridge to Survivor's Crossing? _____

2. What is the actual distance from Starting Place to Death Valley Well? _____

3. What is the actual distance from Skull's Cemetery to the Hidden Treasure? _____

4. Lonesome Lake is 275 m east of Starting Place. On the map, how
many centimeters would Lonesome Lake be from Starting Place? _____

5. What is the actual distance from Bone's Bridge to Poison Cove? _____

6. What is the actual distance from the Starting Place to the Hidden Treasure? _____

Model Room

Have an adult help you with this project.
Pick a room in your house.
Make a scale drawing of the room on the grid paper below.
Mark the doorways.
Draw three pieces of furniture in the room.

Scale: [ ] stands for 1 square foot.

More. . .
Palindromes

Make up and solve your own Palindrome problems

You can start with any number and make a palindrome.
Follow these steps.

Step 1: Pick a number.

Step 2: Reverse the number.

Step 3: Add the numbers.

Step 4: Repeat steps 2 and 3 until you get a palindrome.

$$\begin{array}{r} 58 \\ + \ 85 \\ \hline 143 \end{array}$$

$$\begin{array}{r} + \ 341 \\ \hline 484 \end{array}$$

Work with a member of your family.
Take turns thinking of a number and making it into a palindrome.
Show the work to make three palindromes.

Think of words you know that are palindromes.
Write as many as you can.

Enrichment
Math Grade 6

AMERICAN
EDUCATION
PUBLISHING

Greatest Number

Read each set of rules.
Write the greatest number that meets the rules.

1. Each of the digits 2 through 6 is used once.
   The 4 is in the ones place. _____

2. Each of the digits 5 through 9 is used once.
   The 5 is in the thousands place. _____

3. Each of the digits 1 through 7 is used once.
   The 2 is in the ten thousands place. _____

4. Each of the digits 3 through 8 is used once.
   The 4 is in the hundred thousands place.
   The 6 is in the tens place. _____

5. Each of the digits 1 through 9 is used once.
   The 3 is in the hundred millions place.
   The 5 is in the millions place. _____

6. There are 10 digits.
   There is a 5 in the billions place. _____

7. There are 11 digits.
   There is a 3 in the ten billions place.
   There is a 4 in the ones place.
   There is a 6 in the hundreds place. _____

8. There are 12 digits.
   The digit in the hundred billions place is one
   less than the digit in the hundred millions place.
   The digit in the hundred millions place is one
   less than the digit in the hundred thousands place. _____

Number Rally

Ask someone to play this game with you.
Decide who will play first.
Take turns.

Rules:

■ Pick a number from the number board.
■ Score 1 point for each of the following
that is true:

The number is less than five hundred billion.
The digit in the hundred millions place is less than 5.
The digit in the hundreds place is greater than 2.
The digit in the millions place is odd.
The digit in the billions place is even.
The digit in the hundred thousands place is greater than 6.

■ Record the score and cross off the number.
■ The player with the greater number of points after
four rounds is the winner.

Number Board

163,345,098,072	818,836,792,845
331,459,172,783	956,721,245,996
413,296,356,154	605,925,837,432
202,234,478,299	704,643,782,647

Scoreboard

	Player 1		Player 2	
	Number	**Points**	**Number**	**Points**
1.				
2.				
3.				
4.				
	Total		**Total**	

Cross-Number Puzzle

Add or subtract.
Write the answer in the cross-number puzzle.

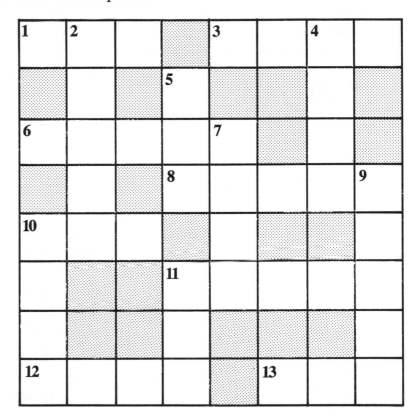

ACROSS

1. 662
       + 98

3. 2,653
       + 5,929

6. 75,995
       − 28,370

8. 70,352
       + 27,809

10. 322
        + 147

11. 88,662
        − 6,469

12. 1,439
        + 5,388

13. 947
        − 575

DOWN

2. 72,885
       − 10,099

7. 9,623
       − 3,791

      1,386
      − 529

4. 8,347
       +   99

9. 4,783
       + 9,609

5. 393
       + 236

      4,904
      − 858

1089

Be a mathemagician.

Cover your eyes.
Ask an adult to follow these directions.

	Yes	**No**

1. Write down a three-digit number. The digit in the hundreds place must be at least 2 more than the digit in the ones place.

    380   ~~329~~

    893   ~~484~~

2. Reverse the digits to write a new number.

    893
    398

3. Subtract.

    893
    −398
    495

4. Reverse the digits in the difference to write a new number.

    495
    594

5. Add.

    495
    +594
    1,089

Now say, "Abrakadabrah, math magic is mine.
Your answer is one thousand eighty-nine."

Ask an adult to pick another number.
See if you can be a mathemagician again.

The Price Is Right

Fill in the missing price so that the bill adds up.

1.

Tennis Pro Shop	
can of tennis balls	$4.00
tennis racket	
2 pairs of shorts	36.98
2 sweatshirts	39.98
Total	**$115.91**

2.

Hit It Right Hardware	
hammer	$9.75
saw	18.20
2 gallons of paint	
paint roller	4.95
Total	**$57.40**

3.

Gourmet Bakery	
2 breads	$2.38
1 dozen cookies	3.00
cake	
6 bagels	1.50
Total	**$15.87**

4.

Carla's Clothes Closet	
scarf	$17.99
blouse	28.49
slacks	
sweater	29.99
suit	89.99
Total	**$201.46**

5.

We've Got It All - Sports	
baseball bat	$14.95
basketball	
catcher's mitt	39.99
table tennis paddles	12.95
ping pong balls	2.99
Total	**$95.83**

6.

Mal's Market	
grapes	$2.19
milk	1.59
cereal	2.79
chicken	7.56
lettuce	.69
cheese	
Total	**$17.81**

Market Hunt

This is an activity for you and someone in your family.

1. Look at a newspaper. Find a grocery store ad. Pick out 4 items that the two of you would like to buy. Use the store prices on the items to complete the bill below.

Item	Price
1.	
2.	
3.	
4.	
Total	

2. Pretend that you each have $20. On the bills below, write 5 items that you think you could buy with your money.

Name of Person _____

Item	Price
1.	
2.	
3.	
4.	
5.	
Total	

Name of Person _____

Item	Price
1.	
2.	
3.	
4.	
5.	
Total	

3. Look at the ad. Find the prices for the items and complete the bills.

Whose total was closer to $20? _____

Odd One Out

In each row, one answer is different.

Estimate to guess which one is different.
Then multiply to check your guess.
Circle the answer that is different.

1.

460	230	920	340
× 200	× 400	× 100	× 300

2.

300	2,500	4,600	600
× 400	× 48	× 25	× 200

3.

1,600	870	990	495
× 99	× 182	× 160	× 320

4.

396	198	792	197
× 68	× 136	× 34	× 134

End-To-End

This is a game for two players.

X _____
Player's Name

O _____
Player's Name

How to Play:
- ■ Take turns
- ■ Pick a number from each sign.
- ■ Multiply the numbers.
- ■ If the answer is on the game board, mark your **X** or **O** on the answer.

The winner is the first player to complete a path connecting its two sides of the game board.

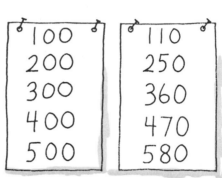

100	110
200	250
300	360
400	470
500	580

GAMEBOARD

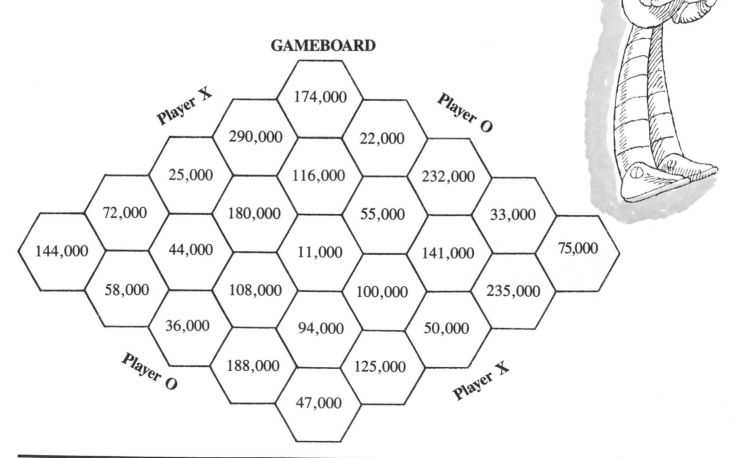

Player X   Player O

174,000

290,000   22,000

25,000   116,000   232,000

72,000   180,000   55,000   33,000

144,000   44,000   11,000   141,000   75,000

58,000   108,000   100,000   235,000

36,000   94,000   50,000

Player O   188,000   125,000   Player X

47,000

Multiplying by a 3-Digit Number

Division Derby

The divisors are on the sign.
Write the divisors in the boxes to make the division
examples correct.
Estimate to make sure the answers make sense.

1. ☐ $\overline{)2{,}688}$ 84

2. ☐ $\overline{)168}$ 3

56	41
92	32

3. ☐ $\overline{)1{,}886}$ 46

4. ☐ $\overline{)5{,}336}$ 58

5. ☐ $\overline{)960}$ 87 R3

6. ☐ $\overline{)707}$ 24 R11

11	63
116	29

7. ☐ $\overline{)6{,}496}$ 56

8. ☐ $\overline{)4{,}725}$ 75

9. ☐ $\overline{)6{,}545}$ 35

10. ☐ $\overline{)16{,}992}$ 472

278	36
52	187

11. ☐ $\overline{)2{,}924}$ 56 R12

12. ☐ $\overline{)32{,}834}$ 118 R30

Dividing by 2- and 3-Digit Numbers

Division Bingo

This is a game for two players, **X** and **O**.
Take turns.

On each turn:
- Pick a number from the divisor sign.
- Pick a number from the dividend sign.
- Divide the dividend by the divisor.
- Find the quotient on the board.
- Make your mark on the quotient.

$$\text{divisor} \overline{)\,\text{dividend}}^{\text{quotient}}$$

The first player with four **X**s or **O**s in a row,
column, or diagonal is the winner.

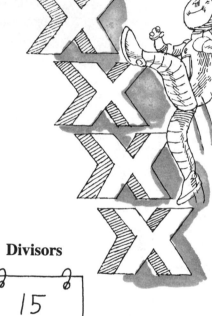

BINGO BOARD

12	72	90	156
180	4	18	78
24	52	120	3
6	360	39	36

Divisors

15
30
45
60

Dividends

180
1080
2340
5400

Dividing by a 2-Digit Number

Join The Group

LESSON
6

Match the labels to the sets of numbers.
Use each label only once.
■ Write the label name on the line.
■ Write the letter of the label on the other line.

I Even numbers	**A** Odd numbers	**A** Factors of 24	**P** Prime numbers
R Multiples of 3	**E** Factors of 36	**L** Multiples of 6	**N** Composite numbers

		Label	**Letter**
1.	{1, 2, 4, 8, 12}	_____	_____
2.	{0, 2, 4, 6 8}	_____	_____
3.	{0, 3, 6, 9, 12}	_____	_____
4.	{2, 5, 11, 17, 31}	_____	_____
5.	{0, 6, 12, 18, 48}	_____	_____
6.	{3, 5, 7, 11, 13}	_____	_____
7.	{4, 6, 8, 10, 15}	_____	_____
8.	{1, 3, 4, 6, 9}	_____	_____

Check: If you labeled the sets correctly, the letters from top to bottom spell the name of a vehicle.

Factor Right

This is a game for two players, **X** and **Y**.

How to Play

Player **X** picks one number on the factor board, records the number on the score sheet, and crosses off the number on the board.

Player **Y** finds all of the factors of that number that are on the board, records the numbers on the score sheet, and crosses off the numbers on the board.

Then player **Y** picks one number on the factor board, records the number on the score sheet, and crosses off the number on the board.

Player **X** finds all of the factors of that number that are left on the board, records the numbers on the score sheet, and crosses off the numbers on the board. If there are no factors left, Player **X** scores no points. Player **X** then picks a number.

This continues until all numbers on the factor board have been crossed off.

Players add all of the numbers on their score sheets.

The winner is the player with the greater total score.

Factor Board

1	2	3	4	5
6	7	8	9	10
11	12	13	14	15
16	17	18	19	20
21	22	23	24	25
26	27	28	29	30

Player X Score Sheet

Player Y Score Sheet

LESSON

7

U.S. Presidents

Write the decimal numbers on the lines in order from least to greatest.
Write the letter of each decimal number under the number.
The letters will spell the name of a U.S. President.

1. The 2nd President of the United States

___ ___ ___ ___ ___

S	0.4
D	0.0012
A	0.0004
M	0.03
A	0.0235

2. The 18th President of the United States

___ ___ ___ ___ ___

T	0.12
N	0.02
G	0.0012
R	0.0021
A	0.003

3. The 33rd President of the United States

___ ___ ___ ___ ___ ___

M	0.36
N	1.4
R	0.0018
T	0.0009
U	0.027
A	1.001

Comparing and Ordering Decimals

Big Events

This is an activity for you and your family.

When did each of these events occur?
Write the event next to the date.

To check your answers, arrange the decimal numbers in order from least to greatest. The order of the decimals gives the order in which the events occured.

Date	Event
1776	_____
1789	_____
1828	_____
1847	_____
1860	_____
1867	_____
1876	_____
1903	_____
1910	_____

0.0078   George Washington elected President of the U.S.

0.0435   Abraham Lincoln elected President of the U.S.

1.3000   Boy Scouts of America founded

1.0200   First plane flight

0.0009   Declaration of Independence signed

0.1201   U.S. buys Alaska from Russia

0.0099   First Webster Dictionary published

0.0102   First stick-on postage stamp

1.0008   Mark Twain publishes *Tom Sawyer*

Comparing and Ordering Decimals

Equal Sums

Draw a line through each sign
so that the sum of the numbers
on one side of the line equals the
sum of the numbers on the other
side.
Write the sum.

1.

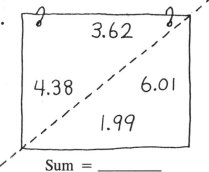

3.62

4.38   6.01

1.99

Sum = _____

2.

6.25   3.45

4.35   7.15

Sum = _____

3.

1.432

6.783

3.104

5.111

Sum = _____

4.

2.4152

2.3784

1.6666

3.127

Sum = _____

5.

16.29   3.5

4.6   6.8

5.19   12.4

Sum = _____

6.

20.1   7.215
0

3.24   7.624

2.021

Sum = _____

Hit The Target

Play this game with a friend.
Make a set of these cards.
Mix up the cards and place them face down.

Rules:
- Turn over a card.
- Both players write the digit that is on the card in one of their 15 boxes.
- Continue to turn over cards and write the numbers in the boxes.
- When the boxes are filled, players put a decimal point in each of their six numbers.
- Players add and compare their sums to the target numbers.
- The player with at least two sums closer to the target numbers is the winner.

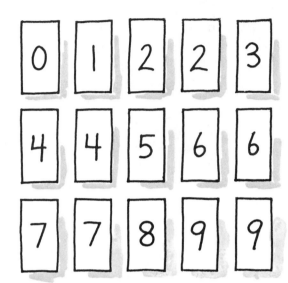

	Target Number	
Player 1		**Player 2**
□ □ □ + □ □	25	□ □ □ + □ □
□ □ □ □ + □	8	□ □ □ □ + □
□ □ + □ □ □	12	□ □ + □ □ □

The winner is _____ .

Adding with Decimals

Snapshot

IN WHAT YEAR WAS THE POLAROID CAMERA INVENTED?

THE YEAR WAS _____ _____ _____ _____ .

1.

16.0476	9.9025
− 5.4218	− 0.0628

The only digit that is in both answers is _____ .
Write this digit in the ones place of the year.

2.

8.973	4.0004
− 2.867	− 0.8125

The only digit that is in both answers is _____ .
Write this digit in the thousands place of the year.

3.

12.283	8.0541
− 11.940	− 2.1056

The only digit that is in both answers is _____ .
Write this digit in the tens place of the year.

4.

4.1856	7.0297
− 1.3884	−2.4309

The only digit that is in both answers is _____ .
Write this digit in the hundreds place of the year.

Zero Out

Play this game with a friend.
Make a set of these cards.
Make the subtraction boxes for each player.

Number Cards

0 1 2 3 4 5 6 7 8 9
0 1 2 3 4 5 6 7 8 9

Subtraction Boxes

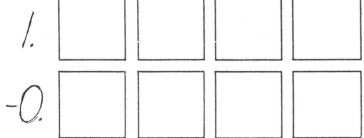

1. ☐ ☐ ☐ ☐

-0. ☐ ☐ ☐ ☐

How to Play:
- Mix up all 20 number cards.
- Turn over 8 cards, one at a time. Each player writes the number on the card in one of the boxes.
- When all 8 boxes have been filled, subtract the decimal numbers.

The winner is the player whose answer is closer to zero.

Subtracting with Decimals

Name The State

First guess the answer.
Then multiply.
To check your guess, write the letters of the
products in the boxes in order, from least to greatest.

IN WHICH STATE WAS PRESIDENT TRUMAN BORN?

S 13.5 $\times$ 3.6	**R** 57.2 $\times$ 8.32	**I** 4.52 $\times$ 2.75	**I** 9.64 $\times$ 92
U 4.36 $\times$ 82.7	**M** 8.4 $\times$ 0.3	**O** 15.2 $\times$ 3.7	**S** 127.5 $\times$ 0.21

IN WHICH STATE WAS PRESIDENT LINCOLN BORN?

K 92.7 $\times$ 8.4	**U** 3.74 $\times$ 4.25	**Y** 83.3 $\times$ 9.8	**N** 5.82 $\times$ 0.7
E 2.56 $\times$ 1.45	**K** 4.32 $\times$ 0.8	**T** 8.75 $\times$ 0.52	**C** 76.3 $\times$ 0.23

Multiplying with Decimals

Multiplication Stand-Off

Play this game with a friend.

Rules:
- Take turns.
- Pick two numbers from the number board.
- Multiply the two numbers.
- Cross out the two numbers on the number board.
- Find the product on the number line. Write the score for the product. When all of the numbers on the number board are crossed out, the player with the greater total score is the winner.

Number Board

1.94	13.6	9.2	3.46
22.6	3.24	8.4	0.98
11.2	0.87	15.8	4.6
7.2	21.32	5.78	19.5

Player 1	Player 2

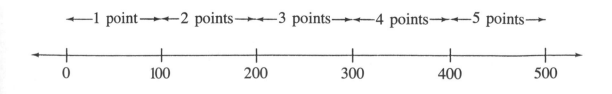

←—1 point—→ ←—2 points—→ ←—3 points—→ ←—4 points—→ ←—5 points—→

```
0        100       200       300       400       500
```

Invention Update

Write the letter of the problem above the answer.
The letters will spell the name of the inventor.

K $6.2\overline{)3.10}$	**R** $1.3\overline{)2.6}$	**J** $2.1\overline{)0.42}$
N $0.23\overline{)6.90}$	**A** $2.4\overline{)9.6}$	**B** $0.12\overline{)3.72}$
I $3.2\overline{)35.2}$	**M** $0.34\overline{)3.4}$	**E** $0.18\overline{)0.39}$

E $0.41\overline{)123}$ **L** $0.92\overline{)184}$

31	2.2	30	0.2	4	10	11	30

300	2	4	30	0.5	200	11	30

Inventor Match

This is a quiz for you and your family.
First guess the inventor of each item.
Then divide to check your guess.
The quotient gives the inventor's name.

Item	Quotient	Inventor
1. jeans	$4.2\overline{)0.882}$ 0.12	Joseph Merlin
2. zipper	$0.28\overline{)8.4}$ 5	Thomas Alva Edison
3. roller skates	$5.3\overline{)0.636}$ 0.21	Levi Strauss
4. computer	$0.16\overline{)0.384}$ 30	Whitcomb Judson
5. electric light	$3.09\overline{)15.45}$ 2.4	Charles Babbage

Dividing with Decimals

Table Teasers

Complete each table.
Add each number at the top to each number at the side.

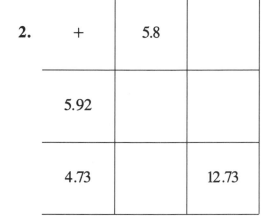

1.

+	2.173	5.946
3.82		
7.04		

2.

+	5.8	
5.92		
4.73		12.73

3.

×	7.3	3.8
5		
		23.18

4.

×		6.31
7.2	16.56	
		29.026

5.

+		5.201
3.45	6.93	
		18.281

6.

×	8.5	
	15.3	
9.1		84.175

Adding, Subtracting, Multiplying and Dividing with Decimals

Score Up

This is a game for you and a friend.
Make a set of these cards.
Mix up the cards and place them face down.

Rules:
- Take turns.
- Pick two cards.
- Use the signs +, −, ×, ÷.
- Write a number sentence.
- Score the number sentence.
- If the answer is 5 or less, score 2 points.
- If the answer is between 5 and 30, score 3 points.
- If the answer is 30 or more, score 1 point.
- Mix up the cards before each player's turn.
- After 5 turns, the player with the greater score wins.

| 7.2 | 3.1 | 15.6 | 0.21 |
| 0.85 | 8.02 | 0.6 | 8 |

Player 1		Player 2	
Sentence	**Points**	**Sentence**	**Points**
TOTAL		**TOTAL**	

The winner is _____ .

Adding, Subtracting, Multiplying, and Dividing with Decimals

Fish Fact

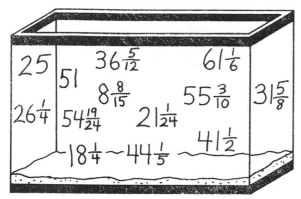

25 51 $36\frac{5}{12}$ $61\frac{1}{6}$
$26\frac{1}{4}$ $54\frac{19}{24}$ $8\frac{8}{15}$ $55\frac{3}{10}$ $31\frac{5}{8}$
$21\frac{1}{24}$
$18\frac{1}{4}$ ~ $44\frac{1}{5}$ $41\frac{1}{2}$

**WHAT IS THE LENGTH OF THE
LONGEST FISH EVER FOUND?**

Add. Write the answer in simplest form.
Cross off the sum in the fish tank.
The number that is left is the answer to the question.

1. $14\frac{2}{3}$
    $+\ 10\frac{1}{3}$

2. $6\frac{1}{5}$
    $+\ 2\frac{1}{3}$

3. $9\frac{3}{4}$
    $+\ 8\frac{1}{2}$

4. $36\frac{5}{6}$
    $+\ 24\frac{1}{3}$

5. $27\frac{3}{8}$
    $+\ 4\frac{1}{4}$

6. $19\frac{2}{3}$
    $+\ 16\frac{3}{4}$

7. $42\frac{3}{10}$
    $+\ 1\frac{9}{10}$

8. $26\frac{1}{6}$
    $+\ 28\frac{5}{8}$

9. $13\frac{6}{8}$
    $+\ 12\frac{1}{2}$

10. $37\frac{2}{5}$
    $+\ 13\frac{6}{10}$

11. $29\frac{1}{2}$
    $+\ 25\frac{4}{5}$

12. $18\frac{3}{8}$
    $+\ 2\frac{2}{3}$

**The longest fish ever found was a whale shark. It was found off
the coast of Pakistan and was _____ feet long.**

Space Quiz

This is an activity for you and your family.
First answer each question.
Then add to check your answers.
The sum gives the answer to the question.

1. Who was the first man to orbit the earth?

$1\frac{7}{8}$ $1\frac{10}{12}$ John Glenn

$+\ \frac{3}{4}$ $2\frac{5}{8}$ Yuri Gagarin

         $1\frac{5}{8}$ Alan Shepard

         $2\frac{2}{8}$ John Flyer

2. Who was the first American in space?

$2\frac{2}{3}$ $6\frac{1}{2}$ Alan Shepard

$+\ 3\frac{5}{6}$ $5\frac{7}{9}$ Dr. Spock

         $5\frac{1}{2}$ John Glenn

         $6\frac{2}{3}$ Neil Armstrong

3. Who was the first American to orbit the earth?

$4\frac{5}{6}$ $8\frac{2}{3}$ Archibald Leach

$+\ 4\frac{5}{6}$ $8\frac{10}{12}$ Orville Wright

         $9\frac{5}{6}$ Thomas Stafford

         $9\frac{2}{3}$ John Glenn

4. Who was the first American to walk in space

$6\frac{1}{2}$ $9\frac{3}{10}$ Edward White, II

$+\ 2\frac{4}{5}$ $8\frac{3}{10}$ Frank Borman

         $8\frac{5}{7}$ Lee Iacoco

         $9\frac{5}{7}$ Gordon Cooper

5. Who was the first man to walk on the moon

$3\frac{11}{12}$ $3\frac{13}{20}$ Charles Conrad

$+\ \frac{2}{8}$ $3\frac{1}{6}$ Thomas Stafford

         $4\frac{17}{24}$ Roger Moore

         $4\frac{1}{6}$ Neil Armstrong

Adding Mixed Numbers

LESSON
14

Hexagon Fractions

There are 3 circles on each side of each hexagon.
Write a fraction in each circle so that the sum
of the 3 circles on a side is the target sum.

1.

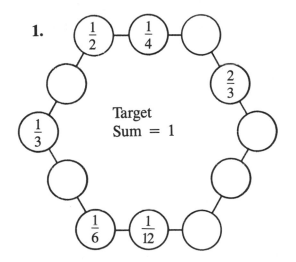

Target
Sum = 1

2.

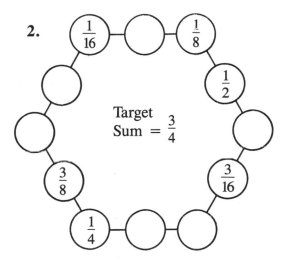

Target
Sum = $\frac{3}{4}$

3.

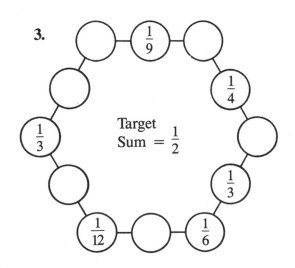

Target
Sum = $\frac{1}{2}$

4.

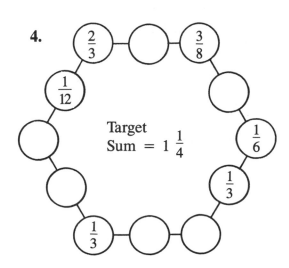

Target
Sum = $1\frac{1}{4}$

Subtraction Action

This is a game for two players.
Make a set of these cards.
Mix up the cards and place them face down.

Rules:

- Each player starts with 10 points.
- Take turns.
  Pick a card.
- Subtract the number on the card from your number of points. Record the number of points that you have left.
- After 5 rounds, the player with the fewer number of points is the winner.

Round	Player 1 Number of Points	Player 2 Number of Points
1		
2		
3		
4		
5		

The winner is _____.

Product Production

Sign:

1	2
3	4
5	6
7	8

Fill in the box with a number from the sign to make the sentence true.
Cross off the number after you use it.

I $\dfrac{1}{2} \times \dfrac{1}{3} = \dfrac{1}{\Box}$

V $\dfrac{2}{3} \times \dfrac{1}{6} = \dfrac{\Box}{9}$

C $\dfrac{3}{8} \times \dfrac{4}{5} = \dfrac{\Box}{10}$

A $\dfrac{8}{9} \times \dfrac{3}{4} = \dfrac{\Box}{3}$

T $\dfrac{2}{5} \times \dfrac{1}{2} = \dfrac{1}{\Box}$

N $\dfrac{1}{\Box} \times \dfrac{1}{3} = \dfrac{1}{24}$

A $\dfrac{3}{5} \times \dfrac{4}{9} = \dfrac{\Box}{15}$

O $\dfrac{2}{7} \times \dfrac{\Box}{2} = 1$

To answer the question, write the letters of the numbers in the boxes in order, from least to greatest.

WHAT DO PEOPLE LIKE TO DO IN THE SUMMER?

___ ___ ___ ___ ___ ___ ___ ___

Fraction Line

This is a game for you and a friend.

To Play:

- Take turns.
- Pick one number from sign A and one number from sign B.
- Multiply the numbers. Reduce the answers to lowest terms.
- Mark the product on the game board with your **X** or **O**.

The first player with four **X**s or **O**s in a row, column or diagonal is the winner.

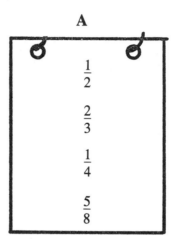

A

$\frac{1}{2}$

$\frac{2}{3}$

$\frac{1}{4}$

$\frac{5}{8}$

B

$\frac{3}{5}$

$\frac{5}{6}$

$\frac{9}{10}$

$\frac{1}{12}$

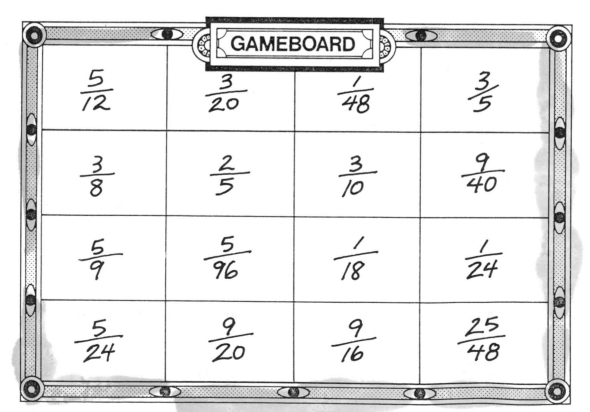

GAMEBOARD

$\frac{5}{12}$	$\frac{3}{20}$	$\frac{1}{48}$	$\frac{3}{5}$
$\frac{3}{8}$	$\frac{2}{5}$	$\frac{3}{10}$	$\frac{9}{40}$
$\frac{5}{9}$	$\frac{5}{96}$	$\frac{1}{18}$	$\frac{1}{24}$
$\frac{5}{24}$	$\frac{9}{20}$	$\frac{9}{16}$	$\frac{25}{48}$

Up And Over

Follow the arrow directions.
Divide up. Divide across.
Complete the square.

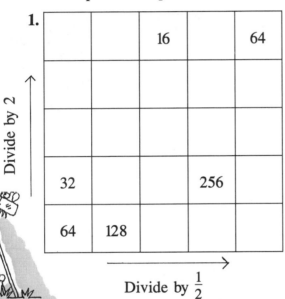

1.

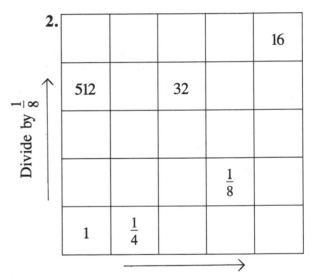

2.

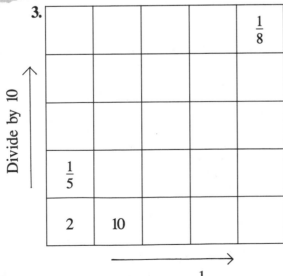

3.

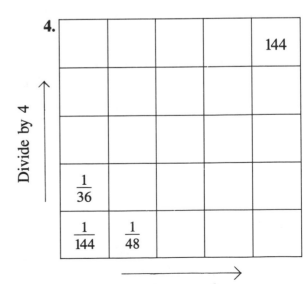

4.

Division Delight

Find someone to play this game with you.
Set a time limit: 2 minutes for each rule.

Each player should:
- Write at least two division examples that fit each rule.
  At least one of the numbers in each example must be a fraction.
- Divide.
- Check the examples with the other player.
- Score 1 point for each example that fits the rule.
- The player with the greater number of points after
  5 rules is the winner.

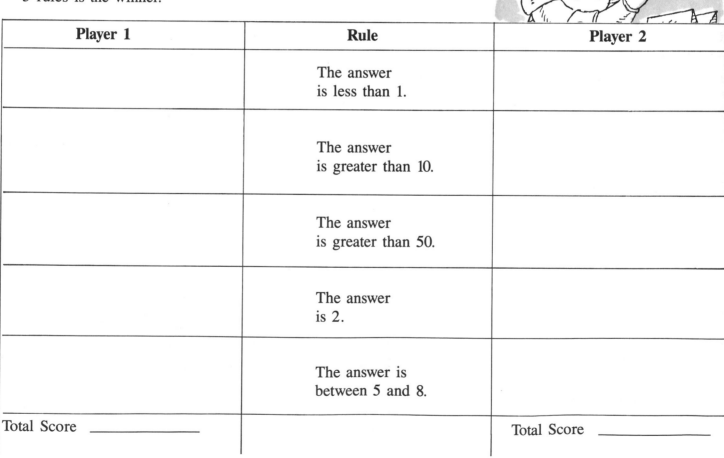

Player 1	Rule	Player 2
	The answer is less than 1.	
	The answer is greater than 10.	
	The answer is greater than 50.	
	The answer is 2.	
	The answer is between 5 and 8.	
Total Score _____		Total Score _____

Dividing Fractions

World Geography

First try to answer the question.
Then check your answer by finding the percent,
fraction, or decimal that is **not** equivalent.

1. Which country is not in South America?

0.25 Brazil $\frac{25}{1000}$ Costa Rica   25% Argentina

2. Which country is not an island?

70% Finland $\frac{7}{100}$ New Zealand   0.07 Greenland

3. Which country is not in Africa?

$\frac{2}{10}$ Zaire   20% Chad   0.02 Turkey

4. Which country's capital does not begin with ''L''?

16% England   0.16 Peru $\frac{1}{6}$ Italy

5. Which country is not in Europe?

5% Mexico $\frac{1}{2}$ Ireland   0.5 Spain

6. Which country's capital does not begin with ''P''?

$\frac{1}{10}$ Greece   1% France   0.01 China

7. Which country is not in Asia?

75% India   0.075 Sweden $\frac{3}{4}$ Japan

Tic-Tac-Toe

Play these games with a friend.

- There is a Tic-Tac-Toe board for each game.

- Find the three numbers in a row, column, or diagonal that are equivalent. One number is a fraction, one is a decimal, and one is a percent.

The winner of each game is the first player to find the tic-tac-toe.

Player A

Game 1

$\frac{1}{3}$	$\frac{1}{4}$	$\frac{1}{2}$
0.3	0.25	0.2
33%	25%	20%

Game 2

$\frac{3}{100}$	$\frac{1}{3}$	$\frac{3}{10}$
0.31	30%	0.13
0.3	$33\frac{1}{3}\%$	3%

Game 3

25%	0.04	$\frac{25}{100}$
0.25	$\frac{4}{5}$	4%
$\frac{2}{5}$	40%	0.4

Game 4

0.4	40%	$\frac{4}{100}$
4	4%	$\frac{1}{4}$
0.04	0.4%	$\frac{4}{10}$

Player B

Game 1

$\frac{1}{5}$	5%	0.2
$\frac{1}{2}$	50%	0.5
$\frac{7}{100}$	70%	0.07

Game 2

80%	$\frac{8}{100}$	$\frac{5}{9}$
0.45	0.8	0.59
45%	8%	$\frac{4}{5}$

Game 3

$\frac{3}{10}$	33%	$\frac{3}{3}$
$\frac{1}{33}$	1	0.3
100%	1%	0.3

Game 4

$\frac{7}{10}$	$\frac{1}{17}$	$\frac{7}{100}$
70%	17%	700%
0.7	0.17	0.07

Writing Fractions, Decimals and Percentages

Challenge

LESSON
18

Write the letter of the answer on the line next to the problem. If the answers are correct, the letters from top to bottom will spell the name for two equal ratios.

_____ **1.** What two numbers are in the ratio 1 to 2 and have a sum of 24?   **O**   66, 33

_____ **2.** What two numbers are in the ratio of 1 to 4 and have a sum of 30?   **R**   6, 24

_____ **3.** What two numbers are in the ratio of 6 to 3 and have a sum of 99?   **O**   18, 12

_____ **4.** What two numbers are in the ratio of 1 to 5 and have a sum of 30?   **N**   27, 72

_____ **5.** What two numbers are in the ratio of 3 to 2 and have a sum of 30?   **R**   110, 40

_____ **6.** What two numbers are in the ratio of 11 to 4 and have a sum of 150?   **P**   8, 16

_____ **7.** What two numbers are in the ratio of 7 to 1 and have a sum of 24?   **P**   5, 25

_____ **8.** What two numbers are in the ratio of 8 to 7 and have a sum of 150?   **O**   45, 55

_____ **9.** What two numbers are in the ratio of 9 to 11 and have a sum of 100?   **I**   80, 70

_____ **10.** What two numbers are in the ratio of 3 to 8 and have a sum of 99?   **T**   21, 3

Check it Out

This is an activity for you and a friend.

You will have to gather some information from your family.

The ratio of the number of people in the United States who are left-handed to the total population is 1:7 or $\frac{1}{7}$.

What is the ratio of left-handed people to the total in your family?

_____

How does your family ratio compare to the ratio for the United States?

_____

Find some ratios of your own.

People with dark hair to the total in your family_____

People with brown eyes to the total in your family_____

People who wear glasses to the total in your family_____

People wearing sneakers to the total in your family_____

How do the ratios in your family compare to those of some other students in your class?

_____

_____

_____

Sale Time!

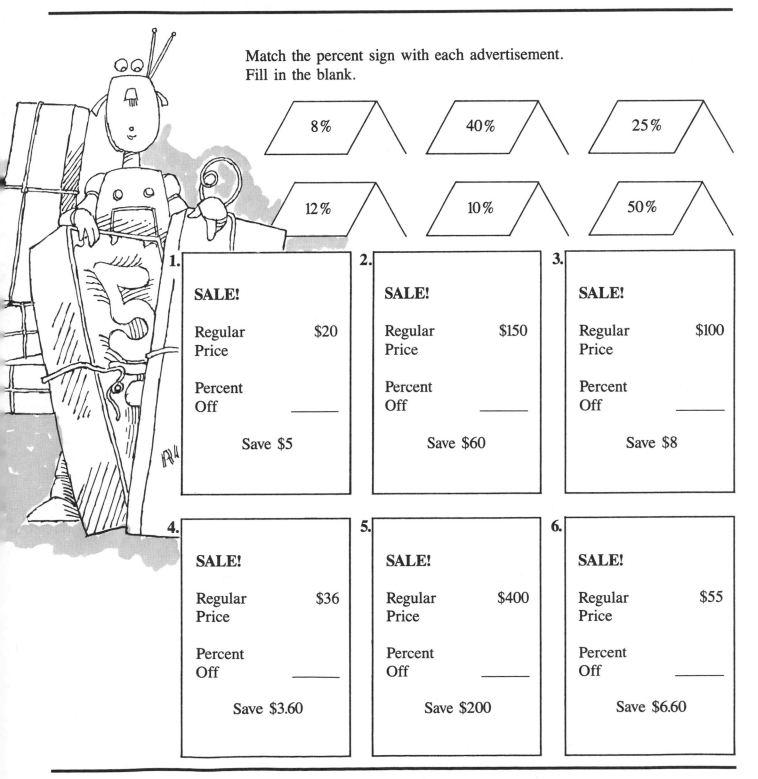

Match the percent sign with each advertisement.
Fill in the blank.

| 8% | 40% | 25% |

| 12% | 10% | 50% |

1.

SALE!

Regular $20
Price

Percent
Off   _____

Save $5

2.

SALE!

Regular $150
Price

Percent
Off   _____

Save $60

3.

SALE!

Regular $100
Price

Percent
Off   _____

Save $8

4.

SALE!

Regular $36
Price

Percent
Off   _____

Save $3.60

5.

SALE!

Regular $400
Price

Percent
Off   _____

Save $200

6.

SALE!

Regular $55
Price

Percent
Off   _____

Save $6.60

Newspaper Ads

Ask someone to do this activity with you.

1. Find a newspaper and a pair of scissors.
2. Look for advertisements that tell the regular price and the percent off.
3. Cut out three of the advertisements and paste them below.
4. List the regular price, the percent off, the amount saved, and the sale price.

regular price _____

percent off _____

amount saved _____

sale price _____

regular price _____

percent off _____

amount saved _____

sale price _____

Percent of a Number

Money Measures

MONEY FACTS		
Coin	**Width**	**Weight**
Penny	19 mm	3 g
Nickel	21 mm	5 g
Dime	17 mm	2 g

Use the information in the table to help you answer these questions.

1. How many dimes are there in a collection of dimes that weighs 150 grams?

_____

2. A collection of nickels is placed in a row end-to-end. The row measures 35.7 centimeters. How many nickels are in the row?

_____

3. A collection of pennies is placed in a row end-to-end. The row measures 1.52 meters. How many pennies are in the row?

_____

4. How many pennies are there in a collection of pennies that weighs 3 kilograms?

_____

5. A collection of dimes weighs 350 grams. What is the total value of the dimes?

_____

6. What is the weight of a collection of nickels that is worth $4.75?

_____

7. How much more is 275 grams of nickels worth than 50 grams of dimes?

_____

8. How much more does $5.98 in pennies weigh than $50.00 in dimes?

_____

Metric Conversions

Ask someone to play this game with you.
You will need a number cube.

1. Take turns.

2. Roll the cube. Move the number of spaces
   shown on the cube.

3. Give the missing number for the space on
   which you land.

4. The first player to reach "STOP" (or beyond)
   is the winner.

<table>
<tr><th colspan="3">FACTS</th></tr>
<tr><td>10mm</td><td>=</td><td>1 cm</td></tr>
<tr><td>100 cm</td><td>=</td><td>1m</td></tr>
<tr><td>1,000m</td><td>=</td><td>1 km</td></tr>
<tr><td>1,000mL</td><td>=</td><td>1L</td></tr>
<tr><td>1,000L</td><td>=</td><td>1kL</td></tr>
<tr><td>1,000mg</td><td>=</td><td>1g</td></tr>
<tr><td>1,000g</td><td>=</td><td>1 kg</td></tr>
</table>

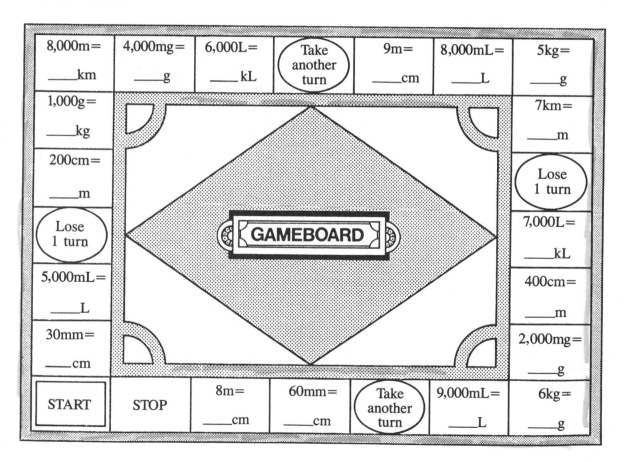

Bills, Bills, Bills

All U.S. paper money is about 6 inches long,
2 inches wide, 0.004 inch thick and weights about 0.03 ounce.
Today, only one-dollar, 5-dollar, 10-dollar, 20-dollar, 50-dollar
and 100-dollar bills are printed.

1. AROUND THE WORLD
The distance around the earth at the equator is about 25,000 miles. How
many dollar bills laid end-to-end, would be needed to wrap around the
earth at the equator? _____

2. A SEARS TOWER OF FIVES
The height of the Sears Tower in Chicago is 1,454 feet. What would be the
total value of the 5-dollar bills laid end-to-end that would equal the height
of the tower? _____

3. MILK BY THE DOLLAR
The weight of a quart of milk is 32 ounces. How many dollar bills
together equal the weight of a quart of milk? _____

4. AN OSTRICH IN TWENTIES
The largest ostrich on record weighed 345 pounds. What would be the
value of a pile of 20-dollar bills equal in weight to that of the ostrich?

_____

5. TABLE TOP DOLLARS
The table for table tennis is 9 feet long and 5 feet wide. How many dollar
bills would be needed to cover the table top? _____

5-10-20: How Much Are You Worth?

This is an activity for you and a member of your family.
Use the facts about paper money on the other side of this page.
Measure to the nearest inch and pound.

Name:		
1. Height		
2. Number of 5-dollar bills laid end-to-end that equal your height		
3. The "value" of your height in 5-dollar bills		
4. Width of your big toe		
5. Number of 10-dollar bills in a pile as thick as the width of your toe		
6. The "value" of your toe in 10-dollar bills		
7. Weight of one shoe		
8. Number of 20-dollar bills that together equal the weight of your shoe		
9. The "value" of your shoe in 20-dollar bills		

Missing Measures

Fill in the missing numbers.

1.

49 yards

28 yards

area = _____ square yards
perimeter = _____ yards

2.

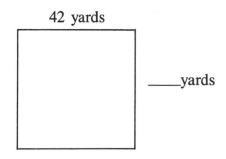

42 yards

_____ yards

area = 1,764 square yards
perimeter = _____ yards

3.

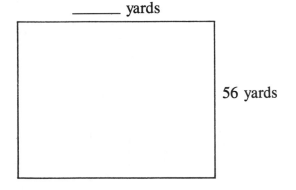

_____ yards

56 yards

area = 3,920 square yards
perimeter = _____ yards

4.

_____ yards

21 yards

area = _____ square yards
perimeter = 210 yards

5.

42 yards   70 yards

_____ yards

area = _____ square yards
perimeter = 168 yards

6.

21 yards   _____ yards

28 yards

area = _____ square yards
perimeter = 84 yards

It's All In The Foot

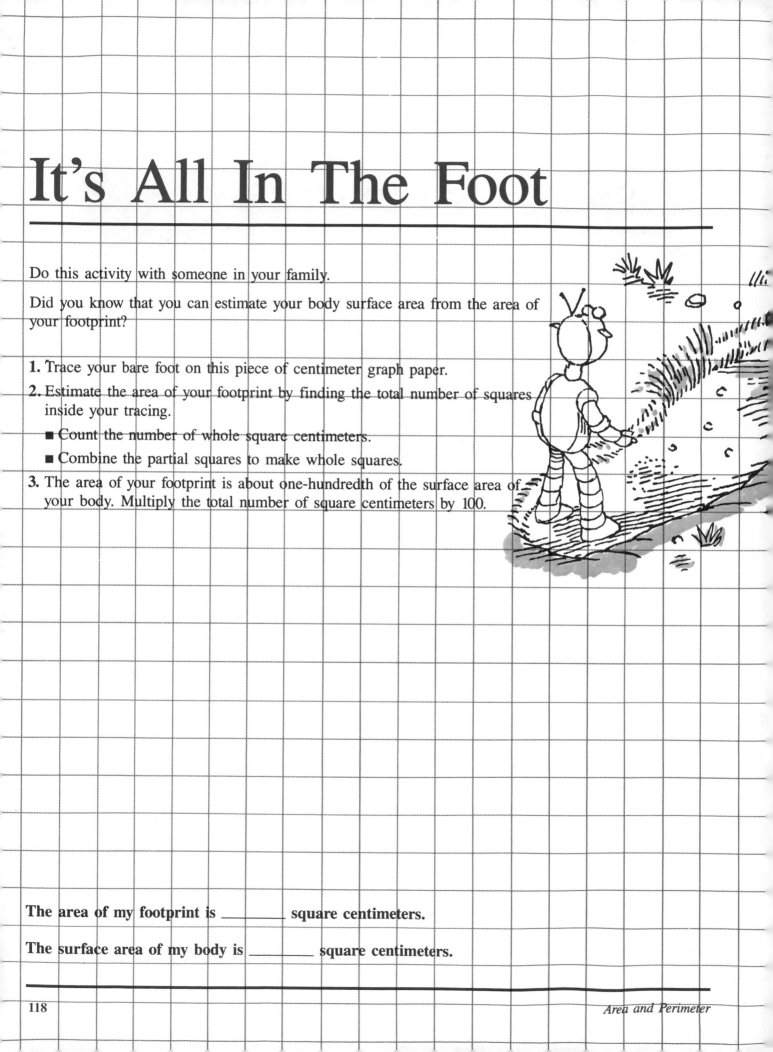

Do this activity with someone in your family.

Did you know that you can estimate your body surface area from the area of your footprint?

1. Trace your bare foot on this piece of centimeter graph paper.

2. Estimate the area of your footprint by finding the total number of squares inside your tracing.

   ■ Count the number of whole square centimeters.

   ■ Combine the partial squares to make whole squares.

3. The area of your footprint is about one-hundredth of the surface area of your body. Multiply the total number of square centimeters by 100.

The area of my footprint is _____ square centimeters.

The surface area of my body is _____ square centimeters.

Block Boggle

Five students used small cubes and glue to build these structures.
The face of each cube has an area of 1 square centimeter.
The volume of each cube is 1 cubic centimeter.

Use the clues to match the students with their structures.
Write the name of the student on the line by the structure.

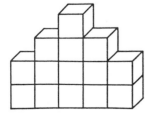

_____

1. **Anna:** "The surface area is 51 square centimeters. The volume is 14 cubic centimeters."

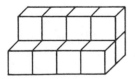

_____

2. **Brett:** "The surface area is 36 square centimeters. The volume is 10 cubic centimeters."

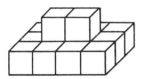

_____

3. **Candia:** "The surface area is 38 square centimeters. The volume is 12 cubic centimeters."

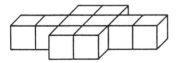

_____

4. **Doris:** "The surface area is 38 square centimeters. The volume is 10 cubic centimeters."

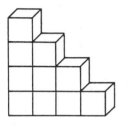

_____

5. **Ethan:** "The surface area is 44 square centimeters. The volume is 14 cubic centimeters."

Measure At The Market

This is an activity for you and your family.

You may have to make a trip to a market to find these boxes.

- Find the five types of boxes listed in the table. Each box must be a rectangular solid.
- Measure the length, width, and height of each box to the nearest inch. Record the measurements in the table.
- Compute the surface area and volume of each box and complete the table.

Type of Box		Width	Height	Volume	Surface Area
1. Toothpicks					
2. Raisins					
3. Crackers					
4. Cereal					
5. Laundry Detergent					

1. Which box has the smallest volume? _____

2. Which box has the largest volume? _____

3. How many times greater is the volume of the largest box than the volume of the smallest box? _____

4. How many of the smallest boxes would fit into the largest box?

_____

Angles, Angles, Angles

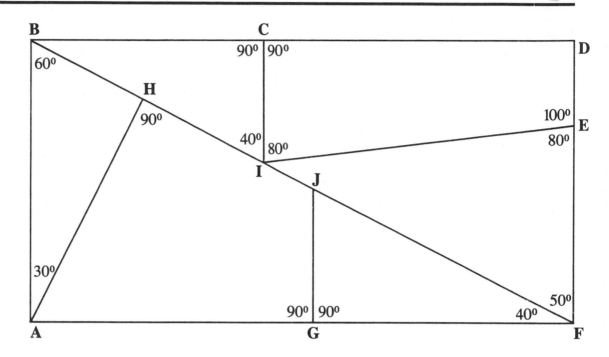

FACTS

The sum of the angles in a triangle is 180^0.
The sum of the angles in a quadrilateral is 360^0.

1. $< AHB$ = _____

2. $< CDE$ = _____

3. $< GJF$ = _____

4. $< EIF$ = _____

5. $< CBI$ = _____

6. $< HJG$ = _____

Right, Acute or Obtuse?

Find something in your family to do this activity with you.

The corners of this piece of paper are 90⁰ angles.
Use the corners to help you identify an angle as **acute, right,** or **obtuse.**

Look for angles in your neighborhood. Find five examples of acute, right, and obtuse angles.
Write the examples below.

REMEMBER

If an angle measures less than 90^0, it is called an **acute** angle.

If an angle measures 90^0, it is called a **right** angle.

If an angle measures more than 90^0, it is called an **obtuse** angle.

---

1. acute angles

2. right angles

3. obtuse angles

Diameter, Circumference and PI

In the figures below, line segment **d** is the **diameter** of the circle.
Line segment **C** is the **circumference.**

■ Measure the line segments to the nearest millimeter
and complete the table.

1.

d

C

2.
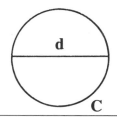
d

C

3.
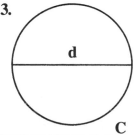
d

C

4.
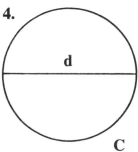
d

C

Circle	Circumference (C)	Diameter (d)	C÷d
1.			
2.			
3.			
4.			
		Average	

5. Find the average of the four quotients to the nearest hundredth and record this number in the table.

6. What is the difference between your average and ℸ (3.14)? _____

Division Dilemma

This is an activity for you and a friend.
Work together. Use $\pi = 3.14$.
Write the letter of the problem on the line above
the answer to solve the dilemma.

**How can you divide 6 potatoes among 10 people
so that each get the same amount?**

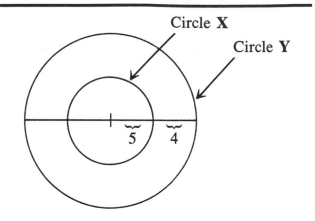

Circle **X**

Circle **Y**

5 4

A Diameter of circle **X**	**K** Circumference of circle X
T Radius of circle **Y**	**O** Area of circle X
M Diameter of circle **Y**	**S** Radius of circle X
P Area of circle **Y**	**D** Circumference of circle Y
H Difference between the circumferences of the circles	**E** Difference between the areas of the circles

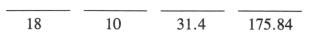

18	10	31.4	175.84

18	10	5	25.12	175.84	56.52

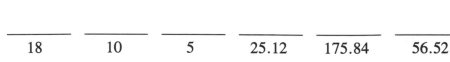

254.34	78.5	9	10	9	78.5	175.84	5

Circles

Bowling Time

The table shows the bowling scores of the Kramer family.

Bowling Scores				
	Week 1	**Week 2**	**Week 3**	**Week 4**
Mr. Kramer	120	110	125	135
Mrs. Kramer	140	102	128	130
Amy Kramer	70	67	70	73
Julio Kramer	90	90	98	100
Jed Kramer	90	85	102	77

1. What is the range of scores for Week 1? _____

2. What is Julio's mean score? _____

3. What is the mean score for Week 4? _____

4. What is the median score for Week 1? _____

5. What is Jed's mean score? _____

6. For which week is the mode 90? _____

7. Who has a mean score of 122.5? _____

8. For which week is the median score 102? _____

9. What is the range of scores for Week 3? _____

10. Which bowler has the greatest range of scores? _____

Measure Up

Find four people to do this activity with you.
Make all measurements to the nearest half-inch.

1. Measure the length of each person's foot.
   Write the lengths below.

   What is the mean length? _____

2. Measure the distance around each person's wrist.
   Write the measures below.

   What is the range of measures? _____

3. Measure the height of each person.
   Write the heights below.

   What is the median height? _____

Face To Face

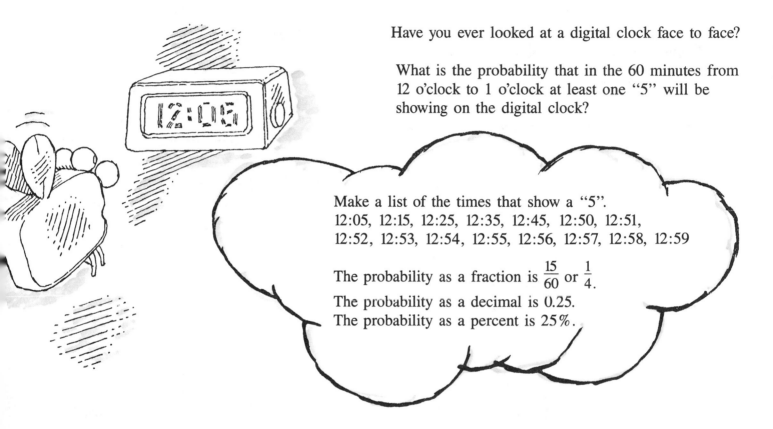

Have you ever looked at a digital clock face to face?

What is the probability that in the 60 minutes from 12 o'clock to 1 o'clock at least one "5" will be showing on the digital clock?

Make a list of the times that show a "5".
12:05, 12:15, 12:25, 12:35, 12:45, 12:50, 12:51, 12:52, 12:53, 12:54, 12:55, 12:56, 12:57, 12:58, 12:59

The probability as a fraction is $\frac{15}{60}$ or $\frac{1}{4}$.
The probability as a decimal is 0.25.
The probability as a percent is 25%.

For each situation about the digital clock, give the probability as a fraction, a decimal and a percent.

1. What is the probability that in the 60 minutes from 3 PM to 4 PM, at least one "6" will be showing? _____

2. What is the probability that in the 60 minutes from 8 AM to 9 AM at least one "2" will be showing? _____

3. What is the probability that in the 60 minutes from 10 AM to 11 AM, at least one "1" will be showing? _____

4. What is the probability that in the three hours from 9 AM to 12 PM at least one "3" will be showing? _____

5. What is the probability that in the five hours from 1 PM to 6 PM at least one "4" will be showing? _____

6. What is the probability that in the 12 hours from 7 AM to 7 PM at least one "2" will be showing? _____

Popular Words

In writing, the 12 words used most often, in order, are:
the, of, and, to, a, in, that, is, I, it, for, as.

Work with someone in your family.
- Choose a passage of 100 words from a novel.
- Make a tally each time you find one of these words.
- Record the total for each word.

1. Rank order the words by total from greatest to least used.

2. Does the order of your list match? _____

3. Which word occurred most often in your tally?

_____

4. What is the probability of that word being in any passage of 100 words?

_____

Novel

Word	Tally	Total
the		
of		
and		
to		
a		
in		
that		
is		
I		
it		
for		
as		

Choose another passage of 100 words.
Take the 100 words from your mathematics textbook.
Record your data in the table. Then rank order the
words from greatest to least by total.

5. Does the order of this list match the order of your

list from the novel? _____ If not, why do you think

that happened? _____

6. From this tally, what is the probability of the word "and"

being in any passage of 100 words? _____

Mathematics Textbook

Word	Tally	Total
the		
of		
and		
to		
a		
in		
that		
is		
I		
it		
for		
as		

The Vote Count

Thirty-four thousand votes were cast for mayor of the city of Handler. The circle graph shows the percentage of votes received by each candidate. Use the data in the graph to complete the table.

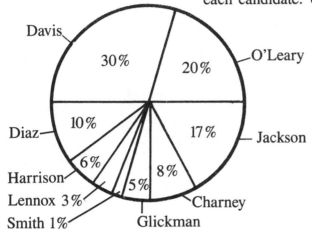

To find the number of votes, change the decimal to a percent, then multiply.

$30\% = 0.30$

$0.30 \times 34,000 = 10,200$

Candidate	Percent	Decimal	Number of Votes
1. Davis	30%	0.30	10,200
2. O'Leary			
3. Jackson			
4. Charney			
5. Glickman			
6. Smith			
7. Lennox			
8. Harrison			
9. Diaz			
Total			

Spend A Hundred

This is an activity for you and a member of your family.

Imagine that you have won a $100 gift certificate
at the Pro Sports Shop. You must spend all $100.
Decide how much money you would spend on each of the items.

The circle graph is separated in 20 sections. Each
section stands for $5. Label the sections for the items.
Then complete the table.

■ Record the number of dollars spent for each item.
■ Write this amount as a fraction of the $100.
■ Write the fraction as a percent.

Item	Number of Dollars	Fraction	Percent
1. T-shirts			
2. Shorts			
3. Bathing suits			
4. Beach towels			
5. Sunglasses			
Total			

■ On which item did you spend the most money? _____
■ If you had won a $1,000 certificate and had spent the same percentage of your money
  on that item, how many dollars would that be? _____

Circle Graphs

Making Generalizations

Look at this pattern. Assume that it continues.

MATHMATHMATHMATHMATHMATHMATHMATHMATH . . . . . .

1. What will be the 40th letter? _____

2. What will be the 99th letter? _____

3. What will be the 956th letter? _____

4. How many Ts will there be in the first 150 letters? _____

Now try this pattern.

GENERALIZEGENERALIZEGENERAL . . . . . .

5. What will be the 76th letter? _____

6. How many of the first 100 letters will be Ns? _____

7. How many vowels will there be in the first 240 letters? _____

8. How many letters are there before the 50th L? _____

Score 12

Ask someone in your family to play this game with you.

Rules:
- Start with a score of 0.
- Take turns.
- Add 1, 2, or 3 to the score.
- The first player to add a number that brings the score to 12 is the winner.

Play five games.
Describe the best way to play the game so that you will always be the winner.

Making Generalizations

Who's Who?

	Nurse	Painter	Decorator	Teacher
Mr. Williams	X			X
Mr. Conrad				
Mrs. Kennedy				
Mrs. Ming				

Mr. Williams, Mr. Conrad, Mrs. Kennedy and Mrs. Ming are neighbors. One is a nurse, one is a painter, one is a decorator, and one is a teacher.

■ Mr. Williams lives between the nurse and the teacher.

■ Mr. Conrad went to school with the painter and the decorator.

■ Mrs. Kennedy had the painter paint her house.

■ Mrs. Ming had lunch with the painter and the teacher.

■ Mr. Conrad and Mrs. Kennedy are not nurses.

What is the occupation of each person?

Use the table to help you organized the information.

Since Mr. Williams lives between the nurse and the teacher, Mr. Williams **cannot** have either of those occupations.

The Xs in the table show this fact.

Mr. Williams is a _____ .

Mr. Conrad is a _____ .

Mrs. Kennedy is a _____ .

Mrs. Ming is a _____ .

Farmer Jack's Problem

Here is a logic problem for you and your family.

Farmer Jack needs to get his fox, his goose, and his
large bag of corn across the river. But, his rowboat only
has enough room for Farmer Jack and either the fox, the
goose, **or** the corn. If Farmer Jack leaves the goose alone
with the corn, the goose will eat the corn. If Farmer Jack
leaves the fox alone with the goose, the fox will eat the goose.
How can Farmer Jack get the fox, the goose, and the corn
across the river?

Make a drawing to show what Farmer Jack takes
with him each time he rows back and forth across the river.

How many one-way trips across the river
does Farmer Jack make? _____

All Aboard

Train #	Rindon	Allentown	Boxford	Canton	Dexter	Eaton	Fairfield	Glennon
10	7:00AM	7:30	7:45	8:05	8:45	9:30	9:42	9:52
23	7:05AM	←		Express			→	9:22
42	8:12AM	8:42	8:57	9:17	9:57	10:42	10:54	11:04
77	8:27AM	8:57	9:12	9:32	10:12	10:57	11:09	11:19
81	9:10AM	9:40	9:55	10:15	10:55	11:40	11:52	12:02PM
84	9:30AM	10:00	10:15	10:35	11:15	12:00PM	12:12	12:22
95	10:05AM	10:35	10:50	11:10	11:50	12:35PM	12:47	12:57
99	10:40AM	11:10	11:25	11:45	12:25PM	1:10	1:22	1:32
106	11:17AM	11:47	12:02PM	12:22	1:02	1:47	1:59	2:09
118	11:58	12:28PM	12:43	1:03	1:43	2:28	2:40	2:50

Use the information in the train schedule to fill in the blanks.

1. "I Left Rindon after 8:30. The trip took 1 hour 45 minutes. I arrived at my destination before 11:30AM. The number of my train is not divisible by 21. I took train # _____ . My destination was _____ ."

2. "I left my hometown before 10AM. I arrived in Fairfield 1 hour 57 minutes later. The number of my train is a multiple of 7 but not a multiple of 6. My hometown is _____ . I took train # _____ ."

3. "I left my hometown after 11AM. My train made two stops before I reached my destination. I was on the train for 97 minutes. I arrived at my destination before 1:30PM. My hometown is _____ . I was not on train #95. I took train # _____ . My destination was _____ ."

4. "I left my hometown and rode the train for exactly two hours. When I arrived, I was about a half hour late for my noon meeting. My hometown is _____ . I took train # _____ . My destination was _____ ."

Setting The Schedule

This is an activity for you and someone in your family.
Make up a train schedule that fits the facts.
Record the time that each train leaves each city.

Facts:

Trains stop at all cities.
Time between cities is the same for all trains.
Lower number trains leave before higher number trains.
No trains leave any city at the same time.
Trains with numbers divisible by 2 leave Arnold between 8AM and 11AM.
Trains with numbers divisible by 3 leave Arnold at 5 minutes after the hour.
■ The time between Minot and Stanton is 15 minutes.
The time between Laramie and Stanton is 35 minutes.

Train #	Arnold	Calder	Elton	Jackson	Laramie	Minot	Stanton
11							
14							
24							
30							
32							
45							
61							
75							

1. How many minutes long is the train ride from Arnold to Stanton? _____
2. How many minutes long is the train ride from Calder to Minot? _____

More. . .
Number Rally

Ask someone to play this game with you.
Decide who will play first.
Take turns.

Rules:

- Pick a number from the number board.
- Score 1 point for each of the following that is true:

   The number is less than five hundred billion.
   The digit in the hundred millions place is less than 5.
   The digit in the hundreds place is greater than 2.
   The digit in the millions place is odd.
   The digit in the billions place is even.
   The digit in the hundred thousands place is greater than 6.

- Record the score and cross off the number.
- The player with the greater number of points after four rounds is the winner.

Number Board

163,345,098,072	818,836,792,845
331,459,172,783	956,721,245,996
413,296,356,154	605,925,837,432
202,234,478,299	704,643,782,647

Scoreboard

	Player 1		Player 2	
	Number	**Points**	**Number**	**Points**
1.				
2.				
3.				
4.				
	Total		**Total**	

Enrichment
Reading Grade 5

AMERICAN
EDUCATION
PUBLISHING

Rumble, Rumble

Read each sentence below.
Use the other words in the sentence to figure out the meaning of the underlined word.
Circle the choice you think gives the correct meaning.

1. If you keep <u>dallying</u>, you will miss the beginning of the movie.

   moving   dawdling   watching

2. The dog raised a <u>clamorous</u> alarm whenever anyone passed in front of the building.

   very loud   beautiful   like a clam

3. The scientist's camera followed the chipmunk into its <u>subterranean</u> den.

   underwater   overhead   undergound

4. The cars were only dented a little, but the drivers were having a loud <u>dispute</u> in the middle of the street.

   change   argument   party

5. The road traced a <u>serpentine</u> path down the side of the hill, winding back and forth many times.

   straight   extremely wide   snake-like

Write your choices from the sentences in order on the blanks in the story.

Rumble, Rumble

Lyndon was _____ over his cereal one

morning when he heard a _____ rumble.

It sounded like it was _____, like huge

stones having an _____. Then suddenly

a _____ crack opened up in the floor.

Read the completed story beginning to yourself.
What do you think happened next?
Finish the story on a separate sheet of paper.

Define It

Play this game with a friend or family member.
Make word cards for these made-up words.

| florigon | grantex | plutick | wringler | filldip | struge |

Put the cards face down.
Take turns.
Choose a card.
Read the word to yourself and decide what you want it to mean.
Then write a sentence using the word on your pad below.
Try to make the sentence show the meaning of the word, but be careful not to give away the meaning.
Have the other player read your sentence.
If the other player figures out the meaning of the word, score 5 points.
If the other player cannot figure out the meaning, score 2 points.
Record your score at the bottom of your pad.
Play until all six words have been used.
The player with the higher score is the winner.

What's a florigon?

Maybe it's a filldip with flowers on it!

Player 1 _____

1.

2.

3.

Score   1   2   3   TOTAL
☐ + ☐ + ☐ = ☐

Player 2 _____

1.

2.

3.

Score   1   2   3   TOTAL
☐ + ☐ + ☐ = ☐

2 What's the Sport?

Each sentence contains a word that needs a prefix.
Write a prefix on the blank so that the sentence makes sense.
Choose from the prefixes in the box.
You may use the prefixes more than once.

re	im	fore	mis	counter	pre	sub	un

1. The coach sat us down to discuss the _____ game strategy.

2. "Betty, last game your shoelaces came _____ done at a critical moment. Make sure they are tied."

3. "In the last game, the playing surface was _____ standard, and both teams suffered."

4. Then the coach began to _____ play the tape of the game.

5. Hollis groaned as she saw her _____ fortunes once again in living color.

6. The coach took out a piece of paper and _____ folded it.

7. "This new play is going to look _____ possible at first."

8. "Carla, you take three steps to the left and then _____ trace your steps after you turn around."

9. "Then, Hollis, you turn _____ clockwise and pass to Carla."

10. "Betty, you fake a trip and _____ gain your balance at the last moment."

11. Carla grinned. "Aha, I can _____ see what will happen next!"

Do you think the team is playing a real sport or some sort of

crazy mixed-up sport? _____

Name the sport. Make up a name if you need to. _____

Prefix Race

Ask someone to play this game with you.
Make two small paper markers to use on the racetrack.
Write each player's name on a marker.
Take turns. Flip a coin on each turn.
If the coin comes up heads, move forward two spaces.
If it comes up tails, move forward one space.
If you land on a word with a prefix, move forward two spaces.
If you land on a word without a prefix, move forward one space.
The winner is the first player to land on FINISH.

Heads = 2 spaces
Tails = 1 space

Prefix = 2 spaces
No prefix = 1 space

START

FINISH

predawn

untied

prepay

nonstop

payment

Passed gas stop. GO BACK 1 SPACE

Need to change tire. LOSE 1 TURN

nonetheless

GAS

disobey

restate

interstate

superhighway

misdeed

Fans cheer you on. TAKE EXTRA TURN

YEA! GO!

impossible

Sun in eyes. Slow down and LOSE 1 TURN.

remake

superior

submarine

physical

More speed needed. GO AHEAD 1 SPACE

missing

disappear

Pyramid Patterns

Read each word on the front of a pyramid.
If the word has a prefix, color the triangle red.
If the word has a suffix, color the triangle blue.
If the word has both a prefix and a suffix, color the triangle green.

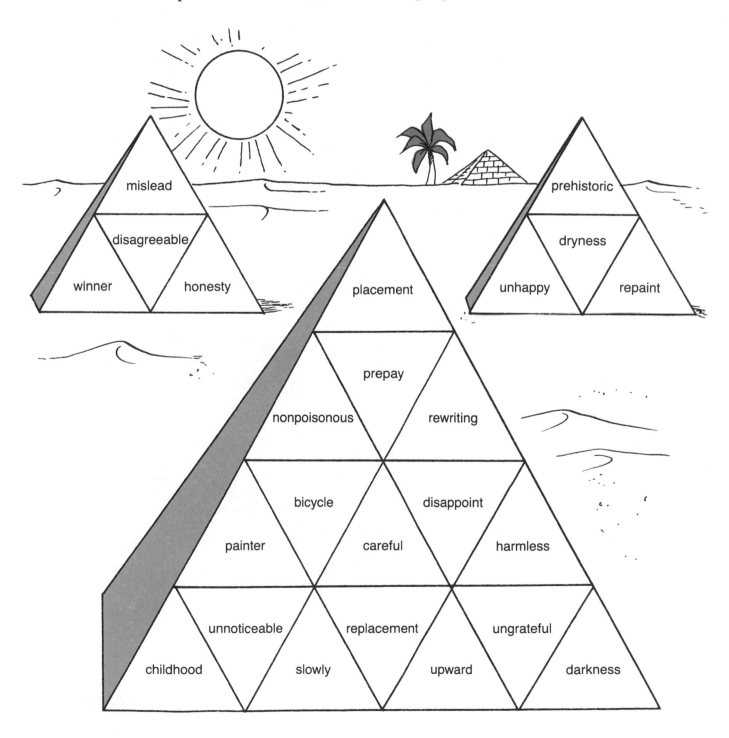

Identifying words with prefixes and suffixes **143**

Toss a Word

Here is a game for you to play with an adult.
Close your eyes and put a pencil point on the box on the left.
Do the same for the box on the right.
Then see if you can make a real word from the prefix or suffix and base word you pointed to.
If you can make a real word, write the word on your list.
If you cannot make a word, point to another prefix, suffix, or base word and try once more to make a real word.
Take turns and play eight rounds.
The winner is the player with more words after eight rounds.

Prefixes and Suffixes

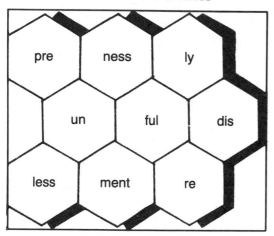

pre   ness   ly

un   ful   dis

less   ment   re

Base Words

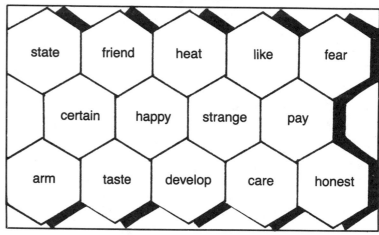

state   friend   heat   like   fear

certain   happy   strange   pay

arm   taste   develop   care   honest

Word Lists

Player 1 _____

Player 2 _____

Word Part Puzzle

Here are some word parts and their meanings.
The word parts can be used to make other words.

tele (distant)	graph (write)	auto (self)	scope (look)	photo (light)	micro (tiny)
port (carry)	scrib, scrip (write)	ology, logy (study)	phono, phone (sound)	bio (life)	

Read each clue below.
Answer with a word that contains one or
more of the word parts in the box.
Write the answer in the puzzle.

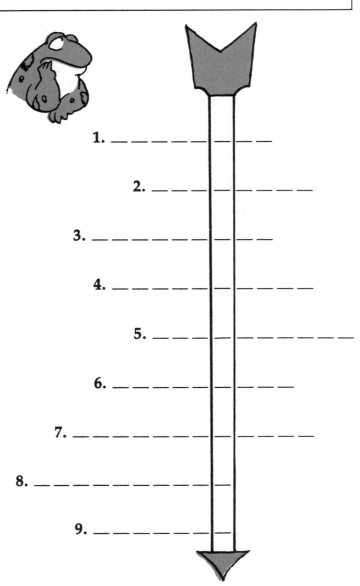

1. If something has a handle and you
   can carry it easily, it is _____.

2. If you do this, people may not be
   able to read what you write.

3. You can get a long-distance call on
   one of these.

4. You can play records on this, but not
   cassettes.

5. Some things are so tiny you need
   one of these to see them.

6. Something that operates all by itself
   is _____.

7. A doctor must write this before you
   can buy some kinds of medicine.

8. Without a camera, you cannot take
   one of these.

9. When you study plant and animal
   life, you study this subject.

1. _ _ _ _ _ _

2. _ _ _ _ _ _

3. _ _ _ _ _ _ _

4. _ _ _ _ _ _ _

5. _ _ _ _ _ _ _ _

6. _ _ _ _ _ _

7. _ _ _ _ _ _ _ _ _

8. _ _ _ _ _ _ _ _

9. _ _ _ _ _ _

Read down from the top box of the puzzle.
What do you call the story of a person's life? _____

Word Factory

Play this game with a friend.
Close your eyes and put a finger on the shelves of boxes.
Have your friend do the same.
Try to make a real word using the two word roots you pointed to.
You may add or take away a syllable to make the word.
If you cannot make a real word, make up your own word.
Write your words on the lists below.
Play until you have six real words and six made-up words.
Then make up meanings for your made-up words.
On separate paper, draw a picture to go with one of your
made-up words.

Maybe a **bibliophone** is a talking book.

aero (air)   audio (hear)   auto (self)   biblio (book)   graph graphy (write, draw)   micro (tiny)   mono (one)   ology logy (study)

phone phono (sound)   photo (light)   port (carry)   scope (look)   scrib scrip (write)   tele (distant)   tri (three)   vid (see)

Real Words	Made-up Words	Meanings

What Is Going On?

Can you figure out this cartoon?
Look at each panel and read what the character is saying.
Then mark the box next to what the character *really* means.

☐ This room is white and full of food.
☐ This room is very cold.

☐ I'm shivering from the cold.
☐ I've grown ears and a black nose.

☐ The furnace is worthless.
☐ The furnace came from the dump.

☐ I have to feed the hamster.
☐ I have a very small memory.

☐ I always liked the way you look.
☐ I need to fasten your clothes.

☐ Don't put paint on your face.
☐ Don't try to be funny.

Make It Colorful

This is a game for two players.
Make fifteen word cards like these.

red	heavy	big	strong	lazy
high	light	hungry	thin	deep
hot	quick	sad	happy	rough

Turn the cards face down.
Take turns.
Select a card and read the word on it to yourself.
Then think of a colorful comparison using the word.
Say your comparison aloud, but say "blank" instead of the word on the card.
If the other player guesses the word on your card, keep the card and score 2 points.
If the other player does not guess the word, return the card face down and lose 1 point.
Record your score on your score card.
Play until all the cards have been used.
The player with the higher score wins.

My hands are as blank as ice.

cold

Score Card

Player 1 _____

TOTAL _____

Score Card

Player 2 _____

TOTAL _____

Raining Cats and Dogs

An idiom is an expression that means something different than the words in it.
The story below is full of idioms.
Read the entire story first.
Then reread it and underline all the idioms you find.

It was raining cats and dogs as Kim and Tomi approached the old wooden house. "This is getting on my nerves," Tomi said.

"Don't be such a scaredy cat," teased Kim. "We're just going to collect paper route money from grumpy Mr. Hendon."

"I know, but just don't shoot off your mouth like last time," mumbled Tomi.

"Well, he really got my goat the way he teased about that hornet's nest on the porch," Kim responded. "Anyway, we're here now. Might as well face the music."

Kim and Tomi went up the steps and rang the doorbell. Nothing happened. "Are we on a wild goose chase?" asked Kim. She rang the bell two more times.

"Hold your horses," shouted a voice from inside. Then there was some loud stomping and rattling.

"Let's call it a day," said Tomi nervously.

"You're not going to chicken out now," said Kim, grabbing her brother's hand.

Finally, the door swung open. A tall wire-haired man stared down at them with darts in his eyes. "Here to rip me off? What are you up to?" he demanded.

"Uh, just collecting money for the Daily Blattle," said Tomi, his knees knocking together.

Mr. Hendon's face suddenly became sunny. "Ah! I thought you were some of those kids who have been giving me a hard time. They were horsing around on the porch roof, and one almost broke a leg when she fell. Scared the pants off me. Well, now, wait right here. I'll get your money in just two winks."

How many idioms did you find? _____

How did you do?   0–5   Try again.   11–15   Good reading!
                   6–10   Not bad.   16 or more   Super!

Now draw a picture for one of the idioms.
Show what the words usually mean, *not* what the idiom means.

Idiom Action

Here is a game to play with one or more friends.
Take turns.
Toss a coin onto the game board.
Read the idiom on which it lands.
If the coin is heads up, explain what the idiom means.
If the coin is tails up, act out the usual meanings of the words in the idiom.
If the idiom you land on has already been explained or acted out, take another turn.
Play until all the idioms have been explained or acted out.

You have a green thumb!

Keep a stiff upper lip.	You're off your rocker.	Get out of my hair.	Stop pulling my leg.
That's the way the cookie crumbles.	You hit the nail on the head.	You put your foot in your mouth.	We're in hot water.
You're making a mountain out of a molehill.	Drop me a line.	Keep this secret under your hat.	It's my turn to take the floor.
Lend me a hand.	We're all in the same boat.	I'll give them a piece of my mind.	Stop beating around the bush.

7 ▸ Crosswords

Read each clue.
Decide what word completes the sentence and fits in the
crossword puzzle.
Write the answer in the puzzle.

Across

2. *Hand* is to _____ as *foot* is to *toe*.

3. *Hot* is to _____ as *cold* is to *ice*.

4. *Easy* is to *simple* as _____ is to *difficult*.

6. *Cow* is to *milk* as *bee* is to _____.

7. *Bicycle* is to _____ as *car* is to *four*.

9. _____ is to *big* as *lowercase* is to *small*.

13. *Carve* is to *knife* as *write* is to _____.

14. *Woman* is to _____ as *man* is to *men*.

Down

1. *Fruit* is to *peach* as _____ is to *carrot*.

2. *Penny* is to *one* as *nickel* is to _____.

3. *Shell* is to _____ as *fur* is to *cat*.

5. *Pizza* is to *food* as _____ is to *toy*.

6. _____ is to *sad* as *up* is to *down*.

8. *Mississippi* is to *river* as *Atlantic* is to _____.

10. *Lead* is to *pencil* as _____ is to *pen*.

11. _____ is to *plane* as *water* is to *boat*.

12. *Year* is to *day* as *hour* is to _____.

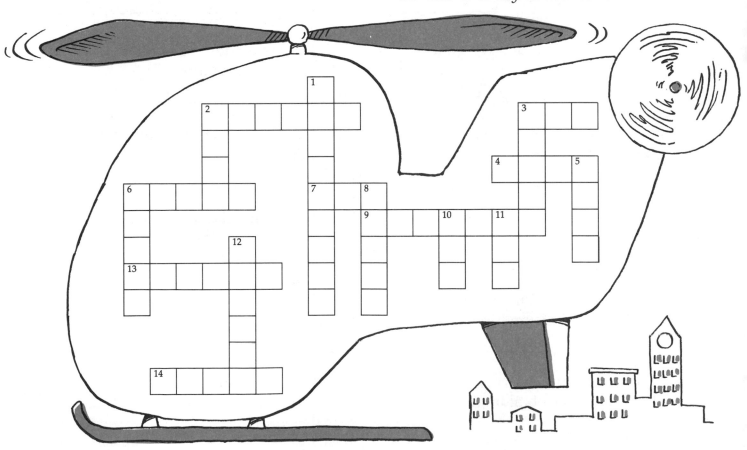

Bingo

Play this game with an adult.
Use strips of paper to make ten word cards like these.

lid	buttons	calf	new	trunk
swim	pounds	microphone	cooler	flying

Mix the cards and lay them out face down.
Take turns.
Choose a card and read the word on it to yourself.
If the word on the card answers a question on your bingo card,
tape the card over the question.
If you cannot use the card, turn it over and put it back with
the rest of the cards.
The first player to cover all five questions says "Bingo" and
wins the game.

My Bingo Card

B	If a young dog is a puppy, what is a young cow?
I	If a radiator is a heater, what is an air conditioner?
N	If shoes need laces, what do shirts need?
G	If milk is measured in quarts, what is meat measured in?
O	If an ancient building is old, what is a modern building?

_____'s Bingo Card

B	If cars are for driving, what are airplanes for?
I	If a person has a nose, what does an elephant have?
N	If a bottle has a top, what does a pot have?
G	If a bird can fly, what can a fish do?
O	If a microscope makes objects bigger, what makes sounds louder?

What's in the Book?

This is the contents page from a book about space flight.

Use the table of contents to answer each item below.
Mark the box in front of your choice.

1. What is the title of the chapter that begins on page 123?
   ☐ Engines and Thrusters ☐ Life Support Systems ☐ Emergencies: Mechanical

2. Chapter 9 probably explains that when hitting warp speed you should be
   ☐ attentive   ☐ carefree   ☐ fearful

3. What are the control groups for?
   ☐ repairing the engine ☐ navigating the ship ☐ viewing the stars

4. How does the book deal with major repairs?
   ☐ covers them in full ☐ does not cover them ☐ briefly covers them

5. Which part of the book is twelve pages long?
   ☐ Minor Repairs   ☐ Overview of Controls ☐ Introduction

6. Which topic would you *not* expect to find in Chapter 4?
   ☐ food and water   ☐ news broadcasts   ☐ oxygen masks

7. A book like this might be helpful when traveling to
   ☐ galaxies   ☐ museums   ☐ airports

What is the title of Chapter 10?
To find out, take the first letter of each of your choices.
Go in order from 1 to 7.
Write the title of Chapter 10 on the contents page.

Space Supplies

Ask a friend or family member to play this game with you.
Cut out fifteen pieces of paper the size of the boxes on the Question Board.
Place one piece of paper over each box.
Take turns.
Uncover one box on the Question Board.
If you think the question can be answered by looking up one of the topics listed in the index, keep the paper.
If the answer cannot be found by looking up one of the index topics, recover the box.
Play six rounds.
The winner is the player with more pieces of paper.

Index

Clothing, 125–210
  breathing masks, 201–210
  cooled, 176–200
  heated, 153–175
  indoor, 125–139
  spacesuits, 139–153
Lawn mowers, 59–79
  atomic, 66–72
  electric, 75–78
  gas, 65
  solar, 60–64

Life support systems, 100–110
  food, 106–110
  oxygen, 103–105
  water, 100–103
  see also Clothing
Payments, 95–99
  credit cards, 98
  interplanetary credit coupons, 97
Shipping, 81–94
  by spacecraft, 86
  by transport beam, 88–94

Question Board

Can I buy an air-cooled life support suit?	Do they sell seeds for space flowers?	Will they take my credit coupons as payment?	What can I buy to cut the grass outside my dome?	Do they sell electric space bikes?
Will they offer the Earth Monster pen for Halloween?	What can I buy to feed my family?	How may I pay for my order?	When is the next sale of spacesuits?	How much will 500,000 gallons of water cost?
Do they carry my favorite brand of peanut butter?	Will they take Glactic Express cards for payment?	What kinds of toys can I buy for my children?	Is it faster to ship by transport beam or spacecraft?	What styles of heated socks do they sell?

9 How Long Was It?

The article below is about dinosaurs.
As you read the article, underline the name of each dinosaur and the part that gives its length.

Dinosaurs varied in size. Some were no bigger than chickens. Others were as tall as trees. If humans had been around, they would have been no match for the larger dinosaurs.

Ornithomimus had a strange combination of features. It had a body like a lizard and a beak like a bird. It was about 12 feet long.

The triceratops had three horns on its face—two over its eyes and one over its nose. At 21 feet in length, triceratops was less than half the size of its sharp-toothed giant enemy, the 50-foot long tyrannosaurus rex. With those three horns, though, triceratops probably had a pretty good chance against the tyrannosaurus.

If the tyrannosaurus was impressively long, it was even more impressive when standing up. It could rear up 25 feet high on its two powerful hind legs. This is about as tall as a three-story building.

The ankylosaurus did not have horns like the triceratops or sharp teeth and claws like the tyrannosaurus. However, it did have protection. Just like a tank, it had heavy armor plates on its back. Ankylosaurus was only 15 feet long, but most enemies probably left it alone.

A giant that no other dinosaurs probably bothered was the plant-eating diplodocus. It was 98 feet long and so heavy that it most likely lived almost its entire life in water.

Now make a bar graph showing the information you underlined in the article.
Write the names of the dinosaurs on the lines at the left.
Then fill in the spaces next to each dinosaur to show how long it was.

LENGTHS OF DINOSAURS

Dinosaur

10   20   30   40   50   60   70   80   90   100
Length in feet

Ocean City

This game is for two or more players.
Look at the map of Ocean City, a small underwater village.
You must get from one side of the village to the other in order
to catch the next submarine home.
First, get some small items to use as markers.
Then make eight game cards like these.

SHARK ZONE

Go North	Go South	Go South	Go East	Go East	Go East	Go West

Put the cards in a bag or box and mix them up.
Take turns. Draw a card and move one box in the direction indicated.
If the road does not go in the direction stated on your card you
lose your turn.
If you get the Shark Zone card, go to the nearest Shark Zone and
follow the directions there.
After each turn, put your card back in the bag or box.
The first player to get to the sub port is the winner.

N

START HERE
Do not cross any heavy black lines.

BEACH
LOSE 1 TURN

NO CROSSING
RESTRICTED AREA

SHARK ZONE
Go play in the park (west end).

OCEAN CITY PARK

Village Fishing site

TROLLEY SERVICE

W

SHARK ZONE
PARK IN PARKING LOT

Enter Here

SUB

E

PORT

PARKING LOT

S

10 ▶ Look Around

Read the guide words on the dictionary pages below.
Then look around your classroom or home for objects whose
names come between the guide words on each page.
On each dictionary page, write the names of three objects you find.
When your pages are complete, number each list of words in
alphabetical order.

babble	buzz
___ _____	
___ _____	
___ _____	

magic	myself
___ _____	
___ _____	
___ _____	

cabin	cycle
___ _____	
___ _____	
___ _____	

pea	puzzle
___ _____	
___ _____	
___ _____	

dairy	dwarf
___ _____	
___ _____	
___ _____	

scar	sword
___ _____	
___ _____	
___ _____	

feast	future
___ _____	
___ _____	
___ _____	

tack	truth
___ _____	
___ _____	
___ _____	

Find It, Use It

Do this activity with an adult.
Make six word cards and three number cards like these.

| 1 | | 2 |

| check | dull | entry | grade | hand | short |

| 3 |

Separate the number cards from the word cards and turn each
group face down.
Choose a word card and a number card.
Find the word on your card among the dictionary entries below.
Then find the definition with the same number as your card.
Make up a sentence using that definition of the word.
Write your sentence on a line in your sentence box.
Return each card face down to its group and mix each group.
Take four turns each.

check (chek), *v.* **1** to examine or search through. *n.*
2 mark made to show that something is true or
correct. **3** written order to a bank to pay money.

dull (dul), *adj.* **1** not sharp or pointed. **2** not exciting
or interesting; boring. **3** not clear or bright.

entry (en'trē), *n.* **1** act of entering. **2** passage or
place by which to enter. **3** item recorded in a list
or book.

grade (grād), *n.* **1** class or level in school. **2** degree
or level of quality or value. **3** number or letter
showing how well one has done; mark.

hand (hand), *n.* **1** end part of the arm below the
wrist. **2** assistance or help. **3** hired worker skilled
at a certain kind or work.

short (shôrt), *adj.* **1** not tall or long. **2** not lasting a
long time. *adv.* **3** in a short manner; abruptly.

❧ **My Sentences** ❧

1. _____
2. _____
3. _____
4. _____

_____'s Sentences

1. _____
2. _____
3. _____
4. _____

11 ▶ The Big Idea

Read the passage below.
For each paragraph, underline the sentence that tells the main idea.

Sometimes people think they have to choose between exercise and fun. For many people, it is more fun to watch television than to run five miles. Yet if you don't exercise, your body gets soft and out of shape. You move more slowly. You may even think more slowly. But why do something that isn't fun? Well, there are ways to exercise *and* have fun.

One family solved the exercise problem by using their TV. They hooked up the television to an electric generator. The generator was operated by an exercise bike. Anyone who wanted to watch TV had to ride the bike. The room with their television must have been quite a sight!

Think of the times you are just spending time with your friends. You get outside and jump rope, play ball, run races, whatever. Soon you are all laughing and having a good time. Many group activities can provide you with exercise and be fun, too.

Maybe there aren't enough kids around after school for group games. Perhaps you are by yourself. Then what? You can get plenty of exercise just by walking, biking, or even dancing. In the morning, walk the long way to the bus. Ride your bike to and from school. Practice the newest dance by yourself. Before you know it, you will be the fittest dancer of all your friends!

What ways can you think of to combine fun and exercise?
Write your ideas here.

_____

_____

_____

_____

_____

_____

Making Headlines

This is an activity for you to do with a friend.
Cut out two short articles, or the first few paragraphs of long articles, from a newspaper or magazine.
Cut off the headlines.
Have your friend do the same.
Tape your articles in the spaces below.
Then read each other's articles.
Write a headline for each article on the line at the top.
The headline should tell the main idea of the article.

My Articles

My Friend's Articles

(headline)

(headline)

(headline)

(headline)

12 > Games for the '90s

Here is a chart of ratings for some new computer games.

COMPUTER GAMES FOR THE 1990s

Title	Type	Memory	Rating
Eat the Dust	Arcade	128 K	++
Fantastica	Adventure	512 K	++
Froddy's Castle	Adventure	320 K	+++
Hockey One-on-One	Sport/Skill	128 K	++
Icicle Breath	Adventure	640 K	◆
Mouse Mountain	Adventure	320 K	$+\frac{1}{2}$
Mouse Race	Maze	128 K	+
Pickle Puss	Maze	384 K	++++
Snake in the Grass	Adventure	320 K	$+++\frac{1}{2}$
Space Defenders	Arcade	512 K	+++
Star Orbits	Arcade	320 K	$++\frac{1}{2}$
Super Oaf	Maze	256 K	++++
Wheels 'n Deals	Sport/Skill	384 K	++

Note Memory requirements in Kilobytes (1024 characters).
Example A 256 K machine will run any program rated at 256 K or less.
Key to Ratings ++++ Stupendous ++ Worth a look ◆ Don't bother
++++ Great + Passable

Use the chart to answer the following questions.

1. What is the top-rated adventure game? _____

2. Which type of game is listed least often? _____

3. Which adventure game would you probably *not* buy if you have

   a 320 K machine? _____

4. How many games are rated "worth a look"? _____

5. How much memory must your machine have to run the two

   top-rated games? _____

6. Which arcade game has the lowest rating? _____

7. If your machine does not have 640 K of memory, why would you

   probably not be disappointed? _____

Choose one of the games listed on the chart.
On separate paper, draw a picture of what you think one or two
screens of the game might look like.
Share your picture with your classmates.

What's Important?

Work with a member of your family.
Sit across from each other with this page between you.
The two passages on the page are identical, so you both can
read the passage at the same time.
Say "go" and start reading the passage.
As you read, underline words or phrases that are important for
answering the question at the beginning of the passage.
When you are finished, compare your answers.
Did you underline the same things?
If not, explain your answers to each other.

What are three things that can affect the sound of a guitar?

A guitar has four basic parts—the body, neck, strings, and screws
that tighten the strings.

The neck and body are made from special woods. The neck must be
strong enough to hold up against the pull of the strings. The body
must be the right shape to give the guitar its special sound. The kind
of wood in the body is also important to the sound.

The strings can be made of nylon, steel wire, or wire wound with
more wire. The thicker strings give the low notes a louder sound. The
thinner strings can move rapidly for the high notes. But the quality of
the sound depends on the material used to make the strings. An all
nylon-string guitar has a mellower tone than a steel-string guitar.

nylon-string guitar has a mellower tone than a steel-string guitar.
the sound depends on the material used to make the strings. An all
thinner strings can move rapidly for the high notes. But the quality of
more wire. The thicker strings give the low notes a louder sound. The
The strings can be made of nylon, steel wire, or wire wound with
of wood in the body is also important to the sound.
must be the right shape to give the guitar its special sound. The kind
strong enough to hold up against the pull of the strings. The body
The neck and body are made from special woods. The neck must be
that tighten the strings.
A guitar has four basic parts—the body, neck, strings, and screws

What are three things that can affect the sound of a guitar?

13 ▶ SQ3R

S You can try the SQ3R method for yourself.
Start with the passage below.
Skim it quickly to get a general idea of what it is about.
Then write a question you think might be answered in the passage.

Q Question: _____

_____

R Now read the passage carefully.
Look for an answer to your question.

Transportation has changed greatly since the founding of our country. At first, of course, the main means of transportation was on foot or by horseback. By the early 1800s, a network of canals crisscrossed the northern states, providing a way to move large amounts of goods around. The railway system took over then, and by 1900 there was a web of rail connections among most cities. With the coming of the automobile and truck, roads became more important, and the rail system almost died. Today, air travel is also important. While shipping by air is too expensive for very heavy items, it has become valuable for sending mail and smaller packages.

Did you find an answer to your question?
Great! Write your answer here.

R Answer: _____

_____

R Your answer is like the Recite part of SQ3R.
The Review part comes when you reread your questions and answers just before a test.

Notable Events

Ask an adult to help you with this activity.
Have the adult choose a passage for you from a newspaper article, magazine article, or one of your schoolbooks.
Then use the SQ3R method for taking notes.
The questions on the note card below will guide you.
Make your answers as clear as you can.
If you know another method, you may use it instead of SQ3R.

Skim the passage. What question or questions do you have?

Read the passage. What answers did you discover?

What other things did you find interesting in the passage?

Now, using just your notes, tell your adult about what you read.
When you study on your own, you can do this Recite step by yourself or with a friend or family member.
If you were to be tested on the information in the passage, your notes would help you with the Review step.

What Was That?

Read this story beginning.

Ella stared out the window. She felt just miserable as the snow continued to pile up outside. It had been snowing for three days straight, and the radio was full of stories about blocked roads, abandoned cars, and downed power lines.

Ella was stranded. There was no school, of course. Mom was trapped in another city, waiting for the weather to clear. Dad kept offering to play games with her, but they had played everything they could think of at least five times. The TV wasn't working, and she couldn't get out to the library to borrow some new books.

Ella let out a deep sigh. As she headed past the window for the kitchen, something caught her eye. A gray form was moving outside. She pressed her face against the window, but only managed to steam it up. She wiped the steam away. What *was* that thing? It was snowing so hard now that she could barely see the trees on the other side of the street.

Suddenly the gray thing came clearly into view. Ella stood up and shouted, "Dad, I'm going out right now!"

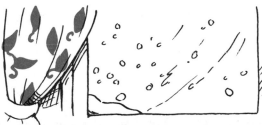

What did Ella see outside the window?
Think of two things Ella might have seen and write them below.
Then write two different endings for the story.
Base each ending on what you said Ella saw.
If you need more room to write, use a separate sheet of paper.

1. Ella saw _____

Ending: _____

_____

_____

2. Ella saw _____

Ending: _____

_____

_____

Round Robin

Do this activity with one or more friends.
Read the story beginnings below.
Choose the one you like best and circle it.
Read your choice aloud.
Then take turns adding sentences to the story.
Keep passing the story around until you agree to end it.
Each person may have several turns.
Continue on separate paper if you need more room to write.
Read the story aloud when you are finished.

The elephant called a meeting of all the animals in the jungle. They had to decide which of them would be the first to talk to this man who thought he was a lion.

Suddenly everything was quiet. Marta held her breath and listened. No sounds came from the rest of the building. All she could hear was the thump, thump, thump of her pounding heart.

The fire-breathing dragon quickly devoured its prey. Then it lumbered forward, turning everything it encountered into an orange ball of fire.

"Follow me," cried Rudy, "we'll head for the cave over there." They rushed forward toward the small opening at the base of the near-by mountain.

The Long and Short of It

Have you ever heard a young child tell a favorite story?
Sometimes the summary is almost as long as the story!
Here is a summary of an old fable.
It is much too long and wordy.
It includes things that are not part of the story.
Read the summary. Then write a better one.
Try to use no more than eight sentences.

Once there were these two characters, and they were the North Wind and the Sun. They were having this argument, see, about which one was stronger. I mean, can you imagine the sun and the wind actually talking to each other? Anyway, they saw this man walking along. He was wearing a big overcoat because it was a kind of cold day. So the Sun said to the Wind—that's the North Wind—the Sun said, "I bet I can make the man take off his coat." Well, the North Wind said, "Oh yeah? I bet I can do it faster." So the Sun said something like, "Be my guest." That means the Sun let the North Wind go first.

So the North Wind got to work blowing cold air down the man's neck. Just like in Chicago, which is supposed to be a really windy city. Anyway, the man just pulled the coat tighter around him, see, and so the Wind blew harder. I mean, that Wind was reeeally blowing! And you know what the man did? Yeah, he just pulled that old coat around him tighter. Pretty soon the North Wind was out of breath. Then the Sun came out, shining so that it got really hot. In about two seconds the man was sweating, wiping his face, and everything. In about three seconds flat the coat was off!

_____

_____

_____

_____

_____

_____

_____

Comic Order

Here is a game activity for you and a friend.
Cut out a favorite comic strip from a newspaper and cut apart the panels.
Have your friend do the same.
Give each other one panel from your comic strip.
Put the rest of the panels from both strips in a bag and mix them up.
Take turns choosing a panel from the bag.
If it goes with the panel or panels you already have, keep it.
If you cannot use the panel, put it back in the bag.
When all the panels have been used, arrange the panels of your comic strip in order.
Then choose one of the completed comic strips and paste it below.
On the lines at the bottom of the page, write a summary of what happened in the strip.

16 ▶ Figure It Out

What can you figure out from each short passage below?
Circle the letter of the conclusion you think is best.
When you are finished, compare your answers with your classmates.
Discuss why you chose each answer.

1. Phillip sank back into his seat, relieved. Dust from the
   exploded meteor swirled past the windows. "That was
   a close call!" he thought.
   a. Phillip is a taxi cab driver.
   b. Phillip is a window washer.
   c. Phillip is a space pilot.

2. The lump under the covers started to move. When it reached
   the end of the bed, a streak of fur raced out and darted
   across the room.
   a. A lumpy bed had come to life and moved around the room.
   b. Someone had made up the bed with a cat inside.
   c. A cat had run into the room and was hiding under the bed.

3. Stella pedaled steadily for the first several laps. She coasted
   when going downhill. Then, as she approached the finish line,
   she gathered all her energy and pumped as hard as she could.
   a. Stella is swimming in a pool.
   b. Stella is lifting weights.
   c. Stella is riding in a bicycle race.

4. "I want to see how quickly you respond," Pedro said to Dana.
   He held the ruler so that the bottom was just between Dana's
   fingers. Then he let go and Dana caught the ruler. "Three
   inches," Pedro said.
   a. Pedro was doing an experiment.
   b. Pedro was measuring Dana's fingers.
   c. Pedro was making rulers.

5. Uri's eyelids began to flutter and droop. He could still hear
   the construction equipment making a racket next door. "Not
   a wink all night. When are they going to stop?" he asked.
   a. Uri had stayed up all night working next door.
   b. Uri had been kept up all night by noisy construction.
   c. Uri was on a construction crew that worked at night.

Ladder Climb

Play this game with a family member or friend.
Use long narrow strips of paper to make eight conclusion cards
like these.

Cars are racing.	Someone is playing ball.	A bear woke up.	Nora is playing tag.
A cat woke up.	Nora is lost.	Runners are racing.	Someone is sneaking up.

Turn the conclusion cards face down.
Take turns.
Turn over a card and read it to yourself.
If the conclusion on the card goes with a sentence on your ladder,
tape the card below the sentence.
If you cannot use the card, turn it back over.
The winner is the first player to complete a ladder.

Player 1 _____

The animal opened its sleepy eyes
after its long winter nap.

Nora ducked from tree to tree as she
laughingly said, "You can't catch me!"

We could hear the racers breathing
hard as they swept past us.

Angelo heard the loud crack of a stick
behind him and turned around, terrified.

Player 2 _____

The animal opened its eyes, stretched,
and then looked for a bowl of milk.

When the trees all began to look alike
to Nora, she started to get scared.

We could hear the roaring whine of the
engines as the racers whizzed by us.

When Angelo heard the crack of the bat,
he faded back into deep right field.

17 ▶ Fable Maze

In each pair of sentences below, one sentence tells a cause and
the other sentence tells the effect.
Mark each sentence **C** for *cause* or **E** for *effect*.

1. ____ The fox leaped into the air with
   its jaws open.
   ____ A bunch of juicy grapes hung high
   up, just out of reach.

2. ____ The lion was trapped in the net,
   unable to move.
   ____ The hunters dropped their net on
   the mighty lion.

3. ____ The moon was always changing
   from thin to full and round.
   ____ The moon's mother could not
   make a gown to fit her.

4. ____ During the race, the hare went
   to sleep under a tree.
   ____ The hare lost the race to the
   tortoise.

5. ____ The fox made the crow want to
   prove it had a lovely voice.
   ____ The crow opened its mouth to
   sing and dropped the cheese.

6. ____ When the weather turned cold,
   the man was freezing.
   ____ The man sold his coat to the
   first person he met on the road.

Now complete the maze.
Begin at START and look at the first pair of sentences.
If the first sentence is the cause, follow the green arrow.
If the first sentence is the effect, follow the black arrow.
Each time you come to a star, use the next pair of sentences to
find out which way to go.

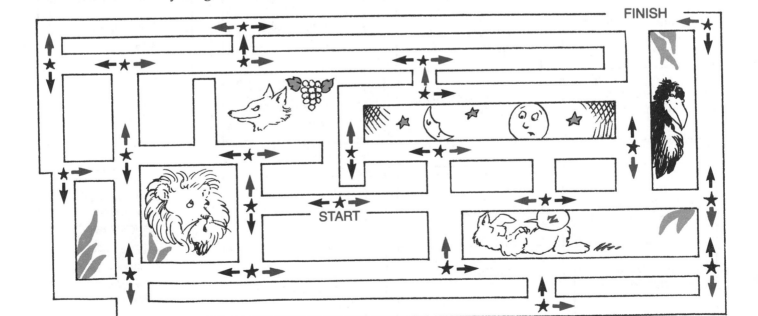

Dominoes

This is a game for you and another player.
Get a watch or clock for keeping time.
Have the other player say "Go" and keep time for two minutes.
Toss a paper clip onto the dominoes.
Find another domino with a cause or an effect that goes with one of the sentences on your first domino.
Put a paper clip on this new domino.
Then find another domino with a cause or an effect that goes with a sentence on the second domino.
Put another paper clip on this new domino.
Keep matching dominoes until the timekeeper says "Stop."
Count your paper clips and take them off the dominoes.
Then let the other player have a turn while you keep time.
The player with more paper clips wins the game.

He dropped the glass.	The fire department came.	She forgot to put film in the camera.	She overslept in the morning.
The forest had been dry for months.	He left his knapsack on the bus.	There was a loud thunderclap.	She was excited about her new camera.

She was late to work.	None of the pictures came out.	A fire broke out.	His knapsack was stolen.
He used too much soap.	She stayed up too late.	They jumped at the sudden noise.	The glass shattered.

He banged on the drums.	He went to the police.	She left the lens cap on the camera.	There was an accident on the freeway.
She called the fire department.	His hands were slippery.	She got stuck in a traffic jam.	Smoke was billowing out of the windows.

18 ▶ Character Words

Read each paragraph below.
Notice what the character says, thinks, feels, and does.
Then look at the words in the middle of the page.
Draw a line from the paragraph to each word that describes
the character.
You may use some words more than once.

Rachel bounded into the room and began shouting. "Guess what everbody! I made the volleyball team! Coach said I'm a natural. She said I have great promise." By now, Rachel had shrugged off her coat, which landed on the floor. She had tossed her books onto the kitchen table, and they had scattered in every direction. "I hope I can do it," thought Rachel. "Everybody thinks I'm such a great player. I hope I don't let them down."

Mel had never been so scared in his life. He stared at the rattlesnake just a foot or so from his left boot. "Freeze, don't move," he kept thinking to himself. "You know what to do. Do nothing. Stay calm. It's only another frightened creature like me," he told himself. The rattler, unable to see Mel unless he moved, finally slithered away. Back at camp, someone asked Mel what he had been doing. "Oh, nothing," Mel said with a smile.

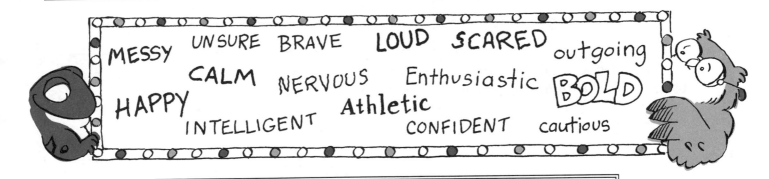

MESSY   UNSURE   BRAVE   LOUD   SCARED   outgoing
CALM   NERVOUS   Enthusiastic   BOLD
HAPPY   INTELLIGENT   Athletic   CONFIDENT   cautious

Lydia really wasn't too sure she was doing the right thing, but anything was worth a try. "Besides," she thought to herself, "I've got a feeling this is going to work out." She held the package tightly, as if it might get away. Finally, the secretary showed her in. At last! She was entering the office of the president of the largest toy company in the world! She looked the president in the eye and said confidently, "I've invented a toy you will just love. It will turn out to be the toy of the century, I'm sure!"

What a Character!

Ask an adult to do this activity with you.

Here are some qualities a character in a story might have.

funny   sloppy   smart   lazy   cheerful   shy   neat   proud

brave   mean   nervous   silly   outgoing   kind   sad   afraid

Write each word on a small card.

Put the cards in a bag and mix them up.

Draw out four cards. Have your adult do the same.

Do not show your cards to each other.

Now work together to create a make-believe character.

Decide whether the character is to be a person, an animal, an object, or an imaginary being.

Think of a name for your character and write it on the line provided.

Then take turns following the directions.

Choose the left side or right side of the page for your answers.

You may end up writing opposite things about your character.

That's OK. An interesting character often has opposite qualities.

Our character's name is _____.

1. Choose one of your word cards. Write a sentence telling what the character **does** because of the quality on the card.

   _____   _____

   _____   _____

2. Choose another one of your cards. Write a sentence telling what the character **thinks** because of the quality on the card.

   _____   _____

   _____   _____

3. Choose another one of your cards. Write a sentence telling what the character **says** because of the quality on the card.

   _____   _____

   _____   _____

4. Use your last card. Write a sentence telling what the character **feels** because of the quality on the card.

   _____   _____

   _____   _____

19 ▶ Who's Telling?

Read each paragraph below.
Decide who is telling the story.

A A character who is in the story.
B A narrator who is not a character in the story.
C A narrator who is also a character, referred to by the word *I*.

Write **A**, **B**, or **C** in front of each paragraph to show who is telling the story.

1. ____ Nancy and Lonnie had not spoken to each other in months. Things had started out innocently enough. Lonnie had teased Nancy about her red hair. She seemed to go along with it for a few days. But then Lonnie found his locker filled with shaving cream. That's when they had this big fight.

2. ____ What could that be crawling along the floor? Kane squinted. Nuts! He had forgotten his glasses this morning. Kane squinted harder, as if by muscle power he could see better. He was startled by a tap on his shoulder. "Kane," said the science teacher. "Where is the mouse you were studying?"

3. ____ The space freighter was hardly gleaming and new. The carpet on the inside was soiled and torn in places. Someone had spilled juice on the computer, and the keys on the keyboard stuck at times. The whole ship smelled funny. "Another pile of junk to pilot," I thought as I signed the work order.

4. ____ The quarrel had to stop. At recess I wandered out into the schoolyard. There was Nancy, talking to some friends. And there was Lonnie, sitting on a bench eating an apple. It was now or never. I caught Lonnie's eye and motioned for him to come over.

5. ____ Free at last! The little creature scooted along the floor over by the wall, hoping the Big Thing that had yanked its tail would not notice. It seemed to be trying to make it to the door. It stopped for a moment, wiggling its whiskers and testing the air for danger.

Which paragraphs could be from the same story?
Write the numbers of the paragraphs that go together.   ____ and ____   ____ and ____

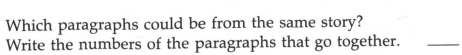

Change It Around

Work with a friend on this activity.

Choose a story with which you are both familiar.

You might choose a movie, TV show, book, fairy tale, or one of the suggestions below.

Talk about how the story was told and who told it.

Then choose a character in the story to retell it in a different way. Here are some examples.

- Have Baby Bear or the porridge tell the story "Goldilocks and the Three Bears."
- Have the hare or the tortoise tell the fable "The Hare and the Tortoise."
- Have one of Columbus's ships tell about the voyage across the ocean.
- Have Paul Revere's horse tell about their midnight ride.

Now work together to develop your story.

Decide how it will be different from the original story.

Then write your story below.

Continue on a separate sheet of paper if you need more room.

When you are finished, read your story aloud.

Take your story to school tomorrow and share it with your classmates.

Title: _____

_____

_____

_____

_____

_____

_____

_____

_____

_____

20 ▷ Picture This

Words can be used to create images, or pictures, in your mind.
Read each pair of descriptions below.
Mark the box at the beginning of the description that creates a
richer and more colorful image in your mind.

☐ It was a cute little dog, but it looked unhappy. It was breathing rapidly, and its tongue was hanging out. As it stared up at me, I wondered if it was asking me to take it home.

☐ The puppy was no bigger than a football. Its eager panting and wagging little tail might have made it look happy. But the sad brown eyes were saying, "I'm lonely. Please take me home."

☐ Dale never knew the wind could shriek like that. The high-pitched whine was like a haunting howl of protest and pain. Trees bent before this shrieking wind, not so much from its force but from its sound.

☐ Dale noticed that the wind was blowing loudly, making an unpleasant sound. It made the trees bend over as it blew. It was almost as if the sound—a kind of high shriek—was the source of the wind's power.

☐ Inside the computer, on a green-colored card, was a web of gold and silver wires. Small black boxes cropped up here and there, along with other things that looked like tiny colored tin cans.

☐ Deep in the inner part of the machine was a jeweled City of Knowledge. On a bright green card, tiny silver and gold highways traveled between cities of square black buildings and brilliant lights.

Choose the description you like best.
In the space below, draw a picture of the image it created
in your mind.

Images, Images

Here is an activity for you and a friend or family member.
Find two pictures that can be cut from a colorful magazine.
The pictures should show the same general thing, such as cars,
people, animals, buildings, or food.
Have your friend or family member do the same.
Then cut out an interesting 2-inch square section from each picture.
Choose one of your picture sections.
Do not tell each other which one you have chosen.
Now write about your picture on the lines below.
Try not to tell just what the picture shows.
Instead, describe the image the picture creates in your mind.

My Picture

_____

_____

_____

_____

_____

_____

_____'s Picture

_____

_____

_____

_____

_____

_____

Now show each other your pictures.
See if you can pick out the one described above.
After you identify each other's picture, tape or paste it in the box
next to its description.

21 ▶ What's Wrong?

Look at each picture below.
Decide what is wrong with the picture.
Write your answer next to the picture.
Then explain what led you to your answer.
When you are finished, compare your answers
with your classmates.

What is wrong: _____

_____

Explanation: _____

_____

What is wrong: _____

_____

Explanation: _____

_____

What is wrong: _____

_____

Explanation: _____

_____

What is wrong: _____

_____

Explanation: _____

_____

What is wrong: _____

_____

Explanation: _____

_____

Topic Recall

Here is a game for two players.
Get a watch or clock for keeping time.
Then look over the topics in the Topic Box.
Write your own topics in the two empty spaces.
Now close your eyes and put a pencil point on the Topic Box.
If you land on a topic that has already been used, point again.
Then start giving facts about the topic or related to the topic.
Have the other player keep time for one minute and count the facts.
Score 1 point for each fact.
Take turns and play five rounds. Keep score below.
The winner is the player with more facts.

These are the facts...

Topic Box

sports stars	explorers	sea creatures	Africa	baseball	wild animals
rivers	astronomy	cooking	computers		insects
birds	flowers	presidents	farm animals	dinosaurs	stars
your state		football	automobiles	pets	money
Asia	music	zoo animals	toys	boats	inventors

Fact Score Sheet	
Player 1	**Player 2**
Round 1	Round 1
Round 2	Round 2
Round 3	Round 3
Round 4	Round 4
Round 5	Round 5
TOTAL FACTS	TOTAL FACTS

22 ▸ Is That a Fact?

A fact is something that can be counted, checked, or tested.
An opinion is what someone thinks or feels about something.
An opinion cannot be counted, checked, or tested.
Here is a Fact-o-Meter machine that separates facts from opinions.
To operate it, just read the restaurant review below.
Write the number of each fact sentence in the Fact Bin.
Write the number of each opinion sentence in the Opinion Bin.
Then add the numbers in each bin.
If the totals are the same, you operated the machine correctly.

1 Fast Food Restaurant Opens in Hagrin Falls

2 I just attended the grand opening of the fifth Chicken Dog restaurant in the Flaptown area. 3 Why these restaurants are so popular is a total mystery to me. 4 Yes, the chicken dog has less fat than a beef or pork dog. 5 And yes, the restaurants are kept so clean that you'd wish they would clean your home. 6 In fact, the Flaptown chain just received a cleanliness award from the Clean Kitchens Association of America.

7 I did try one of the plain grilled chicken dogs without the extras. 8 It was a pretty good dog, and it tasted quite a bit like its beef and pork cousins. 9 However, this plain chicken dog cost $3.25! 10 And the dogs with extras like sauerkraut, cheese, onions, and chili, cost much more. 11 I think the price of the special "Humunga-dog with Everything But the Kitchen Sink" is outrageous. 12 I'm sure you'll agree that seven dollars for a grilled dog, even with all the extras, is pure highway

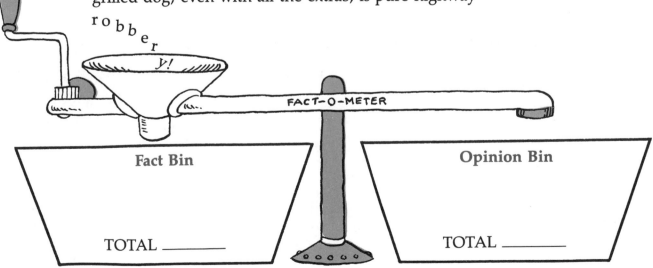

r o b b e r y!

FACT-O-METER

Fact Bin   Opinion Bin

TOTAL _____   TOTAL _____

Scrambled Sentences

Play this game with an adult.
Take turns unscrambling the sentences below.
On each turn, choose a sentence and put a √ in the box.
Then work on separate paper to unscramble the sentence.
Score 2 points if you unscramble the sentence by yourself.
Score 1 point if the other player has to help you.
There is more than one way to unscramble some of the sentences.
As long as your sentence makes sense, it's OK.
Once a sentence is unscrambled, read it aloud.
Then tell whether it states a fact or an opinion.
If both players agree your answer is correct, score 1 more point.
Play until all the sentences have been checked and unscrambled.
The player with the higher score wins the game.

☐ Holland beautiful are tulips everyone in thinks flowers

☐ stories told since vampires about times the have been earliest

☐ Mr. Hank's thousands the computer company saved of dollars

☐ juice better in tastes nothing the orange than morning

☐ happy always is a birthday a occasion

☐ Paris, France are cities in the named there eight United States after

☐ has in movies Ruby Duke in years two starred last the three

☐ a a dog is a trouble of to take than cat care lot more

☐ fly miles can golden a up 100 to eagle per hour

☐ with pizza than better peppers mushroom is pizza

☐ Florida is in place best winter the spend to a vacation

☐ sergeant Army the a Molly Pitcher in was Continental

☐ useful household is tape most the cellophane product

☐ the cat free store offered food opening pet its at grand

My Score

Turn							
1	2	3	4	5	6	7	TOTAL

_____'s Score

Turn							
1	2	3	4	5	6	7	TOTAL

23 ▶ Toasty Toes

An author writes with a purpose.
An author's purpose may be to

Inform (give the reader information),
Entertain (amuse the reader), or
Persuade (convince the reader to do or buy something).

Write **I**, **E**, or **P**, or any combination, in front of each paragraph
to show the author's purpose.

1. _____ Each pair of our electric socks is made of 100% nylon.
Two nine-volt batteries are included. The price is $16.95.

2. _____ The Toasty Toes Company has announced the
development of electric socks. A nine-volt battery is placed at
the top of each sock. Wires run through the socks and heat up
when the battery is turned on. "They work just like an electric
blanket," says Kelsey Foote, president of the company.

3. _____ Martin thought electric socks were a great idea. He wore
them all the time when he went bike riding in the winter. While
he was very pleased with the socks, he was spending a lot of
money on batteries. So he decided to connect the socks to his
headlight generator. Warm feet and free electricity! This setup
worked fine for a while. Then one day Martin started coasting
down a long hill. Faster and faster he went. Suddenly he noticed
his feet were very hot. He slammed on the brakes, tore off his
shoes and socks, and went running through the nearest snowbank.

4. _____ Our electric socks are ideal for people who just can't
seem to get their feet warm enough. The socks are 100% nylon,
so they will last forever. And we even include two batteries so
you can enjoy the socks right away. Just $16.95 a pair.

5. _____ Our nine-volt socks will heat up your feet on the coldest
winter days. Just don't do what Martin Penske did. He connected
his socks to his bike's headlight generator. This worked out OK
until he sped downhill. Picking up speed as he coasted, Martin
began to notice that his feet were burning up. He did no permanent
damage, but he must have been a sight as he ripped off his socks
and plunged his bare feet into a snowbank! Use the socks the way
we suggest and you will be toasty *and* safe. We even throw in a
pair of batteries so you can enjoy these all-nylon socks right out
of the box. The cost is $16.95 plus shipping.

Crazy Catalog

Ask a friend to do this activity with you.
Together, choose one of the products pictured on the catalog page.
Then toss a coin.
If it lands heads up, write a sentence that just gives information about the product.
Have your friend write a sentence that just tries to convince a person to buy the product.
If the coin lands tails up, do the reverse.
You write a sentence that persuades and have your friend write a sentence that informs.
Now use your sentences as part of a catalog entry that tells about the product.
Work together to write an entry that informs, persuades, *and* entertains.
Write your entry on a separate sheet of paper.
Do the activity for two or more different products.

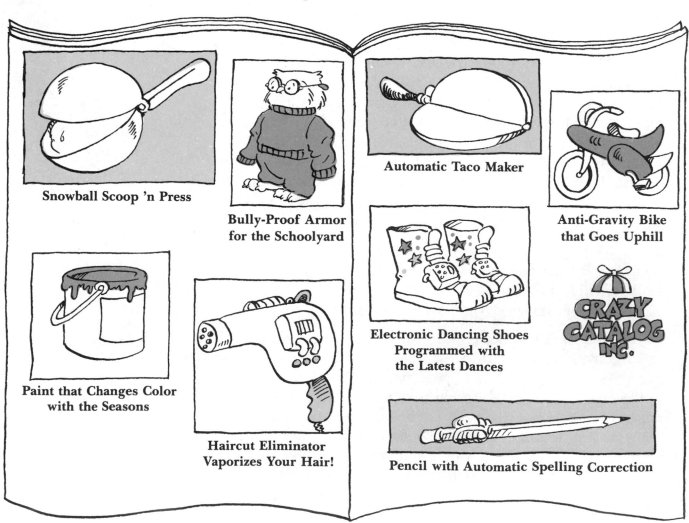

Snowball Scoop 'n Press

Bully-Proof Armor for the Schoolyard

Automatic Taco Maker

Anti-Gravity Bike that Goes Uphill

Paint that Changes Color with the Seasons

Haircut Eliminator Vaporizes Your Hair!

Electronic Dancing Shoes Programmed with the Latest Dances

Pencil with Automatic Spelling Correction

CRAZY CATALOG INC.

Who Wrote It?

When writers want you to buy or do something, they use words to persuade you.

They may use persuasive techniques like the ones used by the advertising agencies named below.

Read what each person is saying about the technique her or his agency uses in its ads.

At the **Bandwagon Agency**, our ads give the impression that everyone has our product. We hope you will want to have it, too.

Bandwagon Agency

The **Testimonial Agency**'s ads contain the words of people who already own the product. We think a satisfied customer is the best advertising.

Testimonial Agency

The **Famous Agency** uses quotes from famous people in our ads. We think their words help get people interested in our products.

Famous Agency

Here at the **Repeaters Agency** we say things over and over in our ads. We want to make sure you don't forget our products.

Repeaters Agency

Now read the ads below.

In the box next to each ad, write the name of the agency that probably wrote it.

Yazah, the famous cartoon frog, says, "I won't let my artist, James, draw me with just any old ink. I demand the best. Only Reptile Inks give the right shade of green."

Get yours while they last. The kids in Nevern are snapping up our new walking book bag right and left. Get the book bag that takes itself to school. The book bag that takes itself home again. But hurry. They won't last long. Don't be the only one left *carrying* your books to school.

Gym Foam Shoes. Sink into the soft padding. Let your feet be cradled by firm support. Gym Foam Shoes. Your feet never had it so good. Gym Foam Shoes. Feel the power. Feel the comfort. Feel the speed. Gym Foam Shoes. Gym Foam Shoes.

When I got my new Audioblast car stereo, I was amazed. Never had I heard sound so realistic. So here I am, telling you about the best car stereo going. Once I was playing a tape of train noises with my windows open and cars stopped to let me go by. *That's* how realistic the sound was!

Identifying persuasive writing techniques   **185**

Sell It

This is an activity to do with an adult or a friend.
Choose one of the ideas in the suggestion box for which
you would like to write an ad, or use your own idea.
Then make notes below.
Work together to write sentences for each persuasive
technique.

Suggestion Box

bucket of steam
never-melt ice cubes
gerbil exercise classes
crooked rulers
dust ball sculptures
Martian "Save Our Planet"
  campaign

Notes for Advertisement

We want to sell:

We want to sell it to:

Everyone has one or does it:

Ask person who has one or does it:

Famous person or people:

Repeating:

Now work together to write an advertisement.
Try to use at least two of the techniques in your notes.
Write your ad on separate paper.
You may also draw a picture to go with your ad.
Take your ad to school tomorrow and read it to your classmates.

Hometown Times

A newspaper editor needs help getting today's articles on the right pages of the Hometown Times.
Here is a guide showing the kinds of articles that appear on each page.

Hometown Times

Page 1 National/ International News	*Page 2* Local News	*Page 3* Business	*Page 4* Letters to Editor Columnists
Page 5 Human Interest Lifestyles	*Page 6* Sports	*Page 7* Editorials	*Page 8* Comics Entertainment

Now read each article below.
Write the letter in the corner of the article on the page guide to show where the article belongs.

 Valley Tigers Play to Tie

In their opening football game this season, the Valley Tigers were unable to defeat their long-time rival, the Orange Lions. Right from the kickoff, . . .

 Stocks Tumble Heavy Trading

Reacting to news that General Ravioli Crimpers had a bad month, the stock market plunged over 40 points. Traders were selling pasta stocks until . . .

 Home At Last

After seventeen months on the road, rock band E. O. Horse and the Riders has finally found a stable. "We made a lot of hay on the road," E. O. said, "so now we will . . .

 Families Make Up

The neighboring Thomps and Pinson families (not their real names) have made peace after eleven years of not speaking to each other. It started . . .

 Phew!

It is time, fellow citizens, to think about closing the landfill site at Mako Industrial Park. The city and this newspaper have received so many complaints . . .

 City Council Approves Budget

Last night's city council meeting proved to be yet one more victory for the Mayor. During her appeal, Mayor Levine explained the basis for new . . .

 To the Editor

Dear Editor:
I would like to point out some colorful errors in your reporting of the closing of our chain of crayon stores. First of all, red is not . . .

 New Peace Plan

In a move that astonished all other nations, the Furminian Parliament approved the Peace Plan with Valvia. Valvian officials applauded the new plan as being the first . . .

Interview

When you interview a person, you ask the person questions to find out information.
Do this activity with a person who agrees to be interviewed.
Have the person pretend to be someone listed in the box.
Then interview that person.
Here are five questions to get you started.
Add your own questions below.
Write the person's answers on the lines provided.

A spy
An inventor
A sports star
A circus performer
The President
The First Lady

Person's Name: _____

1. Where do you live? _____

2. What do you do during the day? _____

_____

3. What do you do when you have free time? _____

_____

4. What are your favorite books, movies, and TV shows? _____

_____

5. What are your favorite sports and games? _____

_____

My questions and answers:

_____

_____

_____

_____

_____

_____

Now use your interview questions and answers to write a newspaper article about your person.
Write your article on a separate piece of paper.
Take your article to school and share it with your classmates.
Decide in which part of a newspaper your article might be printed.

26 ▸ Keep Trying

This scientist's experiment notes are a disaster.
Help the scientist put things in order.
Read the experiment.
Then answer the questions at the end.

Put baking soda and vinegar in bottle.
Put balloon over bottle.
I mean, over bottle <u>opening</u>.

Looks like this ⎯⎯⎯⎯⎯⎯⎯⎯⎯→

Didn't work. Try this.
Put baking soda into balloon.
Put balloon on bottle.
Don't forget the vinegar.
Shake balloon so baking soda drops
into vinegar.

Looks like this ⎯⎯⎯⎯⎯⎯⎯⎯⎯→

Forgot vinegar this time!
Try again.
Success at last!
Balloon fills with carbon dioxide.

Looks like this ⎯⎯⎯⎯⎯⎯⎯⎯⎯→

1. What materials are used in the experiment? _____

_____

2. What is the correct order of steps for the experiment?

    A. _____

    B. _____

    C. _____

    D. _____

3. What is the result of the experiment? _____

_____

Reading science   **189**

Magic Numbers

Here is an activity for you and a friend.
Every person has a magic number from 1 to 9.
Would you and your friend like to know your magic numbers?
Read the directions below.
Then figure out your numbers at the bottom of the page.

First, each letter of the alphabet is given a number from 1 to 9.

A–1	D–4	G–7	J–1	M–4	P–7	S–1	V–4	Y–7
B–2	E–5	H–8	K–2	N–5	Q–8	T–2	W–5	Z–8
C–3	F–6	I–9	L–3	O–6	R–9	U–3	X–6	

Now print your whole name.
Include all your names, but do not use nicknames.
Beneath each letter of your name, write the number for that letter.
Then add all the numbers for each name.
Here is an example.

```
M I C H A E L     O S C A R     H E R N A N D E Z
4 9 3 8 1 5 3     6 1 3 1 9     8 5 9 5 1 5 4 5 8
     33       +      20      +         50          = 103
```

If the total is a number from 1 to 9, that is your magic number.
If the number is more than 9, add the numerals together.
Keep adding the numerals together until you get a one-digit number.
That is your magic number.

For Michael Oscar Hernandez, the magic number is

$$1 + 0 + 3 = \mathbf{4}$$

Now work out your magic numbers.

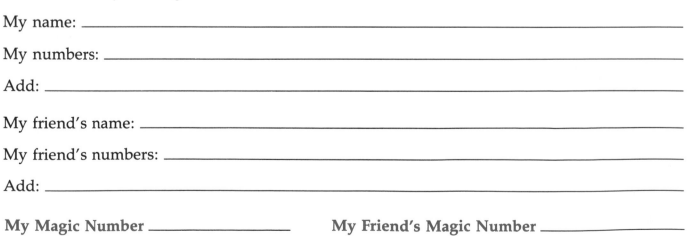

My name: _____

My numbers: _____

Add: _____

My friend's name: _____

My friend's numbers: _____

Add: _____

My Magic Number _____   **My Friend's Magic Number** _____

If your other friends or family members are interested, help
them figure out their magic numbers.

27 ▸ Time Capsule

People who write about history in the future will probably be interested in our everyday lives. How did we live? What did we eat? Why did we wear the clothes we wore? Why did we like the things we did?

Imagine boys and girls your age who live in the year 3000 trying to understand you as you are today. What would they want to know about you? What would you want to tell them?

Write a message to a girl or boy living in the year 3000. Tell about yourself and your everyday life.

_____

_____

_____

_____

Now imagine you are burying a time capsule, not to be opened until the year 3000. The capsule is about the size of a shoebox. How would you fill it? What would you put in it?

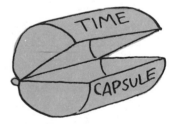

List five things you would put in the time capsule. Tell why you would include each item.

1. _____

_____

2. _____

_____

3. _____

_____

4. _____

_____

5. _____

_____

Where Am I?

Play this game with a family member or friend.

Have the other player close his or her eyes while you toss a coin onto the Geography Board.

Remove the coin and read the name of the place to yourself.

If you land on a place that has already been used, toss again.

Then describe the place aloud, but do *not* name the place.

Make your description as detailed as you can and ask "Where Am I?" at the end.

If the other player guesses the place, score 2 points.

If the other player cannot guess the place, score 1 point.

Take turns and play six rounds. Keep score on a piece of paper.

The winner is the player with more points.

Geography Board

Great Lakes	Pyramids of Egypt	Rocky Mountains	North Pole
Italy	My home town	Amazon rain forest	Sahara Desert
Hawaiian Islands	WILD CARD! Any place you want.	Washington, D.C.	Japan
Capital city of my state	Grand Canyon	Great Britain	Mississippi River

28 ▶ Dear Diary

Some people keep diaries of what they think and do each day.
Here are some diary entries of well-known story characters.
Read each entry.
Write the name of the writer on the line below the entry.

I think I will scream if I have to pick up one more dirty dish or dirty sock. I would never have thought such small people could be so messy. Only one of the seven fellows—Dopey is his name—has any sense of neatness. The rest of them just throw their dirty clothes on the floor when they get back from a day at the mine and stomp around demanding to be fed.

_____

Am I glad that's over! I have never been so embarrassed in all my life. All I really wanted to do was help my papa, but the more I talked the longer and longer my nose got. It's a good thing that nice lady in blue helped me out. I will never tell a lie again. I think.

_____

If I ever get my hands on that kid, I will flatten him! Here I am, minding my own business in my castle in the clouds when this nosey little fellow climbs up a vine and steals my magic hen right out from under my nose. At least I still have the beautiful music of my golden harp to keep me company.

_____

I can't wait until tomorrow. Mother said I could visit Grandmother by myself. Grandmother is sick, so I'm going to bring her a basket of food. I have to go through the forest to get to Grandmother's, but I'm not scared. I love walking in the woods and looking at the trees and flowers. Maybe I will even pick some flowers for Grandmother.

_____

I think I had better stop visiting other people's houses when they are not home. Yesterday I found this adorable little house in the woods. There was this porridge all ready, so I tasted some. Then, by accident, I broke a chair. It was an accident—really! But those bears sure were mad when they came home.

_____

What an exciting day! I sneaked into the garden under the gate and had quite a feast among the carrots and lettuces. It wasn't until I got to the cucumbers that Mr. McGregor noticed me. I have to give him credit though. He is fast! He almost got me in the tool shed, but I escaped with nothing worse than a bad cold from hiding out in a watering can.

_____

This Is Your Life

A biography is the written story of a person's life.
Work with a friend to write each other's biography.
Ask each other the questions below.
Write your answers on this page.
Have your friend write on a separate sheet of paper.

1. When were you born? _____

2. Where were you born? _____

3. Where have you lived since then? _____
   _____

4. Who are the people in your family? _____
   _____

5. Do you have any pets? _____ What are they? _____
   What are their names? _____

6. What are your favorite foods? _____

7. What is your favorite subject in school? _____

8. What activities do you take part in outside of school? ____
   _____

9. What do you like about these activities? _____
   _____

10. What person do you admire most? _____
    Why? _____
    _____

11. If you had a million dollars, what would you do with it? ___
    _____

Now use the information above to write a biography of your friend.
Include other things you know about your friend.
Try to write so people will understand what your friend is like.
Write your story on separate paper.
When you both are finished, read your stories to each other.

Realistic or Fantastic?

Fiction is writing that tells about imaginary characters and events.
Fiction can be realistic. It has real-life characters and events that
could really take place.
Fiction can be fantasy. It has characters that could never live or
events that could not possibly take place.
Read the story beginnings below.
Mark each one **R** for *realistic* or **F** for *fantasy*.

1. ____ Yoko squinted into the microscope
and twisted the focus knob. Suddenly
she gasped. She had never seen anything
so tiny before.

2. ____ Yoko squinted into the microscope.
Two tiny creatures waved at her and
invited her to take a swim in the pond.

3. ____ Yoko squinted into the microscope.
Two tiny creatures were swimming
around in the pond water. They seemed
to be exactly the same.

4. ____ Percy stepped onto the skateboard
and soared into the sky. Soon the people
below looked like little black specs on the
ground.

5. ____ Percy stepped onto the skateboard.
He zoomed down the hill and up the
ramp. As he soared into the sky,
everything was a blur of color.

6. ____ Percy stepped onto the skateboard.
He started the little motor and was soon
putt-putting around the parking lot.

Choose one of the story beginnings you just read and circle it.
Continue the story below.
If you chose a realistic beginning, add other realistic details.
If you chose a fantasy beginning, add other fantasy details.
Use a separate sheet of paper if you need more room to write.
Share your completed story with your classmates.

_____

_____

_____

_____

_____

_____

_____

Distinguishing between realistic fiction and fantasy **195**

Pass It On

Do this activity with two or more friends or family members.
Have each person flip a coin and keep the results a secret.
If the coin comes up heads, write only realistic fiction.
If the coin comes up tails, write only fantasy.
Together, choose one of the pictures on this page as a story starter, or use your own story idea.
Now work on separate paper to write your story.
The first person writes one or two sentences of the story and passes the paper to the second person.
The second person adds one or two sentences, folds the paper so only his or her part shows, and passes it to the third person.
The third person does the same, and so on.
Make sure each person sees only the last person's sentences.
Continue on another sheet of paper if you need to.
Stop after each person has had four turns, or when you all agree to stop.
Then unfold the paper and read the story aloud.
Your story should be quite interesting!

30 > Complete a Poem

The poem below is missing some rhyming words.
Search for the eight missing words in the puzzle.
Look across, down, and diagonally.
Circle each word in the puzzle and write it on a line to the right.
Then read the poem.
Use one of the words you listed to complete each line with a blank.
When you are finished, read the poem aloud with your classmates.
Take turns reading the verses.

Harry Haskins found a rocket.

Put it in his jacket _____.

You should have seen our Harry's face

When he took off for outer _____!

On his way into the sky,

Harry yelled; there was no _____.

So very sudden was his flight

He had no time to be _____.

He wanted to know if he'd be back

In time to get a little _____.

He tried to shout above the racket

That he'd left his lunch in his other _____.

This fact is hard—try to absorb it:

Harry's been placed in permanent _____.

He's very cold, and hungry too,

But he can't complain about the _____.

d	r	s	p	a	c	e	o	t	z	i	l
a	s	w	o	o	a	s	r	v	g	b	u
v	n	s	c	z	l	u	b	c	i	d	a
j	a	c	k	e	t	i	k	t	e	o
r	c	e	e	f	n	p	t	a	b	s	w
w	k	m	t	u	h	a	r	e	p	l	y

_____

_____

_____

_____

_____

_____

Poetry Place

Ask an adult to do this activity with you.
Think of an experience you and the adult have shared.
It could be a game, a meal, a walk—anything.
Take turns writing down words and thoughts that come to you
when you think of the experience.
Use the space below.
Pass this page back and forth quickly at least six times.
Do not take a lot of time to think about what to write.

Now read this poem aloud.

> There's really no trick to writing a poem.
> Just free up your mind and set it to roam.
> Then twist all the words to find ones that rhyme,
> And set up a beat to mark out the time.
> But lines need not rhyme or keep up a beat.
> Your message counts most, so plunge in and have fun!

Work together to write a poem about your shared experience.
Include some of the words and thoughts you wrote in the box above.
Start with one of the words from the box.
Write it one letter under the other down the left side of a sheet of paper.
The first word of each line of your poem should begin with the letter
at the left.
Here is an example of a poem about a tiger at a zoo.

> This cat had stripes
> Icicles of yellow on black velvet
> Growling and pacing on its own little island
> Ears twitching
> Rolling in the grass and napping in the sunlight.

When your poem is finished, practice reading it aloud.
Take your poem to school tomorrow and read it to your classmates.

31 ▶ How It Came to Be

A myth is a story about goddesses and gods, heroes and heroines.
Some myths try to explain how things in nature came to be.
Read the following myths.
Think about what they are trying to explain.

A hole tore open in the sky, and a woman fell out. Two birds
caught her and placed her on a turtle's back. The turtle ordered
the other animals to dive down in the water and bring up some
earth for the woman to live on. Many animals tried and failed.
Finally a toad brought back enough earth for a start. More and
more earth came up, and the woman fashioned the world from
it. To this day, the turtle holds the world on its back.

From a Huron myth

Olorun, the sky god, liked to play on the earth with the other
gods. At that time, the earth was a great swamp, and completely
empty. Olorun wanted to put humans on the earth, but he needed
some dry ground for them. So he told the chief, the Great God, to
make dry land. The Great God took a shell full of dirt from Olorun.
He spread it on the swamp. He also put down a pigeon and a hen.
The pigeon and the hen scratched at the dirt, spreading it around.
Soon the swamp was covered with dry ground.

From a Yoruba myth

There was nothing at first, just the sky and sea. And the Maker
and the Feathered Serpent came together. The Maker was the Sky.
The Feathered Serpent was the Heart of the Sky. And they were
great thinkers. They talked and they thought. Their thoughts were
so powerful that whatever they said became true. So they said,
"Earth!" And there was the earth. So they said, "Mountains and
valleys!" And there were the mountains and the valleys.

From a Quiché Maya myth

What do all the myths above explain? _____

_____

Next to each myth, draw a small picture to illustrate it.

Tall Tales

This is an activity for you to do with a friend.
Choose one of the story starters below and put an X on it.
Then use the story starter as the beginning of a tall tale.
A tall tale is an exaggerated story with parts that are hard
to believe.
Tell your story to your friend.
Just make it up as you go along.
Include at least five exaggerations, the more unbelievable the better.
Take turns and tell each other one or two different tall tales.
When you are finished, work together to write down the tall tale
you both liked best.
You may change it around any way you wish.
Write your story on a separate sheet of paper.
Include a picture that illustrates one of the exaggerated or
unbelievable parts.

> One day I flew so high I crashed into the moon. I knocked a hugh chunk out of it!

The pig was so huge that every time it took a step...

Yolanda leaped onto the gray horse and took off toward the sun in the east for...

One night I wandered into an empty shopping mall and...

Baby Mee Young was barely three years old, yet she was so strong that...

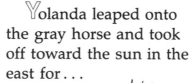

One day the weather turned so hot that the sidewalk...

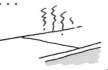

The scientist had created a computer so fast and powerful that only the most...

Jaime reached out his hand and grasped the branch of the tree. As the tree began to shake, Jaime...

The bridge started at Gloria's feet and rose up into the mist. Gingerly she put her foot on the edge...

The horse stopped at the edge of the canyon. It did a little dance and gathered its legs together. Then with a mighty leap...

More. . .
Pass It On

Do this activity with two or more friends or family members.
Have each person flip a coin and keep the results a secret.
If the coin comes up heads, write only realistic fiction.
If the coin comes up tails, write only fantasy.
Together, choose one of the pictures on this page as a story starter, or use your own story idea.
Now work on separate paper to write your story.
The first person writes one or two sentences of the story and passes the paper to the second person.
The second person adds one or two sentences, folds the paper so only his or her part shows, and passes it to the third person.
The third person does the same, and so on.
Make sure each person sees only the last person's sentences.
Continue on another sheet of paper if you need to.
Stop after each person has had four turns, or when you all agree to stop.
Then unfold the paper and read the story aloud.
Your story should be quite interesting!

Enrichment
Reading Grade 6

AMERICAN
EDUCATION
PUBLISHING

1 Figure It Out

Read each item below.
Figure out the meaning of the word in dark print.
Use the context, or other words around the word, to figure out the meaning.
Mark the box next to the choice you think gives the correct meaning.

1. Hey folks! Does it **fatigue** you to watch television? Does watching TV leave you feeling tried? Do your eyelids droop? Do you just drag yourself around?
   ☐ w̲ear out   ☐ m̲ake afraid

2. Now, for the **paltry** sum of just fifty cents, plus shipping, you can have the Sumo TV System.
   ☐ e̲asily seen̲; obviou̲s   ☐ very s̲mall; worthless̲

3. Where you used to sit and watch TV programs for hours, now you can give them a **perfunctory** glance for a couple of minutes and then go do something *really* fun!
   ☐ d̲one perf̲ectly   ☐ done w̲ith littl̲e care

4. Just rush down to our little **emporium.** The place may be hard to find, but the search is worth it because of our large stock.
   ☐ mansion   ☐ s̲tore

5. You may have to **cogitate** for a while as you consider our vast selection of fifty-cent Sumo TV Systems. Take your time. Your decision is important.
   ☐ t̲hink hard   ☐ talk quickl̲y

6. Every **aspiration** you have for freeing yourself from television will be fulfilled by whichever system you choose. Your desires are our command. You couldn't ask for more!
   ☐ w̲ish   ☐ answe̲r

7. Imagine your friends' astonishment when you pass the most **formidable** TV quizzes without having watched any programs.
   ☐ orde̲rly; neat   ☐ t̲ough, har̲d

8. Oh, we almost forgot two small **particulars.** The Sumo TV System is *very* heavy. This brings the shipping charge up to $6,000!
   ☐ specials̲   ☐ d̲etails̲

Now read the question below.
To find the answer, write the underlined letters from your choices in order on the blanks.

What do you do when you *grapple against verbalizations*?

You   __ __ __ __ __ __   __ __ __ __   __ __ __ __ __ __.

Whatchamacallit

Play this game with a friend or family member.
Choose a picture below, but do not tell what you have chosen.
Then make up a sentence describing the part in color.
Use the word *whatchamacallit* instead of the name of the part.
Try to give enough context so the other player can figure out what you are describing.
If the other player guesses correctly, put an X on the picture and score 5 points.
If the guess is incorrect, score 2 points but do *not* mark the picture with an X.
Take turns and play five rounds. Keep score below.
Do not reuse a picture with an X on it.
The player with the higher score wins the game.

rowel	chevron	sprocket	gnomon
lopping shears	rudder	filament	rotating beacon
ruff	caliper	crampon	trowel

Score Sheet	
Player 1	**Player 2**
Round 1	Round 1
Round 2	Round 2
Round 3	Round 3
Round 4	Round 4
Round 5	Round 5
TOTAL	TOTAL

By the Numbers

Read each word.
If the word has a prefix, write the number 1 on the line with the same letter as the word.
If the word has a suffix, write the number 2 on the line with the same letter as the word.
If the word has both a prefix and a suffix, write the number 3 on the line with the same letter as the word.
If the word is just a base word, write a 0 on the line with the same letter as the word.
Then do the subtraction problem.
Write your answer on the lines without letters.

prefix = 1
suffix = 2
prefix and suffix = 3
base word = 0

a. disappearance

b. seldom

c. misname

d. development

e. arrange

f. honestly

g. attraction

h. unstoppable

Now fill in the numbers for the words below.
Then subtract again.
Write your answer on the lines without letters.
The answer is an important date in United States history.

i. refresh

j. notice

k. intercity

l. nonpoisonous

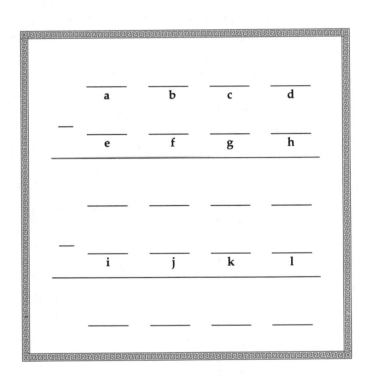

```
        ___  ___  ___  ___
         a    b    c    d
   __  ___  ___  ___  ___
         e    f    g    h
   _____

        ___  ___  ___  ___

   __  ___  ___  ___  ___
         i    j    k    l
   _____

        ___  ___  ___  ___
```

The date is _____.

Why is this date important? _____

_____

Building Words

Here is a game to play with an adult.
Make twelve word cards like these.

| believe | pay | cover | place | kind | happy |
| appear | tire | prove | true | certain | agree |

Put the cards in a pile and turn the pile face down.
Take the top card and read the word on it to yourself.
Then toss a coin onto the building frame.
If the coin lands on PREFIX, add a prefix to the word on the card,
say the new word aloud, and tell what the new word means.
If the coin lands on SUFFIX, add a suffix to the word,
say the new word aloud, and tell what it means.
If the coin lands on BOTH, add both a prefix and suffix,
say the new word, and tell what it means.
Choose your prefixes and suffixes from the tool box.
If both players agree the word and its meaning are
correct, score 5 points.
Then return the card to the bottom of the pile.
Take turns and keep score on a piece of paper.
Play until one player has scored 25 points.

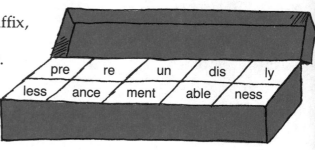

| pre | re | un | dis | ly |
| less | ance | ment | able | ness |

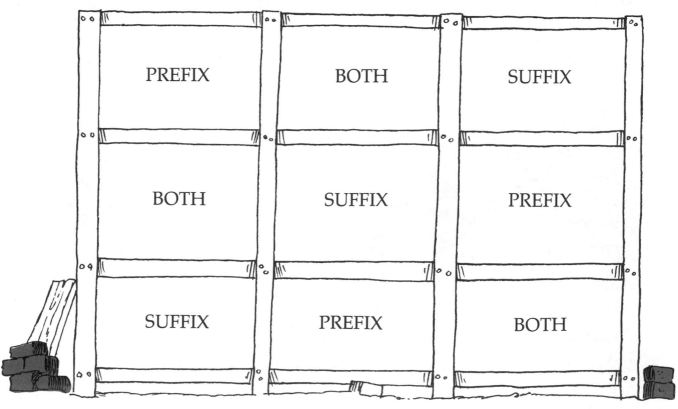

PREFIX	BOTH	SUFFIX
BOTH	SUFFIX	PREFIX
SUFFIX	PREFIX	BOTH

Where Is It From?

Here are some dictionary entries for English words.
Their word origins, or where they came from, are shown on the map.
Read each entry. Then look at the map.
Find the words on the map that give the origin of the entry word.
Write the entry word on the line that connects to its origin on the map.

chow•der (chou′dər), *n.* a thick soup or stew made with fish or shellfish and vegetables.

ka•lei•do•scope (kə lī′də skōp′), *n.* a tube containing bits of colored glass and two mirrors. As it is turned, beautiful, regular patterns are formed by the reflections of the colored glass.

lar•i•at (lar′ē ət), *n.* a long rope with a sliding loop at the end, used for catching cattle, horses, and other livestock.

spa•ghet•ti (spə get′ē), *n.* a food made from flour paste and drawn out into long, thin, solid strings.

waltz (wôlts), *n.* **1** a whirling, gliding dance with three beats to a measure. **2** music for such a dance. *v.* **3** to dance a waltz.

Yan•kee (yang′kē), *n.* **1** a person born or living in New England. **2** a person born or living in the North, especially during the Civil War. **3** any person born or living in the United States.

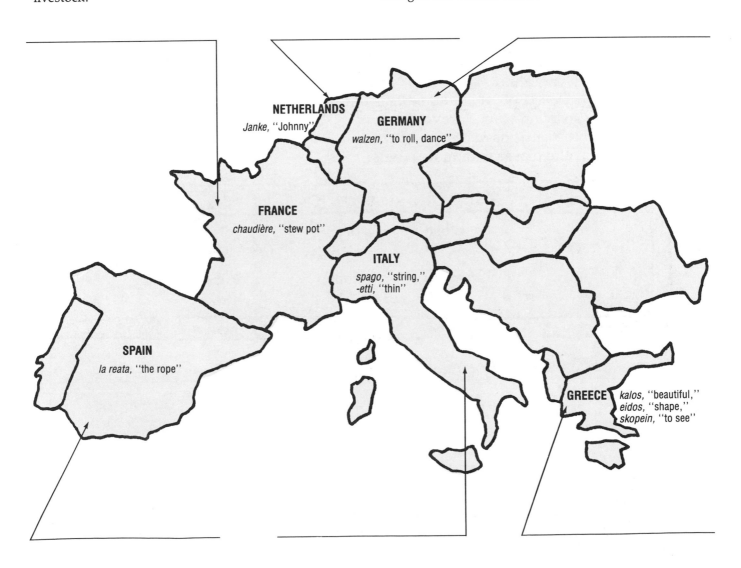

NETHERLANDS
Janke, "Johnny"

GERMANY
walzen, "to roll, dance"

FRANCE
chaudière, "stew pot"

ITALY
spago, "string,"
-etti, "thin"

SPAIN
la reata, "the rope"

GREECE *kalos,* "beautiful,"
eidos, "shape,"
skopein, "to see"

It's Greek to Me

Ask an adult to play this game with you.
Make twelve word cards like these.

autograph	bibliography	microphone	telegraph
telescope	phonograph	biology	autobiography
biography	microscope	telephone	dialogue

Turn the cards face down.
Take turns.
Select a card and read the word on it to yourself.
Then look at the box of Greek roots.
Make up a definition for the word on your card using the
meanings given for the Greek roots.
If the other player figures out your word from the definition,
keep the word card and score 2 points.
If the other player cannot figure out the word, return the card
face down and lose 1 point if your score is not zero.
Record your score on your score card.
Play until all the cards have been used.
The winner is the player with more points.

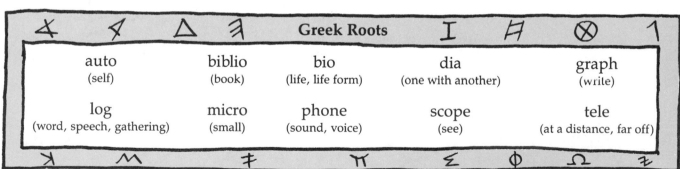

Greek Roots

auto (self)	biblio (book)	bio (life, life form)	dia (one with another)	graph (write)
log (word, speech, gathering)	micro (small)	phone (sound, voice)	scope (see)	tele (at a distance, far off)

Score Card

Player 1 _____

TOTAL _____

Score Card

Player 2 _____

TOTAL _____

Mood Maps

The mood of a story is the feeling the writer tries to create for the reader.
Read each paragraph below.
Circle the word at the right that best describes the mood.

Inez gazed out the window at the soft gray of the rain-filled sky and the brilliant green of the new spring grass. She sighed contentedly and turned to face the room. A cheery, warm fire hissed behind the grate. Her cats, finding her curled up on the window seat, joined her, making a warm nest.

mysterious

cozy

gloomy

A lone gull cried mournfully in the distance as the mist billowed over the sand. Two lonely rocks, black and glistening, seemed to float in the mist. They were guarding the deserted beach from something, but I had no desire to find out what.

angry

excited

sad

Sunlight glanced warmly off the sidewalk and onto Rosemary's face. She felt a surge of life, a surge of energy. Her feet began to move. Soon she was pounding the golden sidewalk and running, running, running. She flung her arms into the air and breathed in the warm promise of spring.

joyous

calm

spooky

Liam felt a cold chill down the back of his neck. The noontime sun did not help warm him. And where the sun could not find a way in, the shadows were dark and cold-looking. One such shadow was formed by the doorway to the damp warehouse.

peaceful

miserable

pleasant

Now choose two of the words you circled.
Write each word in the center of one of the mood maps.
Then reread the paragraph that goes with each word.
Look for specific words that helped create the mood.
Write the words in the boxes on the map.

Mood Maps

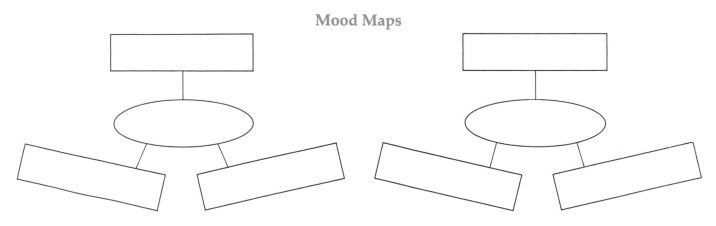

Mood-o-Meter

Do this activity with a friend.
Together, choose one of the moods on the Mood-o-Meter.
Then take turns circling words in the box that could be used to create that mood.

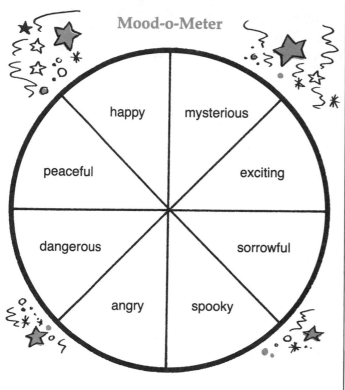

Mood-o-Meter

happy, mysterious, peaceful, exciting, dangerous, sorrowful, angry, spooky

gray	smooth	dull	quickly
slither	rain	brightly	bouncing
blue	soothing	moan	tight
sharp	loud	smile	silvery
strong	green	drooping	crawl
dark	jagged	rough	flat
quietly	tough	storm	cold
creep	tinkling	stink	casually
stroll	bright	cry	black
angrily	hot	jump	laugh
slouch	kind	race	question
sunny	frown	quiet	golden
warm	red	hard	shaking
loudly	soft	run	leap

Now work together to write a paragraph using the words you circled to create the mood you chose.
Write your paragraph on a separate sheet of paper.
Do the activity for two or more different moods given on the Mood-o-Meter.
You may use the words in the box more than once.
When you are finished with all your paragraphs, read them aloud to each other.
Choose the one you like best and draw a picture to illustrate it.

⑤ Patterns of Speech

Writers use similes, metaphors, and personification to make their writing more colorful.
A simile compares two things using the word *as* or *like*.
A metaphor compares two things without using the word *as* or *like*.
Personification compares things by giving human qualities to things that are not human.
Read each sentence below.
Write **S**, **M**, or **P** in front of the sentence to show whether it contains a simile, a metaphor, or personification.

Have you ever played a game where you leap like a frog?

1. ____ When I told Marsha what was in the punch, her face turned as green as grass.

2. ____ Fluffy clouds skipped merrily across the sky.

3. ____ The idea shone through my thoughts like a sunbeam through a dusty room.

4. ____ The new sports car turned out to be a real lemon.

5. ____ When Eli got home, he was as grumpy as a porcupine with an ingrown quill.

6. ____ Gloria was a gazelle, leaping over the hurdles on the way to the finish line.

7. ____ The mountains loomed above us, frowning and threatening.

8. ____ Lars laughed like a hyena at the ridiculous jokes.

9. ____ The animal's eyes were twin stars in the dark forest.

10. ____ The ocean hissed along the sand, whispering the secrets of the deep.

11. ____ Her bike was a time machine, taking her from one history museum to another.

12. ____ Dawn crept quietly into town, careful not to awaken anyone.

Now color the picture.
Find the number of each sentence in the picture.
If the sentence contains a simile, color the triangle blue.
If the sentence contains a metaphor, color the triangle red.
If the sentence contains personification, color the triangle green.

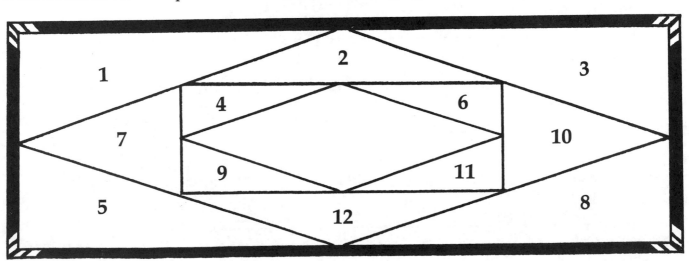

Make It Colorful

This is a game for two players.

Take turns.

Toss a coin or small paper clip onto the game board.

Read the word on which it lands.

If you land on a word that has already been used, toss again.

Then think of a colorful comparison using the word in a simile or metaphor.

If you cannot think of a simile or metaphor, try to make a comparison by personifying the word.

Say your comparison aloud and tell if it contains a simile, a metaphor, or personification.

If the other player agrees with you, score 3 points.

Keep score on separate paper.

The first player to score 18 points wins.

Kelly turned as green as a **pickle** while riding the Killer Twist.

The **pickle** was a blimp floating in the jar.

The slippery **pickle** jumped away as I tried to take a bite.

truck	wind	sandpaper	dog	fence
kitten	tree	steel	glass	engine
door	rocket	marshmallow	bear	candle
rug	bumblebee	storm	rock	bicycle
horse	car	flower	elephant	cloud

6 Laugh Your Head Off

An idiom is an expression that means something different than the words in it.
Read each sentence below and underline the idiom.
Then mark the choice you think gives the meaning of the idiom.
Finally, write the number of the sentence in the box beside the picture that shows a literal, or usual, meaning for the words.

1. Mieko hit the nail on the head when she guessed the correct answer.
   - ○ Meiko was strong.
   - ○ Meiko was right.
   - ○ Meiko was mean.

2. Every spring, Ramón is just itching to get his hands on a baseball bat.
   - ○ Ramón is uncomfortable.
   - ○ Ramón's bat is rough.
   - ○ Ramón can hardly wait.

3. Don't complain about the long ticket lines—we are all in the same boat.
   - ○ We all like to complain.
   - ○ We all like boats.
   - ○ We all have the same problem.

4. The car salesman finally talked turkey with us about the new models.
   - ○ He talked quickly.
   - ○ He talked seriously.
   - ○ He talked occasionally.

5. The audience cracked up when Helen told her jokes.
   - ○ The audience laughed.
   - ○ The audience got angry.
   - ○ The audience left.

6. We polished off all those grapes in about ten minutes.
   - ○ We washed them.
   - ○ We ate them.
   - ○ We picked them.

7. Max, drop me a line once in a while when you're away.
   - ○ Sing to me.
   - ○ Draw me.
   - ○ Write to me.

8. You are barking up the wrong tree if you think I took your book.
   - ○ You are a dog.
   - ○ You are mistaken.
   - ○ You are noisy.

9. Alma really went out on a limb with that suggestion.
   - ○ Alma was wrong.
   - ○ Alma saved a tree.
   - ○ Alma took a chance.

Beehive

Play this game with a friend or an adult.

First, get two different colored crayons or markers.

Then decide who will be Player 1 and who will be Player 2.

Fill in your names and colors on the lines provided.

Now look at the game board.

You are to complete a path between your two sides of the beehive.

Take turns.

Choose a space on your side of the beehive and read the idiom in it.

Then tell what the idiom means and use it in a sentence.

If the other player agrees you used the idiom correctly, color the space.

Keep playing until one player has colored a path connecting her or his two sides of the beehive.

Player 1 _____

Color: _____

Player 2 _____

Color: _____

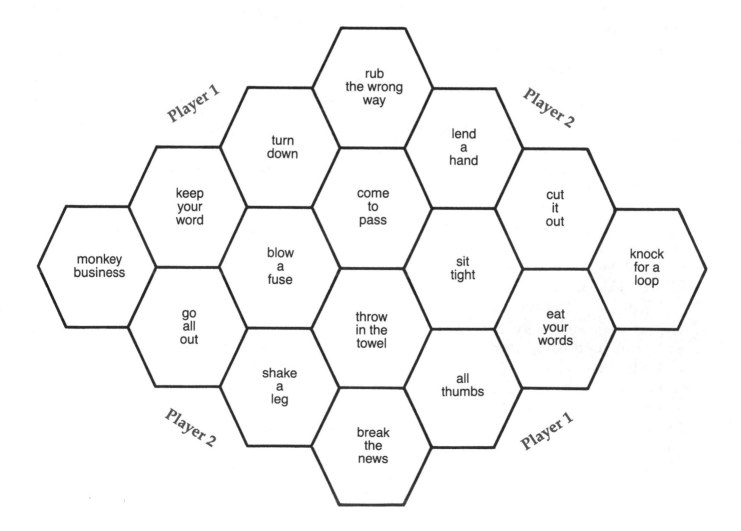

All About Cats

This is the contents page from a book about cats.

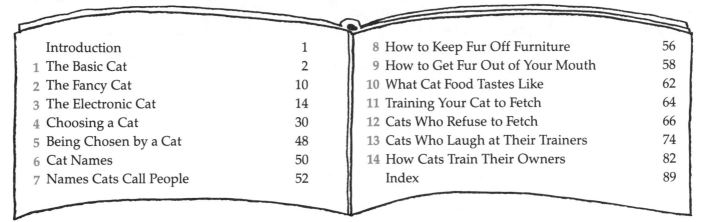

Use the table of contents to answer each question below.
Circle the letter of your choice.

1. On which page would you expect to read about cats that
   cannot be trained at all?
   e. page 65   **f.** page 76   **g.** page 82

2. Based on page counts, which of these topics receives the *least*
   attention in the book?
   d. the fancy cat   **e.** training a cat to fetch   **f.** how cats train their owners

3. Which chapters deal with problems created by cat hair?
   l. chapters 8 and 9   **m.** chapters 1 and 8   **n.** chapters 9 and 13

4. Which chapter probably has information about famous TV cats?
   g. The Basic Cat   **h.** Cat Names   **i.** The Electronic Cat

5. Which pages should you read if you are looking for advice on
   picking a cat?
   c. pages 48–49   **d.** pages 30–47   **e.** pages 52–55

6. Which topic receives the most attention in the book?
   a. choosing a cat   **b.** names cats call people   **c.** being chosen by a cat

7. In which chapter might you find out about feeding a cat?
   c. chapter 2   **d.** chapter 11   **e.** chapter 10

Cats belong to a group of animals that includes lions, tigers,
leopards, panthers, and jaguars.
To find out the name of the entire cat family, write the letters of
your choices in order on the line below.

The cat family is called _____.

Index Race

Ask a friend to play this game with you.
Make twelve number cards like these.
Now look over the index below and become familiar with it.
When you are ready to play, shuffle the number cards, put them in a pile, and turn the pile face down.
Have one player turn over the top card.
Find the question in the Question Box with the same number as the card.
Have the other player read the question aloud.
Then race to see who is first to name the index page or pages that might contain the answer to the question.
The winner makes one mark on his or her tally board.
Play until all the number cards have been used.
The winner of the game is the player with more tally marks.

1	2	3	4	5
6	7	8	9	
10	11	12		

Balinese cat, 26
Bastet (cat-goddess), 10
bathing, 7, 40, 80
bed, 36–37
Birman cat, 26
Bobtail cat, Japanese, 22
body language, 6
Bombay cat, 18
books about cats
  fiction, 82–84
  information, 88
breeders of cats, 33–34
breeds, 14–29
British Shorthair cat, 19

Burmese cat, 20
calico cat, 17, 75
carrier, 36
Carroll, Lewis, 82, 84
cartoons, 77
Cat Fancy, The, 14, 50
"cat" in foreign languages, 64
"cat" in phrases, 62–63
catnip, 39
championship competitions, 48
choosing a cat, 30–35
claws, 3
  clipping, 40
  removing, 42–43

Question Box

1. How do cats communicate with their bodies?
2. How do you say "cat" in Italian or Arabic?
3. Where can I find a picture of a Burmese cat?
4. What is the best way to give my cat a bath?
5. What sort of publication is *The Cat Fancy*?
6. What should I know before choosing a cat breeder?
7. Why should I use a cat carrier to bring home a cat?
8. What kind of bedding is best for cats?
9. What is the best way to clip a cat's claws?
10. How do I enter my prize cat in a competition?
11. What fictional books have been written about cats?
12. How do I tell a calico cat from other cats?

My Tally Board

My Friend's Tally Board

Terrific Toys

The memo below was sent by a salesperson to the sales manager of Terrific Toys, Inc.
As you read the memo, you will notice that the information is not organized very well.

DATE: Friday, June 21
TO: Sales Manager

This week's sales were nothing short of spectacular. I sold 25 of our new Teddy Thunder Bears to Bears for All, another 15 to Fuzzy's Toystore, and surprisingly, 20 of these little bears to Hippo Hurray.
The Hermione Hippo puppet is doing great. Bears for All didn't take any, of course, but I managed to sell 25 to Fuzzy's and another 30 to Hippo Hurray. Hippo Hurray says they just can't keep them in stock!
At Stuffed Things they took 10 Teddys and a half-dozen hippos. They also took 20 Misty Mice and 18 Ollie Octopuses.
My final stop today was Fun 'n Follies. I wound up selling them 15 Teddy Thunders, 30 Hermione Hippos, 40 Misty Mice, and 10 Ollies!
That's it for this week. Next week, on to Waterville.

Help the salesperson organize the information in the memo.
Complete the chart below with the number of toys sold.

	Bears for All	Fuzzy's Toystore	Hippo Hurray	Stuffed Things	Fun 'n Follies	TOTAL
Teddy Thunder						
Hermione Hippo						
Misty Mouse						
Ollie Octopus						

Now make a bar graph showing the sales information on the chart.
Write the names of the toys on the lines at the left.
Then fill in the spaces next to each toy to show how many were sold.

TOYS SOLD—WEEK OF JUNE 17

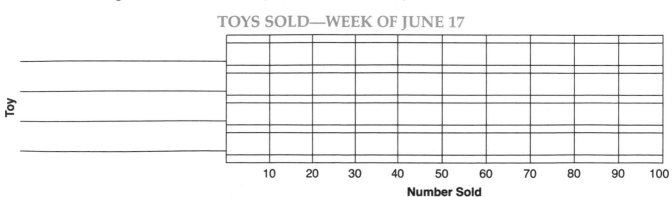

Toy

10 20 30 40 50 60 70 80 90 100

Number Sold

Making a chart and graph **217**

Map It Out

Here is an activity for you and a family member or friend.
Work together to make a map of an imaginary place.
Use one of the places in the suggestion box, or use your own idea.
Make notes about the place before you draw your map.
Write your answers to these questions on separate paper.

Suggestion Box

city on moon
shopping center
solar system
amusement park
forest
ghost town
zoo
car race track

1. What place will you draw?

2. What buildings or other structures will you show on your map?

3. What symbols will you use on your map? What will they stand for?

4. Will your map have streets, roads, or other transportation routes?
   If yes, what will they be? What will they be called?

5. What other things will you show on your map?

Now work together to sketch out your map.
Work on your own paper until you get your map just right.
Then draw your final map below.
Take your map to school tomorrow and share it with your classmates.
Ask them questions based on what is shown on your map.

⑨ Who Are We?

Look at the time line.
It shows what some people think are important events in the development of our planet Earth.
The numbers represent millions of years before the present.

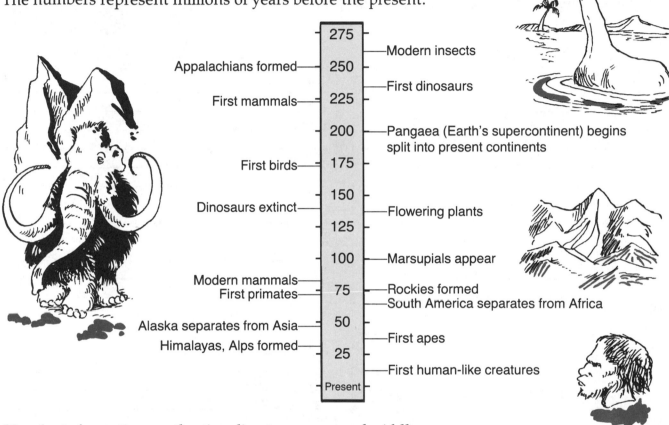

Appalachians formed—250
First mammals—225
First birds—175
Dinosaurs extinct—150
Modern mammals—
First primates—75
Alaska separates from Asia—50
Himalayas, Alps formed—25

275
250
225
200
175
150
125
100
75
50
25
Present

—Modern insects
—First dinosaurs
—Pangaea (Earth's supercontinent) begins split into present continents
—Flowering plants
—Marsupials appear
—Rockies formed
—South America separates from Africa
—First apes
—First human-like creatures

Use the information on the time line to answer each riddle.

1. We were the second major mountain range formed.
   Primates came along just about the same time we did.

   Who are we? _____

2. We were buzzing around before everything. There weren't even any dinosaurs to keep us company.

   Who are we? _____

3. At first we were all one piece of land. Then we drifted apart about 65 million years ago.

   Who are we? _____

4. We never got to eat any flowers. The last of us died out just before the flowers appeared.

   Who are we? _____

5. We are almost as old as the insects. We used to to be taller, but 250 million years of weather have worn us down.

   Who are we? _____

6. Our early models were around for almost 150 million years before the new models appeared.

   Who are we? _____

My Time, Your Time

Do this activity with an adult.
You will each make a time line of what you did during one day.
Together, decide which day you will use.
On that day, keep track of what you do and when you do it.
Then fill in your time lines.
When you both are finished, compare how you spent your time.
Circle any times you did the same things.

My Time Line	_____'s Time Line
6:00 A.M.	6:00 A.M.
7:00	7:00
8:00	8:00
9:00	9:00
10:00	10:00
11:00	11:00
12:00 P.M.	12:00 P.M.
1:00	1:00
2:00	2:00
3:00	3:00
4:00	4:00
5:00	5:00
6:00	6:00
7:00	7:00
8:00	8:00
9:00	9:00
10:00	10:00

Encyclotopics

Read each question below.
Decide where you would find the answer in an encyclopedia.
Circle the letter of your choice.

1. If you wanted to grow avocado pits on a windowsill, under which topic should you look?
   s. Window   **t.** Avocado   **u.** Food

2. To find information about the Cuban revolution of 1959, which topic should you look up?
   e. Cuba   **f.** Revolution   **g.** 1959

3. Information about Rudolph Diesel, the inventor of the Diesel engine, would be found under which topic?
   k. Engine   **l.** Diesel   **m.** Inventor

4. If you wanted to find out if the giant panda of China was really a bear or a raccoon, what should you look up?
   c. Bear   **d.** China   **e.** Panda

5. Under which topic should you look for information on how to plant a vegetable garden?
   t. Plant   **u.** Vegetable   **v.** Gardening

6. If you wanted to write a report on both wild and pet gerbils, under which topic should you look for information?
   h. Animal   **i.** Gerbil   **j.** Pet

7. To find out if World War I was fought only on European soil, which topic should you look up?
   r. Europe   **s.** World War I   **t.** War

8. Under which topic should you look for information on how bats guide themselves in the dark?
   g. Guide   **h.** Flying   **i.** Bat

9. The distance of all the planets from the sun might be found under which topic?
   o. Planet   **p.** Sky   **q.** Sun

10. If you wanted to find out the dates for the twelve signs of the zodiac, which topic should you look up?
    l. Date   **m.** Sign   **n.** Zodiac

11. Which topic should you look up to find out how pictures are sent into our homes for entertainment?

    Write the letters of your choices in order below.

    _____

What Does It Mean?

This is a game for two players.
Take turns.
Choose one of the entries on the dictionary pages below.
Read the word and its two definitions aloud.
One definition is a real one. The other definition is made up.
Write your initials in front of the definition you think is correct.
Play until a definition has been chosen for each entry.

1. **cal•a•mar•i** (kal′ə mer′ē), *n.*
   _____ 1 squid used as food
   _____ 2 a hard growth on a tree

2. **en•dorse** (en dôrs′), *v.*
   _____ 1 to cover with dorse, a kind of fluff
   _____ 2 to sign on the back of

3. **hal•cy•on** (hal′sē ən), *adj.*
   _____ 1 a kind of ancient armor
   _____ 2 calm, peaceful, or carefree

4. **hi•mat•i•on** (hi mat′ē on′), *n.*
   _____ 1 a rectangular cloth worn over the left shoulder
   _____ 2 a loud whine or cry

5. **leaf roll•er** (lēf rō′lər), *n.*
   _____ 1 an insect that nests on a rolled up leaf
   _____ 2 a device for flattening leaves

6. **o•va•tion** (ō vā′shən), *n.*
   _____ 1 something oval or egg-shaped
   _____ 2 approval usually expressed by enthusiastic applause

7. **pe•cu•ni•ar•y** (pi kyoo′nē er′ē), *adj.*
   _____ 1 having to do with money
   _____ 2 having to do with a bird's beak

8. **sheet an•chor** (shēt ang′kər), *n.*
   _____ 1 a large anchor carried as a spare
   _____ 2 a place to tie down sails on a sailboat

9. **shoat** (shōt), *n.*
   _____ 1 the shiny coat of a horse
   _____ 2 a young pig

10. **si•ne•cure** (sī′nə kyùr), *n.*
    _____ 1 a cure for sinus problems
    _____ 2 a job that requires little or no work

Now do this multiplication problem.
The numbers in the answer give the numbers of the correct definitions.
Read the answer from left to right and check the definitions in order from 1 to 10.
Score 1 point for each correct definition with your initials.
Add up your score below.
The player with the higher score wins.

$$
\begin{array}{r}
407040374 \\
\times \qquad 3 \\
\hline
\end{array}
$$

Player 1

Player 2

11 ▶ Thanks, Sun!

A passage may have headings that tell what parts of it are about.
The headings tell the main ideas.
Read each paragraph below.
Make up a heading that tells the main idea.
Write the heading on the line at the top of the paragraph.

```
┌─────────────────────────────────────────────────────────────┐
│                                                               │
│                                                               │
│                                                               │
└─────────────────────────────────────────────────────────────┘
```

_____
(heading)

Eat the sun? Why you would have to be a magician or a monster to do that. Or would you? What is the source of all the energy on Earth? The sun, of course. The plants on Earth get energy from the sun's rays. They use this power from the sun to make the sugar they need to grow and make starches, fats, protein, and vitamins. So when you eat plants—fruits, vegetables, grains—you are eating captured sunshine. Even when you eat meat, you are eating animals that ate plants.

_____
(heading)

What about coal and oil? They provide us with energy, and surely they did not come from the sun. Think again! Millions of years ago, many plants were buried in swamps and bogs. The plants turned to carbon, so now we have coal. Animals that ate the plants also died and were buried. The animals had stored the energy of the sun by eating plants and each other. Their bodies and the plants they ate turned to oil.

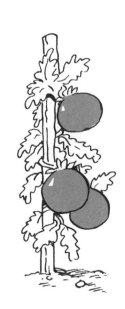

_____
(heading)

Without the sun, we could not breathe. That may sound strange, but it is true. Using only the energy of the sun, plants take water and carbon dioxide and turn them into sugar. The hydrogen in the water combines with the carbon in the carbon dioxide to make the sugar. The oxygen left over from the water enters the air and becomes part of our atmosphere. So take a deep breath and say, "Thanks, plants! Thanks, sun!"

Now reread the passage, including your headings.
Then think of a title for the entire passage.
Write your title in the box at the top of the page.

The Big Idea

Ask a friend to do this activity with you.
Cut out the first few paragraphs from a newspaper or magazine article.
Do not include the headline.
Then cut out a small news picture showing an event taking place.
Have your friend do the same.
Tape your articles and pictures in the spaces below.
Then read each other's article and study each other's picture.
Write a headline that tells the main idea of the article.
Write a caption that tells the main idea of the picture.

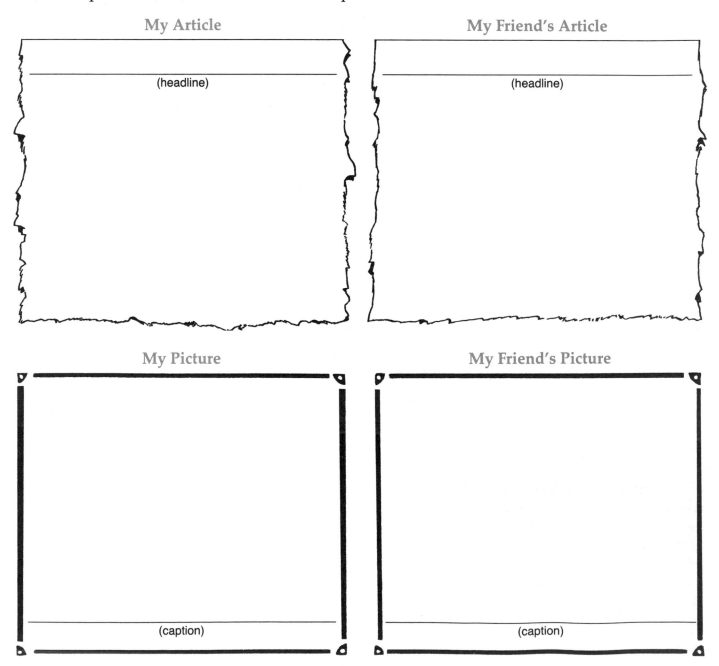

My Article

_____
(headline)

My Friend's Article

_____
(headline)

My Picture

_____
(caption)

My Friend's Picture

_____
(caption)

12 ▶ Yummy, Yummy

The label on a food package often contains a lot of information.
Here is the nutrition label for new Apple Yummies.
Use the label to answer the questions on the right.

ALL NEW! ALL NATURAL!

APPLE YUMMIES

APPLE AND OAT BARS

NUTRITION INFORMATION PER SERVING

SERVING SIZE: 2 BARS
SERVINGS PER PACKAGE: 8

CALORIES 150
PROTEIN. 3g
CARBOHYDRATE 35g
FAT 4g
CHOLESTEROL 0
SODIUM 51mg
POTASSIUM 110mg

PERCENTAGE OF U.S. RECOMMENDED DAILY ALLOWANCE (U.S. RDA)

PROTEIN 6
VITAMIN A . . . . *
VITAMIN C . . . . *
THIAMIN 4
RIBOFLAVIN 5
NIACIN 2
CALCIUM . . . . *
IRON 15
VITAMIN E 12
VITAMIN B6 5
PHOSPHORUS 15
*CONTAINS LESS THAN 2% U.S. RDA

INGREDIENTS: ROLLED OATS, WHOLE WHEAT FLOUR, APPLE JUICE, CRISP RICE, DRIED APPLES, RAISINS, SOY OIL, HONEY, APPLESAUCE, SESAME SEEDS, ALMONDS, CINNA-MON, VANILLA, BAKING SODA

MANUFACTURED BY HWR SNACKS, INC. JAMAICA PLAIN, MA 02130

NET WT. 16oz. (454g)

1. Nutritionists recommend that you have no more than 1000 mg of sodium each day. Is one serving of Apple Yummies a major source of sodium?

____ yes   ____ no

2. RDA stands for Recommended Daily Allowance. How much of your daily iron would you get from eating *two* servings of Yummies?

____ 15%   ____ 2%   ____ 30%

3. How much does each serving of Apple Yummies weigh?

____ 8 oz.   ____ 2 oz.   ____ 16 oz.

4. How many different ingredients give Yummies their apple flavor?

____ 3   ____ 6   ____ 14

5. A serving of Yummies contains less than 2% of the U.S. RDA of which of these nutrients?

____ niacin   ____ vitamin C

____ vitamin A   ____ calcium

6. The label says Apple Yummies are "all natural." Do you agree?

____ yes   ____ no

Why? _____

_____

_____

_____

_____

_____

Which Tools?

Work with a friend or an adult.
Get a regular and colored pencil for each person.
Then sit across from each other with this page between you.
The two pictures on the page are identical.
They both contain kitchen tools, workshop tools, and some other tools.
Using your regular pencils, race to see who is first to circle all
the kitchen tools.
Then use your colored pencils and race to see who is first to put
an X on all the workshop tools.
Compare your pictures and explain any differences to each other.

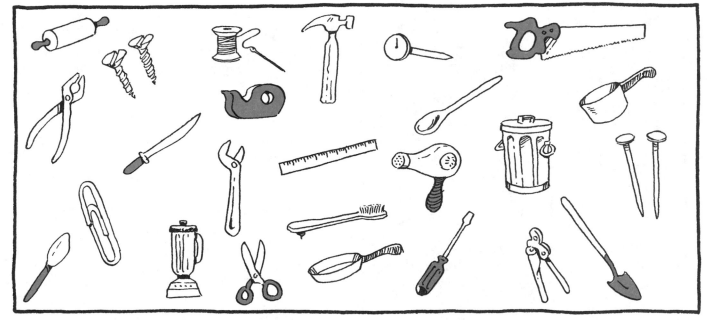

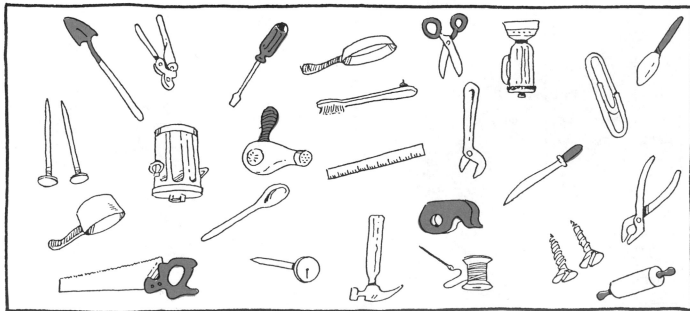

Web of the Senses

Would you like to learn a different way of taking notes?
Start by reading this passage.

You know what your five senses are: sight, taste, touch, hearing, and smell. The most mysterious is probably smell. Scientists are not completely sure about how smell works. They do know, however, that smell is closely related to memory. The smell of something, such as chalk dust, can bring back strong memories. The chalk dust may make you think of your first grade teacher or a time you had to clean all the erasers after school.

Here are some things that are known about the mechanism of smell. You detect smells by breathing air that carries odors. Odors come from tiny particles called molecules that are given off by many substances. These molecules stimulate special cells inside your nose. Tiny hairlike nerve endings, about ten million in each nostril, pick up signals from these cells and rush messages to your brain. Your brain then sorts out these messages and "tells" you what you are smelling.

Now look at the web below.
Complete the top part with the
names of the missing senses.

Now complete the bottom
part to show what the
article says about how
smell works.

```
            SENSES
              |
            smell
         How It Works
              |
    ┌─────────────────────┐
Smell and Memory        Mechanism
```

_____   _____
_____   _____
_____   _____
_____   _____
                         _____
                         _____
                         _____
                         _____

SNIFF   SNIFF

Note It

Ask an adult to help you with this activity.
Have the adult choose a passage for you from a newspaper
article, magazine article, or one of your schoolbooks.
Read the passage and take notes on the card below.

PASSAGE NOTES
Main Idea of Passage:
Most Important Facts:

Now, using just your notes, tell your adult about what you read.
Then reread the passage aloud.
Together, decide if you need to change your notes or add to them.
Make the changes or additions on the card above.
Finally, talk about what else you would like to know about the
topic discussed in the passage.
Write your ideas here.

_____

_____

_____

_____

What Next?

Read each story beginning.
Decide what will happen next.
Write your ideas on the lines provided.
If you need more room to write, use a separate sheet of paper.

The girls and boys stood in a tight knot, whispering and often laughing. Every once in a while, Nanette could hear Carl's loud booming laugh or Rosa's hiccupping giggle. A couple of times, Tommy looked over at her, grinning. Were they laughing at her? Why? Suddenly the bus was there, and its doors wheezed open. The knot untied itself as the boys and girls threaded their way onto the bus. Nanette sighed. Before she could even get herself to begin crossing the street, the doors started to close.

What happened next? _____

_____

_____

The lion crept toward the antelope, moving perhaps an inch at a time. It had to close the distance between them so that the final pounce would be on target. Meanwhile, the antelope grazed peacefully. Was it aware of the lion? Or was it just leading the lion on? It seemed to be tensing its back leg muscles, getting ready for a leap of its own.

What happened next? _____

_____

_____

We gathered around the smoking rock, or whatever it was. It had come down like a flaming streak through the night sky and landed in the vacant lot next to my home. Jane wanted to go right up to it and bang it with a stick, but it was too hot to get that close. So Miguel threw a rock at it. Suddenly a crack appeared, and a fierce red light shone out through it. Then the crack began to widen.

What happened next? _____

_____

_____

Round Robin

Do this activity with two or more friends or family members.
Read the story beginnings below.
Fill in the circle in front of the one you like best.
Then take turns adding to the story.
Start writing on the top stripe below.
When you get to the end of the stripe, give the story to someone else *even* if you are in the middle of a sentence.
Keep passing the story around until each person has had at least four turns.
Continue on separate paper when you get to the bottom of the page.
On the new paper, each person should fill three lines.
Read the story aloud when you are finished.

○ Very, veeery carefully Chuck eased himself out of the tree. He scarcely breathed as he tiptoed past the sleeping creatures.

○ Radole sat down in the master seat. "Now I'll see what this baby can do," Radole muttered as one long tentacle gripped the ship's controls.

○ "There's no such thing as a magic shirt!" declared Laura. Just then, the brand-new shirt started to move. Quickly it slid off the hanger.

15 Capture the Story

Here is a little challenge.
Choose one of the stories listed in the box, or use some other story you know well.
Try to "capture" the story by writing a summary of it in just three sentences.

The Three Little Pigs	The Boston Tea Party	The Hare and the Tortoise
The Story of Columbus	Hansel and Gretel	The Ugly Duckling
The Tale of Peter Rabbit	Snow White and the Seven Dwarfs	The California Gold Rush

Three-Sentence Summary

_____

_____

_____

_____

_____

_____

_____

_____

Here is a stiffer challenge.
Try to write an even shorter summary of the story you just summarized in three sentences.
See if you can "capture" the story in just one sentence.
Here is an example for "Goldilocks and the Three Bears."

While the three bears were out for a walk, Goldilocks entered their home, made a general mess of things, and then fell asleep.

One-Sentence Summary

_____

_____

Now read your one-sentence summary to a classmate.
See if she or he can identify the story.
If not, read your classmate your three-sentence summary.
Have your classmate try again to identify the story.

Comic Order

Here is an activity for you and a friend.

Cut out two comic strips from a newspaper, or use parts of two stories from a comic book you do not mind cutting up.

Cut apart the panels of each strip.

Have your friend do the same.

Then give each other one panel from each of your comic strips.

Mix all the remaining panels together and lay them out face up.

Take turns choosing panels from the group that go with the panels you already have.

When all the panels have been chosen, arrange the panels of your strips in order.

Then decide which completed comic strip you both like best and paste it below.

On the lines at the bottom of the page, write a two-sentence summary of what happened in the strip.

_____

_____

_____

_____

16 ▶ Problems, Problems

Choose three of the stories in the story box, or use some of
your own favorite stories.
For each story, think about these things.
 • The problem or problems that had to be solved.
 • The solution, or how each problem was solved.
 • The climax, or most interesting, exciting moment.
Then write your ideas below.
Here is an example for *Charlotte's Web*.
 Problem: How to keep Wilbur, the pig, away from the slaughterhouse.
 Solution: Charlotte spins webs telling what a great pig Wilbur is.
 Climax: Wilbur is saved, but Charlotte dies at the end of the summer.

Story Box
Cinderella
Peter Pan
Red Riding Hood
Pinocchio
Heidi
Wizard of Oz
Alice in Wonderland
The Hobbit

Story: _____

Problem(s): _____

_____

Solution(s): _____

_____

Climax: _____

_____

Story: _____

Problem(s): _____

_____

Solution(s): _____

_____

Climax: _____

_____

Story: _____

Problem(s): _____

_____

Solution(s): _____

_____

Climax: _____

Solve It

This is an activity to do with an adult.
First, you decide on a character for a story.
Here are some ideas: yourself, your best friend, someone you
saw today, a detective, a reporter, an inventor, an animal.
Next, make up a problem for your character.
Here are some ideas: a car that will not start, missing money,
a mean boss, being lost, being sick, danger of some sort.
Write your character and the problem below.
Then tell your adult about the character and problem.
Have the adult make up a story with a solution to the problem.
Write the solution below.

All of a sudden, the beautiful frog turned into an ugly toad.

My character: _____

The character's problem: _____

_____

My adult's solution: _____

_____

_____

_____

_____

Now have your adult decide on a character and make up a problem.
Then you make up a story with a solution to the problem.
Write the character, problem, and solution here.

My adult's character: _____

The character's problem: _____

_____

My solution: _____

_____

_____

_____

_____

Choose one of the stories you wrote about above.
Together, expand the story and include a climax—the most exciting
or interesting moment of the story.
Write your final story on a separate sheet of paper.
Take your story to school tomorrow and share it with your classmates.

Scan You Find It?

Scanning is a way to read quickly to get specific information.
Sometimes you need to scan slowly and sometimes you need to scan rapidly.
Here are some scanning exercises.
Adjust your scanning speed to the material you are scanning.

1. Which two letters are missing from this alphabet? _____

    A B C D E F H I J K L M N O Q R S T U V W X Y Z

2. Which letters in this alphabet are out of order? _____

    A B C D E F G H J I K L M N O P Q R S T V U W X Y Z

3. What is the phone number of Penelope's Puppy Palace? _____

       Palace Cleaners 723 U.S. Hiway 6 . . . .**555-6666**
       Pandora, Sloan 25 Center Blvd. **555-7652**
       Pelletier, Pat 5 Manor Dr. **555-8090**
       Pendergast, Penelope 18 Ridge **555-8990**
       Penelope, Pietro 88 Rawson Ave **555-7676**
       Penelope's Puppy Palace 78 Mall Rd **555-3647**
       Penenberg Advertising 6370 Station St **555-7355**
       Perelsky, D P 95 S Shawnee **555-8877**

4. Find and circle the phrase "fishing for compliments."

    Tamara went fishing last week, hoping for some compliments on her new fishing hat. Most of the people were fishing for carp. The equipment for fishing included a full complement of rods, reels, sinkers, and bait. Tamara did not care much, for she was fishing for compliments, not carp. She was disappointed when no one complimented her on her new fishing hat.

5. Find and color five numeral 5s in this picture.

Wonder of the World

Work with someone your age or older.
Sit across from each other with this page between you.
The two passages on the page are identical, so you both can
work at the same time.
Say "go" and start scanning the passage for the word *the*.
Circle each *the* you find.
When you both are finished, count only the words you circled.
The winner is the person who circled more words.
Check the bottom of the page to see if the winner found every *the*.

It took fourteen years to build the Brooklyn Bridge. Finished in 1883,
it was, and still is, a wonder of the world. It joins Manhattan and
Brooklyn, and though now there are three other bridges nearby, it is
by far the most beautiful. The bridge represents ideas about beauty
that are very old. It is supported by two giant stone towers. They are
magnificent. Their shape comes from both the temples of ancient Egypt
and the old cathedrals of France. The outline of each tower—the way it
moves slowly in and then pushes out just as it reaches the top—is
Egyptian. The arches in the towers end in the graceful points found in
the taller towers of Chartres, a cathedral in France. It is not easy to bring
together two ideas about beauty that are as different as ancient Egyptian
and old French. Still, the designers of the bridge did so very well.

It took fourteen years to build the Brooklyn Bridge. Finished in 1883,
it was, and still is, a wonder of the world. It joins Manhattan and
Brooklyn, and though now there are three other bridges nearby, it is
by far the most beautiful. The bridge represents ideas about beauty
that are very old. It is supported by two giant stone towers. They are
magnificent. Their shape comes from both the temples of ancient Egypt
and the old cathedrals of France. The outline of each tower—the way it
moves slowly in and then pushes out just as it reaches the top—is
Egyptian. The arches in the towers end in the graceful points found in
the taller towers of Chartres, a cathedral in France. It is not easy to bring
together two ideas about beauty that are as different as ancient Egyptian
and old French. Still, the designers of the bridge did so very well.

Scan this scrambled sentence to find out how many times the word
the is used in the passage.

a times of *the* total used fifteen word the is

Figure It Out

What can you figure out from each short passage below?
Circle the letter of the conclusion you think is best.
When you are finished, compare your answers with your classmates.
Discuss why you chose each answer.

1. Mavis took a deep breath and charged up the steps. Her sample case was heavy and full. "Well," she thought to herself, "the first call is the hardest, they say, so let's get it over with." With that, she rang the doorbell.
   a. Mavis was going to install her first doorbell.
   b. Mavis was starting her first weight lifting class.
   c. Mavis was calling on her first customer.

2. Harold picked up the rock and turned it over in his hand. "Not from around here. Must be from a glacier," he muttered. He made careful notes describing the rock and where he found it. Then he put the rock in his knapsack and hiked on.
   a. Harold is a geologist.
   b. Harold is an arctic explorer.
   c. Harold is a detective.

3. The entire campsite was bathed in a flash of blue-green light, followed almost immediately by a loud rumble. The air felt warm and charged with electricity. "Let's get to the shelter!" Fran shouted. "Our tents won't do us much good."
   a. A power line had come down.
   b. The campsite was on fire.
   c. A thunderstorm had arrived.

4. Elise's taxi stopped in front of the hotel. "Wait here. I'll be right back," she said. The driver shrugged and held out a hand to be paid. Elise started to get out, and the driver started to yell. Elise took out a ten-dollar bill, tore it in half, and handed half to the driver. Then she got out of the taxi.
   a. The ripped bill showed Elise was not pleased with the driver.
   b. The driver had gotten only halfway to Elise's hotel.
   c. The ripped bill was Elise's way of telling the driver to wait.

5. Kenzo put the unusual object on the counter and brought his magnet close to it. The object flew to the magnet and stuck with a clang. "Hmm," said Kenzo, "Just what I thought."
   a. The object was covered with glue.
   b. The object was made of iron.
   c. The object had learned to fly.

Inferring conclusions **237**

Darin and Hettie

Play this game with a friend or family member.
Make nine number cards like these.

| 1 | 2 | 3 | 4 | 5 | 6 | 7 | 8 | 9 |

Put the cards face down.
Take turns.
Turn over a card and read the paragraph below that has the same number as the card.
Then look at the Conclusion Board.
Write your initials in the box that has a conclusion you can draw from the paragraph.
Keep playing until all the number cards have been used.
If one player has initialed three boxes in a row in any direction, that player wins the game.

1. Darin stretched out lazily on the warm blanket. His fingers traced careless patterns in the sand.

2. Hettie stood deep in the shadow of the doorway. They could not see her there, yet she could observe their activities.

3. Darin stood up suddenly. "That's it!" he shouted as he raced to the lab to make adjustments in his experiment.

4. Hettie sat down. "Let's see," she said. "Five across is 'a kind of apple.'"

5. Darin dipped his brush into the paint. An image was taking shape on the canvas.

6. Hettie swung a leg over and grasped the bars. She turned on the motor and the roar of the engine made her heart pound. "Where to this time?" she asked herself.

7. Darin felt the rush of the wind tearing at his clothes. Then whump! He seemed to be jerked upward suddenly. Then he floated down.

8. Hettie said, "One, two, three, four," and the room was suddenly filled with music.

9. Darin said, "Three, two, one, zero," and pressed the red button. The sky was filled with a deafening roar. He watched on the screen as the huge craft sped into the sky.

Conclusion Board

Hettie is conducting an orchestra.	Darin is a scientist.	Hettie is riding a motorcycle.
Darin is painting a picture.	Darin is parachuting from a plane.	Darin is relaxing at a beach.
Hettie is a spy or a detective.	Darin is in charge of a rocket launch.	Hettie is doing a crossword puzzle.

Pictures in My Mind

Words can be used to create images in your mind.
Read each pair of descriptions below.
Put a √ by the one that creates a more interesting and colorful
image in your mind.

Salina looked up at the sky. Gray clouds were moving swiftly overhead. A bunch of Canada geese were flying southward, and Salina could hear their honking.

Salina craned her neck and squinted at the sky. Leaden clouds raced overhead. A "vee" of Canada geese honked along, chasing the clouds southward.

The baby elephant put its trunk between the bars. It was looking for a peanut. Another baby, Jeremy, laughed as the elephant took the peanut from his hand.

The baby elephant's trunk snaked out between the bars, eagerly searching for a peanut. Jeremy, also a baby, giggled as the elephant scooped up the nut from his hand.

Sun streamed hotly into the chilly room. Dolores was curled up in the corner of the overstuffed chair, knees to chin, letting the sun warm both her and the book she was reading.

Dolores sat in the corner of the big, soft chair. The sun shone into the chilly room and on Dolores, warming her. The sun also shone on the book she was reading, warming it, too.

The leader raised a hand, and the band started playing loud, confusing notes. We then tried to sort out the notes, hoping to find a tune we recognized.

The leader raised a hand, and a mountain of notes sped at us at the speed of sound. Our ears started sorting through the rubble, trying to find a recognizable melody.

Choose the description you like best.
In the space below, draw a picture of the image it creates in your mind.

Remembered Images

Do this activity with one or more friends.
Together, study the picture on this page for a few minutes.
Then turn over the page so you no longer see the picture.
On separate paper, each person should write about what he or she remembers from the picture.
Try not to tell just what the picture shows.
Instead, describe the images the picture created in your mind.
When everyone is finished, turn the picture face up.
Then take turns reading each other parts of what you wrote.
After each reading, try to identify the part of the picture described.
You may repeat this activity using other interesting pictures from books and magazines.

20 ▷ What's Wrong?

Look at the picture below.
Use what you know about the world you live in to figure out what
is wrong with it.
Color all the things you find that just cannot be true.

How many things did you find? _____

How did you do?   0–5   Look some more.   11–15   Great!
                   6–10 Pretty good.   16 or more   Fantastic!

Category Challenge

Here is a game for two players.
Get a watch or clock for keeping time.
Then make seven category cards like these.

| animal | vegetable | mineral | person | place | thing | idea |

Put the cards in a bag and mix them.
Draw a card and read the category on it aloud.
Have the other player name something in the category.
Then you try to give three facts about what was named.
Have the other player keep time for up to one minute.
Score 1 point for each fact you give in one minute.
Take turns and play eight rounds.
After each turn, put your card back in the bag.
Keep score below.
The winner is the player with the higher score.

Score Sheet			
Player 1 _____		Player 2 _____	
Round 1	Round 5	Round 1	Round 5
Round 2	Round 6	Round 2	Round 6
Round 3	Round 7	Round 3	Round 7
Round 4	Round 8	Round 4	Round 8
TOTAL		TOTAL	

21 ▶ Sort It Out

A fact is something that can be counted, measured, or checked.
You may not be able to count or measure some things yourself,
but someone has counted or measured them.
An opinion is what someone thinks or feels about something.
It cannot be counted, measured, or checked.
Below is a machine that sorts out facts and opinions.
Read each sentence and mark it **F** for *fact* or **O** for *opinion*.
Then "run" the sentences through the machine.
Write the number of each fact sentence in the part of the Fact
Bin that describes how someone proved the fact.
Write the number of each opinion sentence in the Opinion Bin.

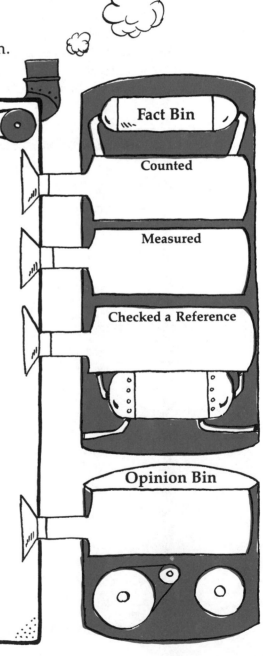

1. _____ The smallest frog ever found was only an inch long.

2. _____ Bananas taste better than apples or pears.

3. _____ There has never been a war in Switzerland.

4. _____ The little girl has 20 baby teeth.

5. _____ The best car ever built was the 1919 Stutz.

6. _____ The average speed of an ocean liner is 33 miles per hour.

7. _____ The first successful typewriter was invented in 1867.

8. _____ The stadium holds 100,001 spectators.

9. _____ Few birds are as beautiful as the flamingo.

10. _____ The tallest waterfall in the world drops 3212 feet.

11. _____ The word *run* has 250 different meanings in English.

12. _____ In 1957, the Russians launched the first Earth satellite.

13. _____ Coin collecting is an exciting and fun hobby.

14. _____ Potatoes consist of about 80 per cent water.

Fact or Opinion?

This is a game to play with an adult.
Make eight game cards, four with **fact** written on them and four with **opinion** written on them.
Mix the cards, put them in a pile, and turn the pile face down.
Take turns.
Toss a coin onto the Topic Board and take the top card.
Do not let the other player see what is written on the card.
If you have a fact card, give a fact about the topic you landed on.
If you have an opinion card, give an opinion about the topic.
Have the other player decide whether you gave a fact or an opinion.
If what the other player decides agrees with what is written on your card, score 5 points.
Record your score on a piece of paper.
Then return the card to the bottom of the pile.
Play until one player has scored 30 points.

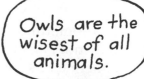

Owls are the wisest of all animals.

Topic Board

sports	music	places	science
history	toys	name your own topic	people
food	current events	school	clothing
animals	movies	jobs	books

Who's Telling?

Read each paragraph below.
Decide who is telling the story.

  A A character in the story.
    The story is seen through this character's eyes and tells
    this character's feelings and reactions to the story.
  B A narrator who is not a character in the story.
    This narrator sees more than any one character could.
  C A narrator who is also a character in the story.
    This narrator is often referred to by the word *I*.

Write **A**, **B**, or **C** in front of each paragraph to show who is
telling the story.

_____ I could feel the crunch of the gravel under my boots as I
hiked up the driveway. Uncle Bill and Aunt Lillian served the best
food in the world, though they did not realize how much I liked it.
They thought all I liked was pizza and burgers, but they always
invited me anyway. It was really no hardship to make the trip to
their house every Sunday for supper.

_____ Jared turned the object over and over in his hand. "Smooth
yet rough. Heavy one minute and light the next," he muttered to
himself. He looked up and saw the alien come through the hatch
of the spacecraft. His face felt hot as the alien cackled, "I see you
have found our little toy."

_____ Martine leaped onto the horse. "Let's go!" she shouted, and
a thousand head of cattle started thundering amid the yips and
whistles of the cowhands. It was a bright, clear day, and no one
sensed that by nightfall they would be in a raging blizzard.

_____ The robot glided into the room on whispering rubber tires. It
turned this way and that, trying to get a fix on where things were
so it would not run into them. Yolanda smiled. Everything seemed
to be going according to plan. Then I picked up a ball and threw it
to the robot.

_____ Rudolph's heart was pounding so hard he thought it might
jump right out of his chest. Could this really be what he had
wanted and worked so hard for? He brushed the hair from his
forehead. Then, his crutches creaking slightly under his hands, he
walked up to accept the award.

Change the Story

Here is an activity for you and a friend.
Choose a favorite story with which you both are familiar.
Talk about how the story was told and who told it.
Then choose a character in the story to retell it in a different way.
Here are some examples.

- Have the sky tell the story "Chicken Little."
- Have the silver dollar George Washington threw across the Potomac tell a story about him.
- Have one of the dwarfs tell the story "Snow White."
- Have the moon tell about the first time a person walked on it.

Now talk about how your story might change when it is told by the character you chose.
Then write your new story below.
At the same time, have your friend write her or his story on a separate sheet of paper.
When you both are finished, read your stories to each other.
Compare your stories to see how they are the same and different.

Title: _____

_____
_____
_____
_____
_____
_____
_____
_____
_____
_____
_____
_____
_____
_____
_____

23 ▶ Sound Blaster

An author writes with a purpose.
An author's purpose may be to

  Inform (give the reader facts and information),
  Entertain (amuse the reader), or
  Persuade (convince the reader to do something or share an opinion).

Read each paragraph below.
Circle **I**, **E**, or **P** to show whether the author's *main* purpose is to inform, entertain, or persuade.

I
E
P
    You won't believe your ears! The new Sound Blaster presents the absolute end in sound reproduction. Sound so real you can reach out and touch it! Rush down to your dealer today. Prepare to be blasted away! Then take home this wonderful little marvel for just $29.95 (plus tax).

I
E
P
    Evelyn put down the new Sound Blaster on the table. She put in a tape, pressed a button, flopped down on her bed, and closed her eyes. Suddenly the room was filled with an unbelievably loud sound. Evelyn's head jerked up and her eyes popped open. She found herself—where?—sliding down the inside of a slippery, bright golden cone. It was a saxophone!

I
E
P
    In our examination of the new Sound Blaster, we found the usual audio system parts. There were standard transistors and tuning circuits, a tape drive, good quality amplifiers, and easy-to-use controls. The one unusual part was a small black box located in one corner. The box was completely sealed and impossible to open. It must be the secret to the Sound Blaster's superior performance, which is achieved without the use of separate speakers.

I
E
P
    Can you believe it? Teenagers all over the country are reporting being transported by their own music systems. Take Doug Johnson, for example. This fourteen-year-old from Passadel was admitted to General Hospital last Friday wide-eyed and babbling about being kidnapped by a bass drum. And then there is Evelyn Ullman of Flin Park, who claims she woke up inside a saxophone. In these cases, and others, the youngsters had been playing the latest model Sound Blaster. There must be something magical about the new model. It is literally taking over everyone on the teenage music scene.

Would you like to own the latest model Sound Blaster?   _____ yes   _____ no

Why? _____

Join Us

Do this activity with a family member or friend.
Together, think up a really strange or unusual hobby.
Here are some ideas: collecting lint from clothes dryers, hiking
around parking lots, taking pictures of out-of-shape paper clips.
Make up a club or an organization for the hobby.
Here are some examples: Fans of Lint United for Fuzz (FLUFF), White
Lines—Parking Lot Hikers Club, Clips Living in Photographs (CLIP).
Then make notes below for a letter or an advertisement inviting
people to join the club or organization.

NOTES FOR LETTER OR AD

Name of club or organization:

Purpose of club or organization:

Where and when meetings are held:

Requirements for joining:

How to persuade people to join:

Other information about club or organization:

Now work together to write your letter or ad.
Use the information in your notes and write on separate paper.
Do your best to make people eager to join.
Try to inform, persuade, *and* entertain them.
Take your letter or ad to school and share it with your classmates.
See if they would like to join your club or organization.

24 ▶ Page One

Here is part of the front page of a newspaper.

Today: Special Section on Vernon History

All the News
All the Time

The Daily Paper

City Edition
Weather: dry, high 60s

VOL. XXX.... No. 3508   *VERNON, MONDAY, MAY 15, 199X*   Copyright © 199X HWR Communications   *35¢*

City Celebrates 150th Anniversary in Style

Talks Open with School Board

Tension High

By CARLOS BARCO
In a tense session that ended in a shouting match, the budget–cutters and taxpayers clashed once again.

Politics as Usual for Mayor

By TERESA JENKS
VERNON, May 14 — Mayor Platero used Vernon's 150-year celebration as a launching pad for a run for the governor's office.

Riverside Park Before Visitors Arrived for Anniversary Celebration

BALLOONS, BANNERS, AND BANDS

FUN FOR ALL AT BIRTHDAY BASH

By LEE SHENG
Sunny weather and several lively brass bands met the thousands of visitors to Riverside Park as Vernon kicked off a week-long celebration of its 150-year history. The festivities still run until 9 o'clock every evening, with a special fireworks display at 9:30 Saturday night. Mayor Platero will make a few remarks before the fireworks begin.

Use the front page to answer each item below.
Mark the box in front of your choice.

1. There are two "ears" on the page. Which one is the weather ear?
   ☐ upper left corner   ☐ upper right corner

2. What is the volume number of the newspaper?
   ☐ 199X   ☐ 35¢   ☐ XXX   ☐ 150

3. One of the headlines is called a skyline. Where would it be?
   ☐ at the very top of the page   ☐ at the top of any story

4. Which do you think belongs on the newspaper's nameplate?
   ☐ HWR Communications   ☐ Vernon   ☐ The Daily Paper

5. A banner headline is an important headline that stretches across the page. Which headline is it?
   ☐ Balloons, Banners, and Bands   ☐ City Celebrates 150th Anniversary in Style

6. A byline gives the name of the person who wrote an article. Which of these is a byline?
   ☐ Mayor Platero   ☐ Tension High   ☐ Teresa Jenks

7. Find the picture caption. Circle it on the newspaper.

News Reporter

Work with a friend on this activity.
Pretend you are reporters who were sent to cover a robbery.
Here are the notes you took at the scene of the crime.
Take a few minutes to review your notes.

Jewelry store broken into.
Stylish Jewelers- 100 High Street.
Alarm didn't go off.
Owner - Jody Hardy.
Discovered early this morning.
Investigated by police - Detective Maria Rao.
$15,000 in diamonds, $25,000 in gold missing.
Burglar seemed to know what to look for.
"I had just paid my insurance and installed alarms. Why me?" - Hardy
"We don't have a suspect yet, but

officers are combing the store for fingerprints and other clues". - Rao
Fifth jewelry store robbery this year.
Hardy blaming police Chief Willy Green.
Green- "We're doing our best. Each robbery was different. We see no pattern".
Glass broken in small window in rear door.
No other damage.
Store closed until Monday, maybe longer.
Meanwhile, Hardy hiring 24-hour guard.
Hardy - "I just don't feel safe anymore".

Now you have to write your article for tomorrow's newspaper.
The instructions below will help you.

1. Write the question words *who, what, where, when, why,* and *how*
   down the left side of a sheet of paper. Work together to find
   information in your notes to answer each question. Write the
   information on your paper.

2. A good news article starts with a "lead"—one or two sentences
   that tell the most important part of the story right away.
   Together, work out a lead for your article and write the final
   version on your paper.

3. Now work together to write your article about the jewelry store
   robbery. Start with your lead and include the answers to the
   question words.

4. Review your article and make any changes that are necessary.
   Then make a final copy.

5. Finally, write a headline for your article. The headline should
   be short, get people's attention, and give information. Try to
   use no more than seven words in your headline. Write it at the
   top of your article.

Take your article to school tomorrow.
Get together with some classmates and read your articles to each other.
Decide whose article should be "printed" in the newspaper.

25 ▶ Air Facts

Since early times, people have tried to explain the world around them. They thought about the workings of their world and came up with explanations that made sense to them.
Here are three things for you to think about and explain.
Write answers that make sense to you.

1. Why does a hot-air balloon rise? _____
   _____

2. What is wind? What causes it? _____
   _____

3. What would happen if a blown-up balloon was put in a freezer? Why?
   _____
   _____

Today, people test their explanations by conducting experiments.
Here are some facts about air that have been tested and proved.

- Air is a mixture of gases.
- Gases are made up of tiny particles called molecules.
- When air is heated, the molecules move about faster.
- The warmer, faster-moving molecules move farther apart from each other and the air becomes lighter.
- When air is cooled, the molecules slow down.
- The cooler, slower-moving molecules move closer together and the air becomes heavier.
- Warmer air rises because it is lighter than the surrounding cooler, heavier air.
- When cooler, heavier air flows toward warmer, rising air, wind is produced.

Now look over your answers to the questions above.
Based on the facts about air, decide if you need to revise your answers.
Write your revised answers here.

1. _____
   _____

2. _____
   _____

3. _____
   _____

The Magic Triangle

In ancient Egypt, builders had a special way of making square corners when marking out fields or planning buildings. They used a "magic" triangle made out of a piece of rope.

Ask a friend to do this activity with you.
You and your friend will find out how a magic triangle works.
First, get a long piece of string and make thirteen equally spaced dark marks on it.
Put the two end marks together and tie a knot where they meet.
Cut off any extra string.
Now you have a loop with twelve equal spaces.
It should look something like this. ——————————→

Next, look around for something with a square corner.
It could be the corner of a floor tile, table top, book, or box.
Put the knot of your loop at the corner and have your friend hold it down.
Then stretch the loop along the two sides of the corner until all three sides of the string are tight.
Slide your hands along the string, keeping the sides tight, until you have a mark in each hand.
You should have a triangle that looks like this. ——————→

How many spaces–places between marks–are on the sides of your corner?   ____ and ____

How many spaces are on the slanted side opposite the corner?   ____

Now measure three other things with square corners.
Record the results below.

	NUMBER OF SPACES ON SIDES OF CORNER		NUMBER OF SPACES OPPOSITE CORNER
Item 1			
Item 2			
Item 3			

If you measured correctly, you should have counted three, four, and five spaces every time.
Anytime you have a triangle with the sides in a three, four, five relationship, you have a triangle with one square corner, or a right triangle.
And a right triangle was the magic triangle the ancient Egyptian builders used to make their square corners!

My Country

A government is the system of rule of a country, state, city, or other group of people.
Governments do not just happen—people invent them.
Imagine you have to set up a government for a new country.
The questions below will help you figure out how the new country should be run.
Continue your answers on a separate sheet of paper if you need more room to write.

1. What is the name of the country? _____

2. Who will be in charge? _____

3. How will the people in charge be chosen? _____
   _____

4. How will the country raise money? _____
   _____

5. How will the country protect itself? _____
   _____

6. How will laws be made? _____
   _____

7. How will laws be enforced? _____
   _____
   _____

8. What laws should the country make? _____
   _____
   _____
   _____
   _____
   _____
   _____
   _____

Who Am I?

Play this game with someone your own age.
Have the other player close his or her eyes while you toss a coin
onto the History Board.
Remove the coin and read the name of the person to yourself.
If you land on a person who has already been used, toss again.
Then tell what you know about the person, but do *not* name the person.
Give as much information as you can and ask "Who am I?" at the end.
If the other player can name the person, score 2 points.
If the other player cannot name the person, score 1 point.
If you do not know anything about the person, score 0.
Take turns and play six rounds. Keep score on a piece of paper.
The winner is the player with more points.

History Board

Theodore Roosevelt	Susan B. Anthony	Frederick Douglass	Sacagawea
Harriet Tubman	Daniel Boone	Amelia Earhart	George Washington Carver
Chief Joseph	Elizabeth Blackwell	Benjamin Franklin	Jane Addams
Clara Barton	John Paul Jones	Sojourner Truth	Abraham Lincoln

27 ▶ Dear Diary

A diary is an account, written each day, of the writer's thoughts and experiences that day.

Here are four imaginary diary entries by people who invented some common everyday objects.

Read each entry and complete the sentence at the end.

The answer is one of the objects pictured on this page.

It occurred to me this morning that there must be an easier way to clean my teeth than with a rag. So I picked out a small bone from a piece of meat and drilled holes in it. Then I tied together some small bunches of short, stiff animal hairs and wedged them into the holes. When I tried it out, it worked like a charm! Why didn't I think of this sooner?

This person invented the _____.

Success at last! Today I tried out the latest version of my platform to hoist the beds in the factory up and down from one floor to another. The addition of the built-in safety device—to keep the platform from crashing down if the pulley rope breaks—was just what was needed. I will test the platform again, but I think I have finally gotten it right.

This person invented the _____.

After months of experimenting, I have found the right adhesive to coat the transparent tape I developed for the refrigerator car manufacturers! The new adhesive is very strong and is practically invisible when applied to the tape. Tomorrow I will take some tape with the new adhesive to the refrigerator car people. Hope they'll be pleased.

This person invented _____.

So many other people have tried to get this machine to work, but I think I have now come up with a way to do it. If I put each letter on an individual bar attached to a keypad, then each letter would hit the paper independently of the others. All you would need to do is push down on the keypads one at a time and they would spell out words. First thing in the morning I will start working on a new model of the machine.

This person invented the _____.

Spoken History

An oral history is a spoken story of past events that happened to a person or nation.

Work with a grandparent or an older adult to prepare an oral history of her or his childhood.

Ask the adult the questions below.

Write the answers on the lines provided.

Use another sheet of paper if you need more writing space.

Be as accurate as you can when you record the answers.

When you are finished, use the information you gathered to tell your adult an oral history of his or her life while growing up.

Q: What was it like where you lived?

A: _____

_____

Q: What was school like?

A: _____

_____

Q: What games did you play?

A: _____

Q: What other things did you like to do?

A: _____

_____

_____

Q: What are your best memories?

A: _____

_____

_____

Q: What else do you remember from your childhood?

A: _____

_____

_____

Realistic or Fantastic?

Fiction may be realistic or it may be fantasy.
A realistic story has real-life characters and events that could really happen.
A fantasy has characters that could never live or events that could not happen in real life.
Read the story beginnings below.
Mark each one **R** for *realistic* or **F** for *fantasy*.

____ The boat sat high in the water, obviously empty after being unloaded. Kyle watched as the five sailors climbed the rigging, making repairs.

____ The boat sat high in the water, a giant hand holding it in place. Kyle could see the five sailors' fearful faces as the giant emerged from the sea.

____ Gena entered the room and saw her dog staring into the fireplace. The old dog turned around. "What are you doing here?" the dog asked.

____ Gena entered the room and saw her dog staring into the fireplace. The old dog turned around. "What are you doing here?" she asked the dog.

____ Jessie walked down the dimly lit corridor. Suddenly a door opened and a man leaped forward, yelling loudly and waving his arms wildly.

____ Jessie walked down the dimly lit corridor. Suddenly a man leaped through a locked door and flew swiftly toward the ceiling.

Choose one of the realistic story beginnings you just read.
Continue the story by adding realistic characters and events.
Use a separate sheet of paper if you need more room to write.

_____

_____

_____

_____

Now choose one of the fantasy story beginnings.
Continue the story by adding fantasy characters or events.
Use a separate sheet of paper if you need more room to write.

_____

_____

_____

_____

Share your completed stories with your classmates.

Finish It for Me

This is an activity for you and a friend.
Begin a realistic or fantasy story below.
Then have your friend finish the story.
If you start a realistic story, your friend should add characters and events to turn it into a fantasy.
If you start a fantasy, your friend should add characters and events to explain away the fantasy.
When your friend is finished, have him or her begin a story.
The story may be realistic or fantasy.
Then you add characters and events to change it into the opposite kind of story.
When you are finished, read your stories aloud to each other.

Did I ever tell you about the space monsters disguised as basketballs?

I bet they just had funny faces painted on them.

My beginning: _____

_____

_____

_____

_____

_____

_____

_____

_____

My friend's ending: _____

_____

_____

_____

_____

_____

_____

My friend's beginning: _____

_____

_____

_____

_____

_____

_____

_____

_____

My ending: _____

_____

_____

_____

_____

_____

_____

29 ▶ Fetch!

A play contains a list of characters, some stage directions, and the characters' words.
The whole story is told by what the characters say and do.
Read the play below.
Then answer the questions at the end.

FETCH!

Cast: MARSHA, A TWELVE-YEAR-OLD GIRL   NINA, ANOTHER FRIEND
DELO, MARSHA'S DOG   A TOY HAMSTER
DWAYNE, MARSHA'S BEST FRIEND

Scene 1

(The friends are in DWAYNE'S *backyard, which has a picnic table.* NINA *has brought a cage with a small toy* HAMSTER *in it. The hamster is connected by a thin black thread to a stagehand off stage. The cage is on the picnic table.* DELO *is sleeping under the table.)*

DWAYNE *(to Marsha)*: When did you get Delo?

MARSHA *(looking fondly at dog under table)*: About a year ago. He was one of those police dogs specially trained to track down things by their smell and bring them back. But he's retired now.

DWAYNE *(sighing)*: I wish I had a dog. But the landlord says no pets allowed unless they live in cages. *(opening door of hamster's cage)* Let's see this hamster you brought me, Nina. *(He picks up the hamster, fumbles, and drops it onto the table.)* Oops! It got away.

NINA: Look out! It's running to the edge of the table. *(She makes a grab for the hamster.)* Oh, no! It's running away!

(All watch as stagehand pulls the hamster off stage.)

1. What is the title of the play? _____

2. How many characters are in the play? _____

3. Where does the action take place? _____

4. What makes the hamster move? _____

_____

5. What do you think will happen next? _____

_____

_____

_____

Radio Play

Here is an activity to do with two or more friends.
There are ideas for a radio play on the radio below.
Together, choose one of the ideas, or use your own idea.
In a radio play, everything that happens is spoken or makes a
sound because the audience cannot see the performers.
Most of the story is told by the characters as they talk to each other.
Sometimes there is a narrator who tells or explains what is happening.
Sound effects are also used to help listeners imagine what is happening.
Talk with your friends to plan your radio play.
Make notes below.

Your spacecraft begins to make strange sounds.

A local toy company is hiring sixth graders to develop new toys.

An explorer is sent to the jungle to recover a lost treasure.

You just discovered a formula for growing bananas instantly.

You and your friends discover a time machine.

The local bank machine has started talking to customers.

Notes for Radio Play

Characters: _____

Setting: _____

Important Events: _____

_____

_____

Outcomes: _____

_____

Now work together to develop your radio play.
On separate paper, write the lines for each character.
Remember to include sound effects and a narrator if you need them
to tell your story.
You do not need stage directions. Just have the narrator tell or
explain what is happening.
When you are finished writing, choose roles and practice reading
your lines and creating the sound effects.
Then gather an audience, such as your family, classmates, or
friends, and put on your play.
You may want to stand behind a screen, sheet, or curtain so the
audience cannot see you.

30 > The Elephant

A poem may tell a story or express the poet's feelings.
A poem also creates strong images through the use of language.
Here is a poem about the wild African elephant.
As you read the poem, pay attention to the images it creates.

THE ELEPHANT

Elephant, who brings death.
Elephant, a spirit in the bush.
With a single hand
He can pull two palm trees to the ground.
If he had two hands
He would tear the sky like an old rag.
The spirit who eats dog,
The spirit who eats ram,
The spirit who eats
A whole palm fruit with its thorns.
With his four mortal legs
He tramples down the grass.
Wherever he walks
The grass is forbidden to stand up again.

Yoruba people, Africa

1. What is the elephant's "hand"? _____

2. Why is the grass "forbidden to stand up again"? _____

   _____

3. How do the Yoruba people feel about the elephant? _____

   _____

4. How is the Yoruba view of the elephant different from your own
   feelings about elephants?

   _____

   _____

Now think about your own experiences with elephants.
Where have you seen them? What did they look like?
How did they move? What did they make you think of?
Write six words you would use to describe your experiences
with elephants.

_____   _____   _____

_____   _____   _____

Create a Poem

Ask a family member to do this activity with you.
Find some old magazines and newspapers that you may cut up.
Together, go through the magazines and newspapers and cut out any words or phrases that appeal to you.
Cut out twenty-five or more words and phrases.
Then work together to write a poem.
Start by arranging the words and phrases to create images and express thoughts and feelings.
Look for unusual combinations that help you "see" or think about things differently.
Keep rearranging the words and phrases until you have the poem just the way you like it.
Then tape or paste your final poem below.
When you are finished, practice reading your poem aloud.
Take your poem to school tomorrow and read it to your classmates.

Wow! Look at that poem!

Looks like you were cut out to be a poet.

31 ▶ What Does It Explain?

Some myths try to explain how things in nature came to be.
Read the following myth.
As you read, think about what the myth is trying to explain.

Long, long ago, cats liked their whiskers short. The shorter the whiskers, the more beautiful the cat. Cats who thought their whiskers were too long regularly cut their whiskers short.

The cats did not have much to do. People thought they were pretty and they fed the cats whenever the cats were hungry. Then one day a farmer who kept some cats said, "You are not earning your keep. You must start catching mice for me. They are eating all my grain."

The cats thought this would be fun. They liked chasing things. But they found out that the mice slept all day and ate the grain at night. The cats had to chase the mice in the dark.

The mice turned out to be very smart. If a cat started chasing a mouse, it would scamper through a hole in a wall. The cat, not being able to see, would try to follow and bang its face against the wall. Some mice got so clever they could lead a cat into a hole just big enough for the cat to get stuck in.

"We need something to keep us from diving into holes that are too small," the cats said to one another. One young cat had an idea. She hid for a few days and let her whiskers grow until they were just as long as the width of her body. "Next time I chase a mouse, I will stop if I feel my whiskers scrape on the sides of the hole," she thought to herself.

The whiskers worked! The next time a mouse led this particular cat into a hole, she stopped just in time. When the curious mouse came out to find out why the cat was not crying in pain, the cat pounced on it!

The whiskers proved to work so well that all the cats decided to let their whiskers grow. The whiskers grew just as long as the cats were wide. Now the cats could have their fun, and the farmer got rid of the mice.

What does the myth explain? _____

_____

Write a title for the myth that expresses what it explains.

_____

Next to the myth, draw a picture to illustrate it.

Whoppers

Do this activity with an adult or a friend.
Have your adult or friend choose one of the story starters below.
Then you use the story starter as the beginning of a tall tale.
A tall tale is an exaggerated story.
It often contains whoppers—lies so outrageous and unbelievable they make people smile.
Tell your tall tale to your adult or friend.
Just make it up as you go along.
Be sure to include at least five whoppers.
Then you choose a different story starter and have your adult or friend use it as the beginning of a tall tale.
When your adult or friend is finished, decide which tall tale you both liked better.
Work together to write down the tale.
You may change it around any way you wish.
Write your tale on a separate sheet of paper.
Include a picture that illustrates one of the whoppers.

The box contained the most colorful shirt Luis had ever seen. He put it on and right away . . .

I warned Janice what would happen, but she insisted. As I handed her the balloons . . .

No one really believed Harry had become so strong until . . .

One day the sun became so huge and bright that . . .

Roy had become so sticky from the molasses that . . .

I thought Lian was just an ordinary baby until one day I found her . . .

Melba gently put her hand on the book. Suddenly the room was filled with . . .

Last night the wind blew so long and so hard that . . .

Fast? You haven't seen fast until you have seen . . .

Enrichment

MATH and READING

Grades 5 & 6
Answer Key and Teaching Suggestions

AMERICAN EDUCATION PUBLISHING

OVERVIEW

ENRICHMENT MATH was developed to provide children with additional opportunities to practice and review mathematical concepts and skills and to use these skills in the home. Children work individually on the first page of each lesson and then with family members on the second page. Every lesson presents high interest activities designed to heighten children's awareness of mathematical ideas and to enrich their understanding of those ideas.

ENRICHMENT MATH consists of 31 two page lessons for grade levels 5 and 6. At each grade level *ENRICHMENT MATH* covers all of the important topics of the traditional mathematics curriculum. Each lesson is filled with games, puzzles and other opportunities for exploring mathematical ideas.

AUTHORS

Peggy Kaye is the author of *Games For Math* and *Games for Reading*. She spent ten years as a classroom teacher in New York City public and private schools, and is today a private tutor in math and reading.

Carole Greenes is Professor of Mathematics at Boston University. She has taught mathematics and mathematics education for more than 20 years and is a former elementary school teacher. Dr. Greenes is the author of a K-8 basal math series and has also written for programs such as *Reach Program, Trivia Math* and the *TOPS-Problem.*

Linda Schulman is Professor of Mathematics at Lesley College . For the past 12 years, she has taught courses in mathematics and mathematics education. Prior to her work at the college level, Dr. Schulman taught elementary school. She is the author of a basal mathematics textbook as well as of other curriculum programs including *TOPS-Problem Solving Program, The Mathworks* and *How to Solve Story Problems.*

WHY ENRICHMENT MATH?

Enrichment and parental involvement are both crucial parts of children's education. More school systems are recognizing that this part of the educational process is crucial to school success. Enrichment activities give children the opportunity to practice basic skills and that encourages them to think mathematically. That's exactly the kind of opportunity children get when doing *ENRICHMENT MATH.*

One of the important goals of *ENRICHMENT MATH* is to increase children's involvement in mathematics and mathematical concepts. When children are involved in mathematics activities, they become more alert and receptive to learning. They understand more. They remember more. Games, puzzles, and "hands-on" activities that lead to mathematical discoveries are guaranteed to get children involved in mathematics. That's why such activities form the core of each *ENRICHMENT MATH* lesson.

Another important goal of *ENRICHMENT MATH* is to provide opportunities for parents to become involved in their children's education. Every *ENRICHMENT MATH* lesson has two parts. First, there is a lesson that the children do on their own. Second, there is a game or an activity that the child does with an adult. *ENRICHMENT MATH* doesn't ask parents to teach children. Instead the program asks parents to play math games and engage in interesting math activities with their children.

Published in 1995 by AMERICAN EDUCATION PUBLISHING
© 1991 SRA/McGraw-Hill

HOW TO USE ENRICHMENT MATH

Each *ENRICHMENT MATH* section consists of 31 lessons on perforated sheets. On the front of each sheet, there is an activity that the child completes independently. On the back there is a follow-up activity for the child to complete with an adult. These group activities include games, projects, puzzles, surveys and trivia quizzes. The front and back pages of a lesson focus on the same mathematical skill.

Activities may be done at the time the skills are being taught to provide additional practice, or used at a later date to maintain skill levels.

Within each level, the lessons are organized into four or five sections. These sections correspond to the major mathematical topics emphasized at the particular grade level. This means you can quickly locate a lesson on whatever topic you want at whatever level is appropriate for your child.

Also available from American Education Publishing—

THE COMPLETE BOOK OF PHONICS

The most thorough and comprehensive guide to phonics available and an essential guide for reading success. Featuring full-color, kid-appealing illustrations and exercises, special review pages, writing activities, answer key, and much more!

• 352 pages • All-color • $14.95 each

TEACHING SUGGESTIONS
Grade 5
Optional Activities

A TIP FOR SUCCESS

Your student will find *ENRICHMENT MATH* Grade 5 assignments enjoyable and easy to understand. Although each lesson has simple and easy-to-read instructions, you may wish to spend a few minutes explaining some lessons before assigning the material. You might even do some of the activities prior to giving the assignments. Many of the activities can liven up an at-home math session and will prepare your child for even greater success.

Part One: Place Value and Operations with Whole Numbers

Students are expected, by this grade level, to have mastered their basic addition, subtraction, multiplication, and division facts, although there are always a number who have not done so and a greater number who would benefit from additional practice. *ENRICHMENT MATH* Grade 5 devotes the first seven lessons to operations with whole numbers.

The activities in these lessons are designed to make practice with basic operations on whole numbers interesting if not fun. Some of the acitivities can be used not only at the beginning of the year but also throughout the year to practice and maintain skills. The activity *Palindromes*, for example, can be used throughout the year by simply writing a number and asking your child to use addition to find the palindrome. You might use this activity at the beginning of a math session or anytime there are a few extra minutes in the day. The game *The Big Difference* is another activity that can be pursued any time during the year by children who need additional practice with subtraction.

A lesson that provides practice in addition and division is the one entitled *Average Facts*. The lesson also helps children learn how to gather, organize, and report data. After this lesson has been utilized, you may wish to suggest that your child work on projects involving the same skills. For example, you can suggest that your child find the average length of a forearm (from the elbow to the tip of the fingers) in the family or find the average number of students in a classroom in their school.

Because place value is an important concept in all computational work with whole numbers, you may wish to develop variations of the game *Pick and Score*. For example, each player draws 4 of the 9 cards and then forms the greatest and least numbers possible. Practice with computation could be included if, in each case, they find the difference between the two numbers. The winner could be either the one with the greatest difference or the one with least difference.

Part Two: Operations with Fractions and Probability

The first lesson in this section provides activities related to a subskill involved in addition and subtraction of fractions and mixed numbers: finding or identifying equivalent mixed numbers and improper fractions. Then the next two lessons address the addition and subtraction of fractions without common denominators. Before assigning the activity *Boxing Fractions* for independent work you may wish to discuss the lesson. Begin by writing the numbers 1, 1, 3, and 3 and ask your child to use the numbers as numerators and denominators to name two fractions whose sum is $\frac{2}{3}$. ($\frac{1}{3} + \frac{1}{3} = \frac{2}{3}$) Then write the numbers, 1, 1, 2, and 4 and ask your child to use these numbers to name fractions who sum is $\frac{3}{4}$. Help your child see that the notion of equivalent fractions is involved in the exercise because the answer is $\frac{1}{2} + \frac{1}{4}$ since $\frac{2}{4} + \frac{1}{4} = \frac{3}{4}$.

The game *Toss a Fraction* is an example of many activities and games in *ENRICHMENT MATH* Grade 5 that can be performed throughout the year whenever time permits or you judge your child's need for such practice and maintenance. Additional cards for this particular game can be created, if you wish, but note that they must be multiples of 2 x 3.

Before assigning the last lesson in this section for independent work, make sure your child understand how to find probability. First, count the number of possible events that can occur. Then, count the number of desired events that can occur. Finally, use a fraction to show the probability: The number of desired events is the numerator and the number of possible events is the denominator. For example, when drawing a card from a deck of regular playing cards, the number of possible events is 52. The number of aces if 4. Therefore, the probability of drawing an ace is 4 out of 52, or $^4/_{52}$.

Part Three: Decimals

The six lessons in this section include finding equivalent decimals for fractions, examining place-value concepts with decimals, and then adding, subtracting, multiplying and dividing decimals.

The game *Close to the Target* is a good activity to help develop an understanding of place value in decimals. The game will help your child recognize that the place-value pattern in decimals is the same as it is in whole numbers, and that the decimal point is not a place but a device used to identify the ones place in the decimal. The game should be played before introducing operations with decimals and can be repeated throughout the year whenever you determine that your child will benefit from the activity.

You may want to introduce the lesson *Missing Points* by writing a few multiplication exercises on a separate piece of paper, such as 3.21 x 7.14. Then demonstrate how, by multiplying only the whole number parts, 3 x 7 = 21, a good estimate of the product can be found. Finally, ask your child to explain how the estimate can be used to correctly place the decimal point in the product if the digits of the product in correct order are 2 2 9 1 9 4.

Part Four: Measurement and Geometry

The first two of the six lessons in this section deal with metric units and customary units of measure respectively. The activity on *Body Measures* can be used to discuss the difference between a unit (anybody's foot) and a standard unit (a foot that is exactly 12 inches long). You might also discuss that all of the units mentioned in this activity are names of standard units, although some of them are seldom if ever used anymore by the average person.

The lessons on *Picture Puzzle* and *Size It* involve finding both the perimeter and the area of geometric figures to help children recognize important differences in these two measurements.

Part Five: Problem Solving

The last six lessons in *Enrichment Math* Grade 5 deal with problem solving and provide many opportunities for children to use a variety of problem-solving strategies. You might wish to help your child recognize that there often is more than one way to solve a problem by using the first problem in *Drawing Conclusions* to illustrate. For example, you can suggest the strategy of acting it out by having family members of three different heights play the parts of Nicole, Kimberly, and Barbara. Another strategy that can be used is draw a picture. Your child can draw vertical lines to represent the three people in the problem. Guess and check is a third possible strategy where your child might guess either Barbara or Kimberly as the taller and then check to see if this leads to any contradiction. Note that guess and check, because it is an important and useful strategy for solving many real-life problems, is given specific attention in the second lesson in this section.

The remaining lessons deal with problems where data is supplied in tables, graphs, and in maps or scale drawings. The lesson on *Tree Diagrams* helps children learn a procedure to use when the question involves a number of choices.

Answer Key
Grade 5–ENRICHMENT MATH

page 11: 1. $486+593=1079$
2. $795+6201=6996$
3. $9432+9=9441$
4. $3268+78=3346$
5. $826+7321=8147$
6. $2047+5177=7224$
7. $3428+6590=10,018$
8. $37+68942=68,979$
9. $84926+485=85,411$
10. $3286+53216=56,502$
11. $1047+39520=40,567$
12. $26439+38643=65,082$

page 12: answers will vary
answers will vary. Ex. pop, tot, mom, dad

page 13: 1. 170 2. 3,857 3. 12,496
4. 8,341 5. 21,598 6. 35,251
7. 45,027 8. 72,746

page 14: answers will vary

page 15: 1. A; 5408 2. A; 1036 3. A; 5400
4. A; 1626 5. B; 13,707
6. C; 28,905 7. B; 12,614
8. C; 27,435 9. D; 32,784
10. D; 31,056 11. A; 5932
12. B; 15,365

page 16: answers will vary

page 17:

^{1}1	^{2}2	3	^{3}7	5	0		
	$^\cdot$0		1			^{4}4	8
^{5}2	0	9	1	^{6}6		8	
	$^\cdot$0		^{7}7	8		^{8}9	^{9}9
^{10}2	0	6	7	0			4
^{11}6	0		^{12}4	0	7	5	2
	7			0			8
^{13}2	4	3		^{14}7	8	4	

page 18: answers will vary

page 19: 1. 39; 92; 9 2. 140; 71; 1
3. 143; 216; 1 4. 105; 325; 5

page 20: answers will vary

page 21: 1. 3; T 2. 40; A 3. 13; I
4. 72; L 5. 31; B 6. 87; A
7. 22; C 8. 58; K

page 22: answers will vary

page 23:

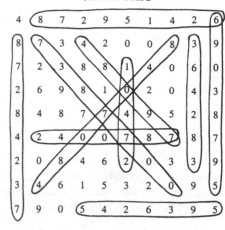
Number Board

page 24: answers will vary

page 25: 1. $\frac{5}{3}$ New Delhi   2. $\frac{11}{5}$ Paris
3. $\frac{27}{8}$ Madrid   4. $\frac{11}{6}$ Oslo
5. $\frac{13}{7}$ Buenos Aires   6. $\frac{11}{4}$ Tokyo
7. $\frac{10}{3}$ Budapest   8. $\frac{25}{6}$ Athens
9. $\frac{9}{5}$ Rome   10. $\frac{15}{7}$ Canberra
11. $\frac{23}{8}$ Peking

page 26: answers will vary

page 27: 1. $\frac{1}{2}+\frac{1}{3}$ 2. $\frac{1}{2}+\frac{3}{4}$ 3. $\frac{1}{3}+\frac{1}{5}$ 4. $\frac{3}{5}+\frac{1}{10}$
5. $\frac{2}{3}+\frac{3}{4}$ 6. $\frac{1}{4}+\frac{9}{10}$ 7. $\frac{1}{6}+\frac{7}{8}$ 8. $\frac{5}{6}+\frac{2}{9}$

page 28: answers will vary

page 29:

1.

$\frac{7}{8}$	$-$	$\frac{3}{8}$	$=$	$\frac{1}{2}$
$-$		$-$		$-$
$\frac{1}{4}$	$-$	$\frac{1}{8}$	$=$	$\frac{1}{8}$
$=$		$=$		$=$
$\frac{5}{8}$	$-$	$\frac{1}{4}$	$=$	$\frac{3}{8}$

2.

$\frac{9}{10}$	$-$	$\frac{2}{5}$	$=$	$\frac{1}{2}$
$-$		$-$		$-$
$\frac{3}{10}$	$-$	$\frac{1}{5}$	$=$	$\frac{1}{10}$
$=$		$=$		$=$
$\frac{3}{5}$	$-$	$\frac{1}{5}$	$=$	$\frac{2}{5}$

3.

$\frac{2}{3}$	$-$	$\frac{1}{5}$	$=$	$\frac{7}{15}$
$-$		$-$		$-$
$\frac{2}{5}$	$-$	$\frac{1}{15}$	$=$	$\frac{1}{3}$
$=$		$=$		$=$
$\frac{4}{15}$	$-$	$\frac{2}{15}$	$=$	$\frac{2}{15}$

4.

$\frac{3}{4}$	$-$	$\frac{1}{3}$	$=$	$\frac{5}{12}$
$-$		$-$		$-$
$\frac{1}{2}$	$-$	$\frac{1}{6}$	$=$	$\frac{1}{3}$
$=$		$=$		$=$
$\frac{1}{4}$	$-$	$\frac{1}{6}$	$=$	$\frac{1}{12}$

page 30: answers will vary

page 31: 1. 13 2. 4 3. 15 4. 10 5. 100
6. 102 7. 52 8. 144 9. 755
10. 275

page 32: answers will vary

page 33:

1. Multiply by 1/4 (vertical) / Multiply by 2 (horizontal)

1/64	1/32	1/16	1/8	1/4
1/16	1/8	1/4	1/2	1
1/4	1/2	1	2	4
1	2	4	8	16
4	8	16	32	64

2. Multiply by 10 (vertical) / Multiply by 1/5 (horizontal)

50,000	10,000	2000	400	80
5,000	1000	200	40	8
500	100	20	4	4/5
50	10	2	2/5	2/25
5	1	1/5	1/25	1/125

3. Multiply by 2 (vertical) / Multiply by 1/8 (horizontal)

128	16	2	1/4	1/32
64	8	1	1/8	1/64
32	4	1/2	1/16	1/128
16	2	1/4	1/32	1/256
8	1	1/8	1/64	1/512

4. Multiply by 1/3 (vertical) / Multiply by 1/2 (horizontal)

20/27	10/27	5/27	5/54	5/108
$2\frac{2}{9}$	$1\frac{1}{9}$	5/9	5/18	5/36
$6\frac{2}{3}$	$3\frac{1}{3}$	$1\frac{2}{3}$	5/6	5/12
20	10	5	$2\frac{1}{2}$	$1\frac{1}{4}$
60	30	15	$7\frac{1}{2}$	$3\frac{3}{4}$

page 34: 1. $\frac{8}{15}$ 2. $\frac{2}{5}$ 3. $\frac{1}{4}$ 4. $1\frac{5}{9}$ 5. $4\frac{1}{4}$

page 35: 1. $\frac{1}{9}$ 2. $\frac{5}{9}$ 3. $\frac{3}{9}$ or $\frac{1}{3}$ 4. $\frac{8}{9}$ 5. $\frac{4}{9}$
6. A 7. B 8. C 9. C 10. B
11. C 12. B

page 36: answers will vary

page 37: Column 1: 0.5; 0.25; 0.3; 0.04; 0.4
Column 2: 0.6; 0.75; 0.8; 0.46; 0.9
Column 3: 0.85; 0.18; 0.7; 0.02; 0.24
Column 4: 0.2; 0.1; 0.16; 0.15;
BECAUSE IT WILL SQUEAL

page 38: answers will vary

page 39: 1. 5.73 2. 72.4 3. 24.37
4. 2.86 5. 4.824 6. 3.275

page 40: answers will vary

page 41: 1. $\frac{0.009}{T}$, $\frac{0.057}{A}$, $\frac{0.231}{X}$, $\frac{0.406}{I}$
2. $\frac{0.007}{T}$, $\frac{0.01}{R}$, $\frac{0.082}{A}$, $\frac{0.299}{I}$, $\frac{0.6}{N}$
3. $\frac{0.001}{A}$, $\frac{0.004}{I}$, $\frac{0.005}{R}$, $\frac{0.016}{P}$, $\frac{0.018}{L}$, $\frac{0.097}{A}$, $\frac{0.107}{N}$, $\frac{0.871}{E}$

page 42: 0.003 MATCH; 0.01 LAWN MOWER;
0.012 SAFETY PIN; 0.02 CARPET
SWEEPER; 0.029 BALL POINT PEN;
0.209 ZIPPER; 0.294 AIR
CONDITIONING; 0.412 AUTOMATIC
TOASTER; 0.42 LONG PLAYING
RECORD

page 43:

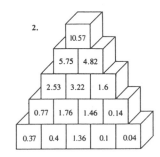

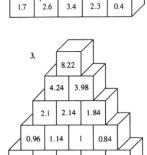

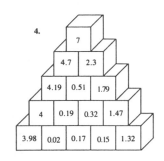

page 44: answers will vary

page 45: 1. 18.2 2. 10.3 3. 17.6
4. 377.25 5. 3.14 6. 167.2
7. 28.98 8. 142.1 9. 139.46
10. 1.17 11. 1.8 12. 1.74
13. 34.06 14. 25.6 15. 429.8
16. 302.6 17. 1867.32 18. 59.1
19. 4.488 20. 76.255

page 46: answers will vary

page 47: 1. 3; 1.2 2. 2; 1.2 3. 5; 1.2 4. 6;
1.2 5. 4; 1.2 6. 7; 1.2 7. 2; 2.41
8. 9; 2.41 9. 5; 2.41 10. 6; 2.41
11. 8; 2.41 12. 3; 2.41

page 48: 1. 203.1 2. 15.43 3. 122.1
4. 68.4 5. 9.69 6. 139.4
7. 7.08 8. 8.12 9. 11.17; 100.9

page 49: 1. 6; 3 2. 16; 8 3. 8; 4 4. 10; 5
5. 18; 9 6. 14; 7 7. 28; 14

page 50:

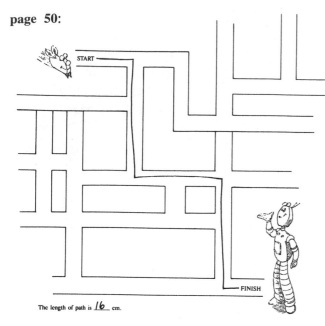

The length of path is _16_ cm.

page 51: 1. =   2. >   3. >   4. <
     5. =   6. <   7. =   8. >
     9. >   10. <   11. <   12. =
     13. >   14. >   15. =
     16. >

page 52: answers will vary

page 53: 1. 2; 1   2. 1; 3   3. 4; 1   4. 3; 3
     5. 6; 3   6. 8; 1

page 54: answers will vary. Possible answers given.

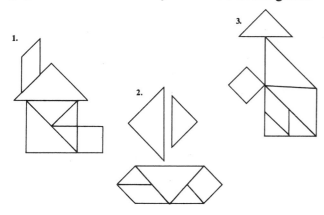

page 55: 1. Ben   2. Sara   3. Jack   4. Rosa
     5. Mele   6. Elliot

page 56: answers will vary

page 57: 1. B;   2. D   3. A   4. C   5. E

page 58: answers will vary

page 59: 1. 6; 0; 0   2. 2; 4; 0   3. 0; 3; 2
     4. 6; 4; 0   5. 3; 4; 2   6. 2; 5; 2

page 60: answers will vary

page 61: 1. Barbara   2. Saturday   3. Jon
     4. 5 years old   5. $4.50   6. squash
     7. 1:00pm   8. Tricia

page 62: answers will vary

page 63: 1. 14; 35   2. 28; 23   3. $\frac{14}{19}$; 23
     4. 35; $\frac{28}{23}$ 5. $\frac{14}{35}$; 19   6. $\frac{14}{19} \div 23$; $\frac{28}{35}$

page 64:

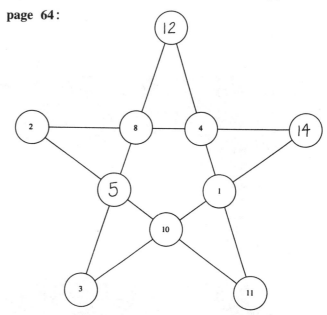

page 65: 1. Entertainment   2. Transportation
     3. School Supplies, Transportation
     4. Savings, Food, Entertainment
     5. $6   6. $9   7. $10.50   8. $10.50
     9. $162

page 66: answers will vary

page 67: 1. 3:00pm   2. $27.00   3. $6.40
     4. 4   5. $44.20   6. 7:00am
     7. $6.75   8. 10

page 68: answers will vary

page 69: 1.

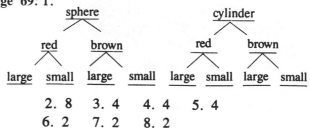

     2. 8   3. 4   4. 4   5. 4
     6. 2   7. 2   8. 2

page 70: 1. answers will vary.   2. 9
     3. answers will vary   4. 12

page 71: 1. 250cm   2. 125m   3. 175m
     4. 11cm   5. 475m   6. 875m

page 72: answers will vary

TEACHING SUGGESTIONS
Grade 6
Optional Activities

A TIP FOR SUCCESS

Your child will find *ENRICHMENT MATH* Grade 6 assignments enjoyable and easy to understand. Although each lesson has simple and easy-to-read instructions, you may wish to spend a few minutes explaining some lessons before assigning the material. You might even do some of the activities prior to giving the assignments. Many of the activities can liven up an at-home math session and will prepare your child for even greater success.

Part One: Operations with Whole Numbers and Number Theory

Because the concept of place value is pervasive in all of the computational procedures or algorithms for operating with whole numbers, an understanding of this concept is essential to success with such computation, and the first lesson in *ENRICHMENT MATH* Grade 6 provides activities to help insure this success. The next four lessons then focus on operations with whole numbers.

Beginning with this grade level, children will be expected to be proficient with all operations on whole numbers. Therefore, during the year ample opportunity should be provided to practice and make permanent the skills required to add, subtract, multiply, and divide whole numbers. Although four of the lessons in this section provide such practice, you may choose to follow up the lessons with ones of similar nature to be used for practice and maintenance throughout the year. For example, after using *Cross-Number Puzzle*, you can ask your child to design his or her own puzzles for others to solve. *The Price is Right* and *Market Hunt* can also be used to launch a project where children find prices in newspaper advertisements and use them to write their own problems for others to solve. Such projects have the additional benefit of providing insight into problem solving with whole numbers that comes from writing your own problems for others to solve.

Part Two: Decimals

Once again, *Enrichment Math* Grade 6 recognizes the importance of understanding the concept of place value to success in computation, not only with whole numbers but also with decimals, and this section begins with a lesson that focuses on the concept. Once children recognize that the place-value pattern in decimals is merely an extension of the same pattern in whole numbers and that the decimal point serves only as a device to identify the ones place, those students who are skillful with operations on whole numbers should have minimum difficulty with operations on decimals.

To provide more practice with addition of decimals after playing the game *Hit the Target*, your child can create additional games merely by assigning new target numbers for the three given on the game sheet. To establish some parameters, tell your child that each target number can be any number they choose as long as it is between 0 and 900. For more practice with subtraction of decimals, your child can play the game *Zero Out* using the same rules given on the game sheet or varying the rules by common agreement. These games, as well as other activities in *Enrichment Math* Grade 6, can be used throughout the year any time.

Part Three: Fractions, Proportions, and Percents

The major focus of the seven lessons in this section is on fractions. With increased attention being given to the metric system and its relationship to decimals, some say that attention to fractions is no longer as important as it once was. However, they would be wrong to conclude this. One can readily see the application of fractions to such real-life activities as measurement with customary units, and since many young people and adults are and will continue to be active in do-it-yourself projects involving customary units, proficiency in this area is important. However, an understanding of fractions and operations on fractions is equally important in many other applications such as those that involve ratio, proportion, percent, and probability. And, of course, future success in mathematics courses such as algebra, with its considerable concentration on rational expressions, requires an understanding of the concepts and mastery of the skills related to fractions.

The first four lessons in this section focus on operations with fractions and mixed numbers by providing interesting activities involving addition, subtraction, multiplication, and division. Then the focus changes to identifying equivalent fractions, decimals, and percents. To provide motivation for these activities, you may want to indicate to your child that computation can often be simplified by being able to choose from two equivalent numbers. For example, to find 25% of 160, it would be easier to multiply 160 by $\frac{1}{4}$ than to multiply by 0.25.

Part Four: Measurement and Geometry

The first two of the six lessons in this section focus on metric units and customary units of measure respectively. The first lesson with its attention to money facts will be of particular interest to the many children interested in coin collecting. As a follow-up project, interested children may want to research similar data about coins that once were used by people but no longer are in circulation, such as the two-cent piece and the three-cent piece. An excellent source available in most libraries is R.S. Yeoman's *A Guide Book of United States Coins*, published each year by Western Publishing Company.

Note that the lesson on *Missing Measures* deals with both perimeter and area simultaneously. This has been done deliberately to help children better appreciate the differences between these two measurements and the units used to find them.

The lesson *All in the Foot* utilizes a relationship between the surface area of one's foot and the total surface area of the body. Some children may be interested in exploring the possibility of there being other relationships. For example, they might measure the forearm (distance between elbow and the finger tips) of family members and compare it with their own height to see if any relationship exists. If the ratio is virtually the same for all the family, and it will be, then a relationship does exist.

Part Five: Statistics, Probability, and Problem Solving

The first of the six lessons in this book presents activities where children find two different measures of central tendency–the mean or average and the median or middle score–and the range of the data.

The second lesson deals with probability. Before assigning this lesson, you may want to make sure that your child understands how to find probability by using a number to illustrate. When a number cube is rolled, there are 6 possible outcomes. If you want to roll a specific number, there is only 1 way this can be done. So, the probability of rolling a specific number is 1 out of 6, or $\frac{1}{6}$. Probability is a ratio of the number of favorable outcomes to the total number of possible outcomes. As a follow-up to *Popular Words*, in order to further illustrate the use of probability to predict, you could have your child make a tally chart for the number of times each letter of the alphabet appears in different paragraphs. Then use the results to predict which letter will appear most often in another paragraph chosen at random from a book.

The lesson *Making Generalizations* helps children use the important problem-solving strategy of looking for patterns. The game *Score 12* is an entertaining and challenging application of this strategy. The lesson *Who's Who* and *Farmer Jack's Problem* helps children recognize how making a table or drawing can be a useful strategy for solving non-routine problems. The last lesson begins with a fairly familiar problem of reading data from a schedule in *All Aboard*, but then turns the problem around by asking children to make a schedule in *Setting the Schedule*, thereby requiring them to think more deeply and insightfully about this type of real-life situation.

Answer Key
Grade 6–ENRICHMENT MATH

page 75: 1. 653,214 2. 95,876
3. 7,625,431 4. 487,563
5. 395,876,421
6. 5,999,999,999
7. 39,999,999,694
8. 799,899,999,999

page 76: answers will vary.

page 77:

¹7	²6	0		³8	5	⁴8	2
	2	⁵6			4		
⁶4	7	6	2	⁷5		4	
	8		⁸9	8	1	6	⁹1
¹⁰4	6	9		3			4
0			¹¹8	2	1	9	3
4							9
¹²6	8	2	7	¹³3	7	2	

page 78: answers will vary

page 79: 1. 34.95 2. 24.50 3. 8.99
4. 35.00 5. 24.95 6. 2.99

page 80: answers will vary

page 81: 1. 92,000; 92,000; 92,000; (102,000)
2. 120,000; 120,000; (115,000); 120,000
3. 158,400; (158,340); 158,400; 158,400
4. 26,928; 26,928; 26,928; (26,398)

page 82: answers will vary

page 83: 1. 32 2. 56 3. 41 4. 92 5. 11
6. 29 7. 116 8. 63 9. 187
10. 36 11. 52 12. 278

page 84: answers will vary

page 85: 1. Factors of 24; A
2. Even Numbers; I
3. Multiples of 3; R
4. Prime Numbers; P
5. Multiples of 6; L
6. Odd Numbers; A
7. Composite Numbers; N
8. Factors of 36; E

page 86: answers will vary

page 87: 1. $\dfrac{0.004}{A}, \dfrac{0.0012}{D}, \dfrac{0.0235}{A}, \dfrac{0.03}{M}, \dfrac{0.4}{S}$
2. $\dfrac{0.0012}{G}, \dfrac{0.0021}{R}, \dfrac{0.003}{A}, \dfrac{0.02}{N}, \dfrac{0.12}{T}$
3. $\dfrac{0.009}{T}, \dfrac{0.0018}{R}, \dfrac{0.027}{U}, \dfrac{0.36}{M}, \dfrac{1.001}{A}, \dfrac{1.4}{N}$

page 88: 0.0009 0.0078 0.0099 0.0102
0.0435 0.1201 1.0008 1.0200 1.3000;
Declaration of Independence signed; George Washington elected President of the U.S.; First Webster Dictionary published; First stick-on postage stamp; Abraham Lincoln elected President of the U.S.; U.S. buys Alaska from Russia; Mark Twain publishes Tom Sawyer; First plane flight; Boy Scouts of America founded.

page 89: 1. 8 2. 10.6 3. 8.215 4. 4.7936
5. 24.39 6. 20.1

page 90: answers will vary

page 91: 1948 1. 10.6258; 9.8397; 8
2. 6.106; 3.1873; 1
3. 0.343; 5.9485; 4
4. 2.7972; 4.5988; 9

page 92: answers will vary

page 93: MISSOURI 48.6; 475.904; 12.43; 886.88; 360.572; 2.52; 56.24; 26.775
KENTUCKY 778.68; 15.895; 816.34; 4.074; 3.712; 3.456; 4.55; 17.549

page 94: answers will vary

page 95: 0.5; 2; 0.2; 30; 4; 31; 11; 10; 2.2; 300; 200
BENJAMIN FRANKLIN

page 96: 1. 0.21 2. 30 3. 0.12 4. 2.4 5.5

page 97:

1.
+	2.173	5.946
3.82	5.993	9.766
7.04	9.213	12.986

2.
+	5.8	8
5.92	11.72	13.92
4.73	10.53	12.73

3.
×	7.3	3.8
5	36.5	19
6.1	44.53	23.18

4.
×	2.3	6.31
7.2	16.56	45.432
4.6	10.58	29.026

5.
+	3.48	5.201
3.45	6.93	13.08
13.08	16.56	18.281

6.
×	8.5	9.25
1.8	15.3	16.65
9.1	77.35	84.175

page 98: answers will vary

page 99: 1. 25 2. $8\frac{8}{15}$ 3. $18\frac{1}{4}$ 4. $61\frac{1}{6}$

5. $31\frac{5}{8}$ 6. $36\frac{5}{12}$ 7. $44\frac{1}{5}$ 8. $54\frac{19}{24}$

9. $26\frac{1}{4}$ 10. 51 11. $55\frac{3}{10}$

12. $21\frac{1}{24}$; $41\frac{1}{2}$

page 100: 1. $2\frac{5}{8}$ 2. $6\frac{1}{2}$ 3. $9\frac{2}{3}$ 4. $9\frac{3}{10}$ 5. $4\frac{1}{6}$

page 101:

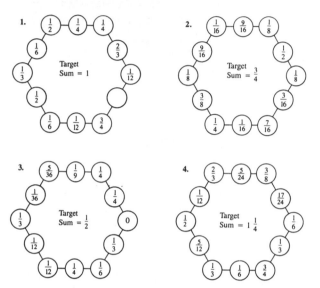

page 102: answers will vary

page 103: 6; 1; 3; 2; 5; 8; 4; 7

VACATION

page 104: answers will vary

page 105:

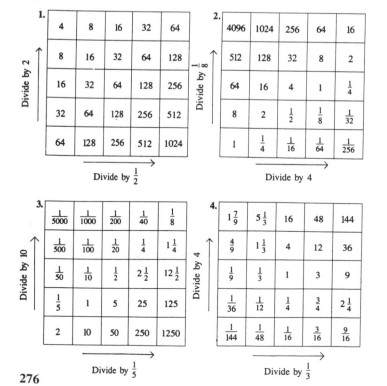

page 106: answers will vary

page 107: 1. Costa Rica 2. Finland 3. Turkey
4. Italy 5. Mexico 6. Greece
7. Sweden

page 108:

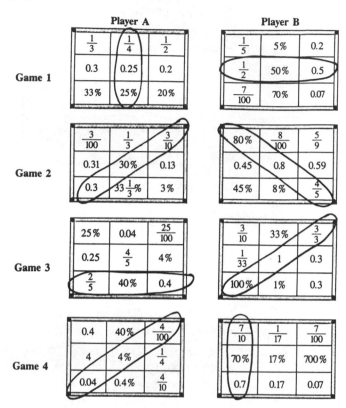

page 109: PROPORTION

page 110: answers will vary

page 111: 1. 25% 2. 40% 3. 8% 4. 10%
5. 50% 6. 12%

page 112: answers will vary

page 113: 1. 75 dimes 2. 17 nickels
3. 80 pennies 4. 1000 pennies
5. $17.50 6. 475 grams
7. $0.25 8. 794 grams

276

page 114:

8,000m = __8__ km | 4,000mg = __4__ g | 6,000L = __6__ kL | Take another turn | 9m = __900__ cm | 8,000mL = __8__ L | 5kg = __5000__ g

1,000g = __1__ kg

200cm = __2__ m

Lose 1 turn

5,000mL = __5__ L

30mm = __3__ cm

7km = __7000__ m

Lose 1 turn

7,000L = __7__ kL

400cm = __4__ m

2,000mg = __2__ g

GAMEBOARD

START | STOP | 8m = __800__ cm | 60mm = __6__ cm | Take another turn | 9,000mL = __9__ L | 6kg = __6000__ g

page 115: 1. 264,000,000 2. $14,540
3. approximately 1067
4. $3,680,000 5. 540

page 116: answers will vary

page 117: 1. area = 1372 square yards;
perimeter = 154 yards
2. 42 yards; perimeter = 168 yards
3. 70 yards; perimeter = 252 yards
4. 84 yards; area = 1764 square yards
5. 56 yards; area = 1176 square yards
6. 35 yards; area = 294 square yards

page 118: answers will vary

page 119: Brett; Ethan; Doris; Candia; Anna

page 120: answers will vary

page 121: 1. 90° 2. 90° 3. 50° 4. 50°
5. 50° 6. 130°

page 122: answers will vary

page 123: answers will vary

page 124: MAKE MASHED POTATOES

page 125: 1. 70-140 2. 94.5 3. 103 4. 90
5. 88.5 6. week 1 7. Mr. Kramer
8. week 3 9. 70-128 10. Mrs. Kramer

page 126: answers will vary

page 127: 1. $\frac{6}{60}$ or $\frac{1}{10}$; 0.1; 10%
2. $\frac{15}{60}$ or $\frac{1}{4}$; 0.25; 25%
3. $\frac{60}{60}$ or 1; 1; 100%
4. $\frac{45}{180}$ or $\frac{1}{4}$; 0.25; 25%
5. $\frac{120}{300}$ or $\frac{2}{5}$; 0.4%; 40%
6. $\frac{270}{720}$ or $\frac{3}{8}$; 0.375; 37.5%

page 128: answers will vary

page 129: 2. 20%; 0.20; 6,800
3. 17%; 0.17; 5,780
4. 8%; 0.08; 2,720
5. 5%; 0.05; 1,700
6. 1%; 0.01; 340
7. 3%; 0.03; 1,020
8. 6%; 0.06; 2,040
9. 10%; 0.10; 3,400
Total: 100%; 1.00; 34,000

page 130: answers will vary.

Total: $100; $\frac{100}{100}$; 100%

page 131: 1. H 2. T 3. H 4. 37 5. A 6. 10
7. 1200 8. 496

page 132: answers will vary. The best way to play so that you will always win is to 1) play second and 2) add a number that will bring the score to a multiple of 4.

page 133:

	Nurse	Painter	Decorator	Teacher
Mr. Williams	X	O	X	X
Mr. Conrad	X	X	X	O
Mrs. Kennedy	X	X	O	X
Mrs. Ming	O	X	X	X

Mr. Williams is a painter; Mr. Conrad is a teacher; Mrs. Kennedy is a decorator; Mrs. Ming is a nurse.

page 134: Farmer Jack with goose.
Farmer Jack
Farmer Jack with fox.
Farmer Jack with goose.
Farmer Jack with corn.
Farmer Jack
Farmer Jack with goose.
Farmer Jack makes 7 one-way trips across the river.

page 135: 1. #81; Dexter 2. Boxford; #77
3. Canton; #99; Fairfield
4. Allentown; #95; Eaton

page 136: answers will vary.

OVERVIEW

ENRICHMENT READING is designed to provide children with practice in reading and to increase their reading abilities. The major areas of reading instruction—word skills, vocabulary, study skills, comprehension, and literary forms—are covered as appropriate at each level.

ENRICHMENT READING provides a wide range of activities that target a variety of skills in each instructional area. The program is unique because it helps children expand their skills in playful ways with games, puzzles, riddles, contests, and stories. The high-interest activities are informative and fun to do.

Home involvement is important to any child's success in school. *ENRICHMENT READING* is the ideal vehicle for fostering home involvement. Every lesson provides specific opportunities for children to work with a parent, a family member, an adult, or a friend.

AUTHORS

Peggy Kaye, the author of *ENRICHMENT READING*, is also an author of *ENRICHMENT MATH* and the author of two parent/teacher resource books, *Games for Reading* and *Games for Math*. Currently, Ms. Kaye divides her time between writing books and tutoring students in reading and math. She has also taught for ten years in New York City public and private schools.

WRITERS

Timothy J. Baehr is a writer and editor of instructional materials on the elementary, secondary, and college levels. Mr. Baehr has also authored an award-winning column on bicycling and a resource book for writers of educational materials.

Cynthia Benjamin is a writer of reading instructional materials, television scripts, and original stories. Ms. Benjamin has also tutored students in reading at the New York University Reading Institute.

Russell Ginns is a writer and editor of materials for a children's science and nature magazine. Mr. Ginn's speciality is interactive materials, including games, puzzles, and quizzes.

WHY ENRICHMENT READING?

Enrichment and parental involvement are both crucial to children's success in school, and educators recognize the important role work done at home plays in the educational process. Enrichment activities give children opportunities to practice, apply, and expand their reading skills, while encouraging them to think while they read. *ENRICHMENT READING* offers exactly this kind of opportunity. Each lesson focuses on an important reading skill and involves children in active learning. Each lesson will entertain and delight children.

When children enjoy their lessons and are involved in the activities, they are naturally alert and receptive to learning. They understand more. They remember more. All children enjoy playing games, having contests, and solving puzzles. They like reading interesting stories, amusing stories, jokes, and riddles. Activities such as these get children involved in reading. This is why these kinds of activities form the core of *ENRICHMENT READING*.

Each lesson consists of two parts. Children complete the first part by themselves. The second part is completed together with a family member, an adult, or a friend.

ENRICHMENT READING activities do not require people at home to teach reading. Instead, the activities involve everyone in enjoyable reading games and interesting language experiences.

Published in 1995 by AMERICAN EDUCATION PUBLISHING
© 1991 SRA/McGraw-Hill

HOW TO USE HOMEWORK READING

Each *ENRICHMENT READING* section consists of 31 two-page lessons. Each page of a lesson is one assignment. Children complete the first page independently. They complete the second page with a family member, an adult, or a friend. The two pages of a lesson focus on the same reading skill or related skills.

Each level is organized into four or five units emphasizing the major areas of reading instruction appropriate to the level of the book. This means you will always have the right lesson available for the curriculum requirements of your child.

The *ENRICHMENT READING* lessons may be completed in any order. They may be used to provide practice at the same time skills are introduced at school, or they may be used to review skills at a later date.

The games and activities in *ENRICHMENT READING* are useful additions to any classroom or home reading program. In many cases, your child's answers will vary according to his or her own thoughts, perceptions, and experiences. Always accept any reasonable answers your child gives.

Also available from American Education Publishing—

MASTER SKILLS SERIES SKILL BOOKS

The Master Skills Series is not just another workbook series. These full-color workbooks were designed by experts who understand the value of reinforcing basic skills! Subjects include Reading, Math, English, Comprehension, Spelling and Writing, and Thinking Skills.

• **88 pages**   • **40 titles**   • **All-color**   • **$5.95 each**

TEACHING SUGGESTIONS
Grade 5
Optional Activities

A TIP FOR SUCCESS

Children using Grade 5 of *ENRICHMENT READING* will find the directions easy to read, understand, and follow. Even so, you may want to spend a few minutes explaining each assignment. You might also do some of the activities and play some of the games. Children are more likely to be successful with the assignments if they are familiar with them, and the games and activities will fill their reading time with fun and learning.

Vocabulary

The Vocabulary unit contains seven lessons designed to help children build and expand their vocabularies. Most children using Grade 5 will have been exposed to the basic skills used in vocabulary building including context clues, affixes, root words, word derivation, figurative language, and analogies. The activities and games in this unit provide children with opportunities for additional practice using these skills in ways that are interesting and fun.

The first lesson focuses on context clues. After your child becomes familiar with the game *Define It* (page 140), you may want to use it throughout the year to give your child practice in getting meaning from context. Each time the game is used, let your child make up new words for the word cards.

The second and third vocabulary lessons deal with prefixes and suffixes. You may wish to develop home versions of *Prefix Race* (page 142) and *Toss a Word* (page 144) to use throughout the year. Some spaces on each game board may be left blank and filled in with words from your child's reading materials each time the games are played.

Children often enjoy making up similes and metaphors, and activities that encourage them to create these kinds of comparisons also help them stretch their imaginations. After your child completes *What Is Going On?* (page 147), he or she may want to help the frog and owl get out of the refrigerator by adding panels to the cartoon. Be sure to remind your child that the speech he or she makes up for the characters should contain metaphors or similes.

After your child completes *Raining Cats and Dogs* (page 149), challenge him or her to find idioms in other stories and books. Having children act out idioms will also help them recognize the difference between figurative and literal language. *Idiom Action* (page 150) may be played at home and expanded to include idioms children find in their reading materials.

After completing *Crosswords* (page 151), some children may want to try their hands at making up their own analogy crossword puzzles. Your child's puzzles may be copied and distributed for other family members to complete.

Study Skills

The Study Skills unit contains three lessons covering parts of books, graphs, maps, and dictionary skills. The first lesson takes advantage of children's interest in space travel and space exploration to provide them with practice using a table of contents and an index. Once children have played the *Space Supplies* (page 154) game, try this variation in which children race to see who can find an index reference first. Make sure each child has a copy of the same book. Then ask questions based on the book. After each question, have children search the index for the page or pages that might contain the answer. The first child to name the correct page reference wins the round.

In *How Long Was It?* (page 155), children are asked to make a bar graph. To prepare for this activity, you may want to review with your child how to complete a simple bar graph. Children who are interested in dinosaurs may also want to expand their graphs to include the lengths of additional dinosaurs. Before you assign *Ocean City* (page 156), make sure your child has had some experience locating objects and following directions on a map.

A thorough understanding of alphabetical order and the parts of a dictionary is crucial to developing good dictionary skills. *Look Around* (page 157) reviews the purpose of guide words and may be adapted to provide children with practice in using other reference books that have guide words, such as encyclopedias. *Find It, Use It* (page 158) may also be played at home. Let your child choose his or her own entry words, make word cards for the words, and make number cards for the definition. When your child plays his or her games, he or she will be increasing their vocabularies as well as practicing their dictionary skills.

Comprehension

The Comprehension unit contains thirteen lessons covering the major aspects of comprehension appropriate to Grade 5. The first three lessons focus on finding main ideas and details and on taking notes. Find main ideas in paragraphs and then extending the ideas can be a powerful comprehension tool for readers of all abilities. *The Big Idea* (page 159) provides children with opportunities to extend the ideas in a paragraph about exercise, and may spark an interest in fitness. To adapt *Making Headlines* (page 160) for at home use, try this variation. Tape short articles and their headlines on opposite sides of cards. Vary the articles according to your child's interests and abilities. Then let your child choose articles, write headlines, and check his or her answers. In *Games for the '90s* (page 161), children glean details from a chart of imaginary computer games. To provide your child with additional practice, repeat the activity with charts from consumer magazines and special-interest magazines that review products. Page 161 will also prompt some imaginative thinking and artwork. Let children who are interested develop some of the imaginary games listed on the chart, including pictures to show what the game screens look like. After your child completes *SQ3R* (page 163) and before you assign *Notable Events* (page 164), review the SQ3R method with your child. Your child may also be encouraged to use this method with any materials from which he or she needs to take notes.

Children often enjoy making up endings for stories. Both *What Was That?* (page 165) and *Round Robin* (page 166) can easily be extended by creating additional story beginnings. Children can also be notoriously long-winded when summarizing stories. In *The Long and Short of It* (page 167), children must compress a wordy summary into just a few lines. After your child completes the activity, challenge him or her to write summaries in limited spaces. You could try having your child write his or her summaries on index cards or even on blank business cards. In Lesson 17, two familiar types of activities, mazes and dominoes, are used to provide children with practice in distinguishing causes and effects. When *Dominoes* (page 172) is assigned as homework, make sure your child understands he or she is to go from one domino to another based on cause-and-effect relationships between statements on the dominoes.

Change it Around (page 176) can be adapted for use with any story in your child's reading experiences. Once children get the hang of retelling stories from another point of view, they can have wonderful imaginative fun with this kind of activity. Children also have fun with the kind of activity in *What's Wrong?* (page 179). You might extend the "what's wrong" concept, perhaps on April Fool's Day, by having your child become walking "what's wrongs." On the appointed day, have your child wear one or more things that are wrong, such as mismatched socks or shoes, a pair of gloves indoors, one pants leg rolled up, a watch around an ankle, and so on. Award a silly prize to the child who notices and lists the most wrong things by the end of the day.

Forms of Writing

The Forms of Writing unit contains eight lessons that help children develop appreciation for several different forms of written material including newspaper, science, mathematics, geography, diaries, poetry, and mythology.

In Lesson 24, children tackle the language of advertising. If children are unfamiliar with persuasive writing techniques, you may wish to help them identify these techniques in newspaper and magazine ads before you assign *Who Wrote It?* (page 185). After children complete *Hometown Times* (page 187), a home version of the newspaper guide can be created and hung on a wall or bulletin board.

Keep Trying (page 189) presents a simple science experiment which you may want to let your child do at home. Even though it is quite safe, do not let your child do the experiment wihout supervision.

Dear Diary (page 193) introduces children to diary entries and also provides them with additional experiences with summarizing story plots and retelling stories from another point of view. After children finish the page, they may enjoy writing fictitious diary entries for their own favorite story characters. Then let pairs of children exchange entries and try to guess what character "wrote" each entry.

How It Came to Be (page 199) introduces children to three different myths about the origin of Earth. Children may be interested in trying to find myths on this topic from other cultures and comparing them to those on page 199.

Page 139 1. dawdling 2. very loud 3. underground 4. argument 5. snake-like; dawdling, very loud, underground, argument, snake-like; story endings will vary

Page 140 Sentences and results will vary.

Page 141 1. *pre*game 2. *un*done 3. *sub*standard 4. *re*play 5. *mis*fortunes 6. *un*folded 7. *im*possible 8. *re*trace 9. *counter*clockwise 10. *re*gain 11. *fore*see; answers will vary

Page 142 Results will vary.

Page 143 *Red:* mislead, unhappy, repaint, prepay, bicycle, disappoint *Blue:* winner, honesty, dryness, placement, painter, careful, harmless, childhood, slowly, upward, darkness *Green:* disagreeable, prehistoric, nonpoisonous, rewriting, unnoticeable, replacement, ungrateful

Page 144 Words and results will vary.

Page 145 1. portable 2. scribble 3. telephone 4. phonograph 5. microscope 6. automatic 7. prescription 8. photograph 9. biology; biography

Page 146 *Possible real words:* aerography, audiology, autograph, bibliography, micrology, microphone, microscope, monograph, phonograph, photograph, photography, telegraph, telegraphy, telephone, telephoto, telescope, trilogy; made-up words, meanings, and pictures will vary

Page 147 *Top row:* This room is very cold. I'm shivering from the cold. *Middle row:* The furnace is worthless. I have a very small memory. *Bottom row:* I always liked the way you look. Don't try to be funny.

Page 148 Answers and results will vary.

Page 149 *Underline:* raining cats and dogs, getting on my nerves; scaredy cat; shoot off your mouth; got my goat, face the music; on a wild goose chase; Hold your horses; call it a day; chicken out; wire-haired, darts in his eyes, rip me off, up to; knees knocking together; suddenly became sunny, a hard time, horsing around, Scared the pants off, in two winks; results and pictures will vary

Page 150 *Possible meanings—Top row:* be brave or do not show any emotion, you are nuts or crazy, stop bothering me, stop teasing or kidding me *Second row:* that's the way things go sometimes, you are right or you guessed right, you said something embarrassing or you said the wrong thing, we are in trouble *Third row:* you are making something seem more important than it is, write to me, do not tell anyone this secret, it is my turn to speak *Bottom row:* help me, we are all in the same circumstance or situation, I will tell them what I think or I will scold them, say what you mean

Page 151

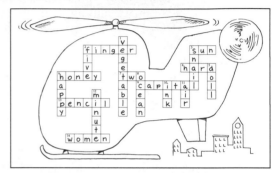

Page 152 *My Bingo Card:* B–calf, I–cooler, N–buttons, G–pounds, O–new *Adult's Bingo Card:* B–flying, I–trunk, N–lid, G–swim, O–microphone

Page 153 1. Life Support Systems 2. attentive 3. navigating the ship 4. does not cover them 5. Introduction 6. news broadcasts 7. galaxies; Landing

Page 154 Results will vary.

Page 155

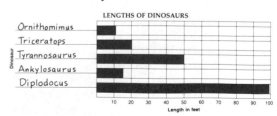

Page 156 Results will vary.

Page 157 Answers will vary.

Page 158 Sentences will vary.

Page 159 *Underlined sentences:* Well, there are ways to exercise *and* have fun. One family solved the exercise problem by using their TV. Many group activities can provide you with exercise and be fun, too. You can get plenty of exercise just by walking, biking, or even dancing; ideas will vary

Page 160 Articles and headlines will vary, but headlines should focus on the main ideas of the articles.

Page 161 1. Snake in the Grass 2. Sport/Skill 3. Mouse Mountain 4. four 5. 384 K 6. Eat the Dust 7. The only 640 K game has the lowest rating; pictures will vary

Page 162 *Possible underlined phrases:* body must be the right shape, kind of wood in the body, material used to make the strings

Page 163 Questions and answers will vary.

Page 164 Questions, answers, and notes will vary.

Page 165 Answers and story endings will vary.

Page 166 Stories will vary.

Page 167 Summaries will vary, but should tell the basic plot of the story.

Page 168 Comic strips and plot summaries will vary.

Page 169 1. c 2. b 3. c 4. a 5. b

Page 170 *Player 1:* A bear woke up. Nora is playing tag. Runners are racing. Someone is sneaking up. *Player 2:* A cat woke up. Nora is lost. Cars are racing. Someone is playing baseball.

Page 171 1. E, C 2. E, C 3. C, E 4. C, E 5. C, E 6. E, C

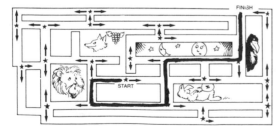

Page 172 Results will vary.

Page 173 *Possible lines between:* Rachel—messy, unsure, loud, outgoing, nervous, enthusiastic, happy, athletic, bold; Mel—brave, scared, calm, intelligent, cautious; Lydia—unsure, brave, scared, nervous, enthusiastic, bold, intelligent, confident

Page 174 Answers will vary.

Page 175 1. B 2. A 3. C 4. C 5. A; 1 and 4, 2 and 5

Page 176 Stories will vary.

Page 177 *Top pair:* description at left *Middle pair:* description at right *Bottom pair:* description at right; pictures will vary

Page 178 Pictures and descriptions will vary.

Page 179 *Possible answers—Top picture:* cave dwellers fighting dinosaur; humans and dinosaurs did not live at same time *Second picture:* photographer taking picture of George Washington; camera not yet invented at time of Washington *Third picture:* thermometer in boiling water shows almost 312°; temperature should be 212°F or 100°C *Fourth picture:* magnet picking up carrot; carrot is not magnetic (not made of iron or steel) *Bottom picture:* tigers eating grass and leaves; tigers are meat eaters

Page 180 Answers will vary.

Page 181 *Fact Bin:* 1, 2, 4, 6, 7, 9, 10 *Total:* 39 *Opinion Bin:* 3, 5, 8, 11, 12 *Total:* 39

Page 182 *Possible answers:* Everyone in Holland thinks tulips are beautiful flowers.—opinion; Stories about vampires have been told since the earliest times.—fact; Mr. Hank's computer saved the company thousands of dollars.—fact Nothing tastes better in the morning than orange juice.—opinion; A birthday is always a happy occasion.—opinion; There are eight cities in the United States named after Paris, France.—fact; Ruby Duke has starred in two movies in the last three years.—fact; A dog is a lot more trouble to take care of than a cat.—opinion; A golden eagle can fly up to 100 miles per hour.—fact; Mushroom pizza is better than pizza with peppers.—opinion; The best place to spend a winter vacation is in Florida.—opinion; Molly Pitcher was a sergeant in the Continental Army.—fact; Cellophane tape is the most useful household product.—opinion; The pet store offered free cat food at its grand opening.—fact

Page 183 1. I 2. I 3. E 4. I, P 5. I, E, P

Page 184 Sentences and catalog entries will vary.

Page 185 *Yazah:* Famous Agency *Book Bag:* Bandwagon Agency *Gym Foam Shoes:* Repeaters Agency *Audioblast:* Testimonial Agency

Page 186 Notes, ads, and pictures will vary.

Page 187 *Page 1:* H *Page 2:* F *Page 3:* B *Page 4:* G *Page 5:* D *Page 6:* A *Page 7:* E *Page 8:* C

Page 188 Answers and newspaper articles will vary.

Page 189 1. a bottle, a balloon, baking soda, vinegar 2. A. put vinegar in the bottle B. put baking soda in the balloon C. put open end of balloon over neck of bottle D. shake baking soda out of balloon into bottle 3. Carbon dioxide is produced and this gas inflates the balloon.

Page 190 Magic numbers will vary.

Page 191 Answers will vary.

Page 192 Descriptions will vary.

Page 193 *Left column:* Snow White, the Giant, Goldilocks *Right column:* Pinocchio, Red Riding Hood, Peter Rabbit

Page 194 Answers and biographies will vary.

Page 195 1. R 2. F 3. R 4. F 5. R or F 6. R; stories will vary

Page 196 Stories will vary.

Page 197 pocket, space; reply, polite; snack, jacket; orbit, view

d	r	s	p	a	c	e	o	t	z	i	l
a	s	w	o	o	a	s	r	v	g	b	u
v	n	s	c	z	i	u	b	c	i	d	a
j	a	c	k	e	t	i	k	t	e	o
r	c	e	e	f	n	p	t	a	b	s	w
w	k	m	t	u	h	a	r	e	p	l	y

Page 198 Poems will vary.

Page 199 the origin of Earth; pictures will vary

Page 200 Tall tales and pictures will vary.

TEACHING SUGGESTIONS
Grade 6
Optional Activities

A TIP FOR SUCCESS

Children are sure to enjoy using Grade 6 of *ENRICHMENT READING* because it is filled with enjoyable and imaginative activities and games. Although the directions for each lesson are easy to read and understand, you may want to spend a few minutes reviewing them. Feel free to play the games and do the activities before assigning them. The games and activities will prepare children for success with their homework as well as provide them with worthwhile reading experiences.

Vocabulary

The Vocabulary unit contains six lessons designed to help children build and expand their vocabularies. Most children using Grade 6 will have been exposed to the basic skills used in vocabulary building. The activities and games in this unit provide children with opportunities for additional practice using these skills in ways that are interesting and fun.

The first lesson focuses on context clues. After children become familiar with the game *Whatchamacallit* (page 204), you may want to use it throughout the year to give children practice in getting meaning from context. Encourage children to find and label pictures of unusual objects. Each time children play the game they may choose their own selection of pictures for the game board.

Lesson 2 provides children with practice in identifying and forming words with affixes. Several variations of *Building Words* (page 206) may be played throughout the year. Additonal word cards may be made using words from children's reading materials, and prefixes and suffixes may be added to the tool box. Children may vary the number of word cards and affixes each time they play the game. The formation of non-sense words could also be allowed as long as children's definitions reflect the meanings of the base word and affix.

If your child seems interested in word origins after he or she completes *Where Is It From?* (page 207), you might hang up a large outline map of the world and have your child add words and their origins to it as he or she comes across new words in his or her reading.

Mood Maps (page 209) is a very subjective activity, and all answers should be accepted as long as your child can reasonably explain his or her choices. The activity in *Mood-o-Meter* (page 210) may be done numerous times throughout the year using the words on page 210 and/or new words added by your child.

Once children have an understanding of figurative language, they often enjoy making up their own comparisons. After students play *Make It Colorful* (page 212), the game may be played at home and expanded to include more than two players and words added by your child. The game in *Beehive* (page 214) may also be adapted for home use. Reproduce the hexagon grid on a large, glossy sheet. Then use an erasable crayon or marker to fill the spaces with idioms. The idioms may be changed as your child finds new idioms in his or her reading materials.

Study Skills

The Study Skills unit contains four lessons covering parts of books, charts, graphs, maps, time lines, and reference books. The first lesson takes advantage of the almost universal appeal of cats to provide children with practice using a table of contents and an index. Once children have played the *Index Race* (page 216) game, try this variation in which children race to find information in their own books. Make sure each child has a copy of the same book. Then ask questions based on the book. After each question, have children search the index for the page or pages that might contain the answer.

When you assign *Terrific Toys* (page 217), explain to children that the memo, chart, and graph are three different ways of representing the same information. You may want to use this activity as a starting point for more practice in charting and graphing information. Children may chart or graph information about themselves, the subjects they are studying, or special projects. Before you assign *Map It Out* (page 218) as homework, make sure your child has the basic map skills necessary to draw readable maps.

The time line activities in Lesson 9 have many possible extensions. You may wish to have children develop ongoing time lines for long-term class projects, and children may be encouraged to make time lines for past events in history, science, sports, and so on. After children complete *Encyclotopics* (page 221), let them use an encyclopedia to find the answers to the questions and information about the topics on the page. Children may also make a variation of the dictionary game in *What Does It Mean?* (page 222). Have teams of children find unusual words and write down correct and made-up definitions. Then let each team present its words and definitions to another team.

Comprehension

The Comprehension unit contains thirteen lessons covering the major aspects of comprehension appropriate to Grade 6. The first three lessons focus on finding main ideas and details and on taking notes. The activity in *Thanks, Sun!* (page 223) may be adapted to a variety of reading materials, especially textbooks. Reproduce passages from your child's textbooks and have him or her write paragraph headings and titles. To adapt *The Big Idea* (page 224) for home use, try this variation. Mount several short news articles and news pictures on cards and place the cards in a box. Let your child search through the box, choose one or more cards, and write headlines or captions. To extend *Yummy, Yummy* (page 225), ask your child to find ingredient and nutrition labels from food packages. Have your child choose labels from comparable or similar products and then compare and evaluate the ingredients, nutrients, and so on. Page 225 may also be used as the starting point for further study of nutrition and how to make healthy food choices. After your child completes *Web of the Senses* (page 227) and *Note It* (page 228), you may want to explore with your child a variety of note-taking methods. Encourage your child to experiment, using his or her subject-area materials, with different ways of recording and remembering information. Webs, semantic maps, outlines, and lists are just some of the possibilities.

Writing brief, informative plot summaries is often a challenge for children. For additional practice, a variation of *Comic Order* (page 232) may be used as needed. Prepare several envelopes containing cut-apart comic strips. Your child may then choose an envelope, arrange the panels in order, and write a plot summary. Change the comic strips often and encourage your child to contribute to the collection. Analyzing story plots may also be challenging for children. Before assigning *Problems, Problems* (page 233), review with your child how to identify the problem, solution, and climax of a story.

When *Scan You Find It?* (page 235) is assigned, make sure your child understands that scanning involves examining something quickly and closely, but it does not mean reading every word or looking at every detail. After your child completes Lesson 17, have him or her devise his or her own visual puzzles for family members to scan.

Pictures in My Mind (page 239) may be used to stimulate some imaginative artwork. Encourage your child to draw pictures of the images their favorite books, movies, or TV shows left in their minds. The kind of activity in *What's Wrong?* (page 241) will also stimulate imaginative artwork. After children complete the page, challenge them to draw their own "what's wrong" pictures with as many "wrong" things as they can think of to include.

Change the Story (page 246) can be used with almost any story. A favorite rewritten story may also be turned into a play, puppet show, or tape recording and shared with family members.

Forms of Writing

The Forms of Writing unit contains eight lessons that help children develop appreciation for several different forms of written materials. In *Page One* (page 249), children are introduced to some technical terms for parts of a newspaper front page. After children complete the page, have them identify these parts on the front page of as many different local newspapers as you can provide. You may also wish to explore a real newspaper further, noting where various features are found, where the most important stories appear, and so on.

Before you assign *The Magic Triangle* (page 252), you may want to go over the directions with your child to make sure he or she understands what to do. After your child completes *My Country* (page 253), have him or her share and discuss his or her answers. This page may also be used as a lead-in to a discussion of how smaller groups, such as a team, club, class, and school, are "governed." Although all the people in *Who Am I?* (page 254) are covered in most fifth grade social studies curriculums, you may wish to review briefly a few facts about each person before you assign the page.

After children complete *Dear Diary* (page 255), they may enjoy writing diary entries for real people or fictional characters they admire. You may also want to use the page to interest your child in keeping his or her own diaries or journals. The *Spoken History* (page 256) activity could also be used as a tie-in to a study of local history.

If your child enjoys the actvity in Lesson 29, encourgage him or her to read and put on more plays. You might also try to arrange a trip to a radio station. Even though the station most likely does not broadcast plays, your child will be fascinated to discover how news and music are broadcast.

Create a Poem (page 262) encourages children to explore free-form poetry. Children may enjoy working together to create additional poems. In Lesson 31, children read a myth and create tall tales. Myths and tall tales are often used to express truths about human nature and to explain relationships between people and their world. You may want to extend this lesson by inviting your child to find and tell myths and tall tales from his or her own cultural background.

Answer Key
Grade 6–Enrichment Reading

Page 203 1. wear out 2. very small; worthless 3. done with little care 4. store 5. think hard 6. wish 7. tough; hard 8. details; wrestle with words

Page 204 Results will vary.

Page 205

$$3012$$
$$-0223$$
$$2789$$
$$-1013$$
$$1776$$; It is the year the Declaration of Independence was signed.

Page 206 Words and results will vary.

Page 207 *chowder:* France *kaleidoscope:* Greece *lariat:* Spain *spaghetti:* Italy, *waltz:* Germany *Yankee:* Netherlands

Page 208 Definitions and results will vary.

Page 209 cozy, sad, joyous, miserable; mood maps will vary

Page 210 Paragraphs and pictures will vary.

Page 211 1. S 2. P 3. S 4. M 5. S 6. M 7. P 8. S 9. M 10. P 11. M 12. P *Blue:* 1, 3, 5, 8 *Red:* 4, 6, 9, 11 *Green:* 2, 7, 10, 12

Page 212 Answers and results will vary.

Page 213 1. hit the nail on the head–Meiko was right. 2. just itching–Ramón can hardly wait. 3. we are all in the same boat–We all have the same problem. 4. talked turkey–He talked seriously. 5. cracked up–The audience laughed. 6. polished off–We ate them. 7. drop me a line–Write to me. 8. barking up the wrong tree–You are mistaken. 9. went out on a limb–Alma took a chance.

Page 214 *Possible meanings:* rub the wrong way–irritate, turn down–refuse, lend a hand–help, keep your word–do as you promised, come to pass–happen, cut it out–stop it, monkey business–mischief, blow a fuse–become angry, sit tight–wait

patiently, knock for a loop–astonish or surprise, go all out–be enthusiastic, throw in the towel–give up or admit defeat, eat your words–admit you spoke wrongly, shake a leg–hurry, all thumbs–clumsy, break the news–reveal something

Page 215 1. f 2. e 3. l 4. i 5. d 6. a 7. e; Felidae

Page 216 1. page 6 2. page 64 3. page 20 4. pages 7, 40, 80 5. pages 14, 50 6. pages 33–34 7. page 36 8. pages 36–37 9. page 40 10. page 48 11. pages 82–84 12. pages 17, 75

Page 217

	Bears for All	Fuzzy's Toystore	Hippo Hurray	Stuffed Things	Fun 'n Follies	TOTAL
Teddy Thunder	25	15	20	10	15	85
Hermione Hippo		25	30	6	30	91
Misty Mouse				20	40	60
Ollie Octopus				18	10	28

TOYS SOLD—WEEK OF JUNE 17

Page 218 Maps will vary.

Page 219 1. Rockies 2. Modern insects 3. South America and Africa 4. Dinosaurs 5. Appalachians 6. Mammals

Page 220 Time lines will vary.

Page 221 1. l 2. e 3. l 4. e 5. v 6. i 7. s 8. i 9. o 10. n 11. television

Page 222 *Correct definitions:* 1. 1 2. 2 3. 2 4. 1 5. 1 6. 2 7. 1 8. 1 9. 2 10. 2; 1,221,121,122

Page 223 Headings and titles will vary, but should focus on the main ideas of the paragraphs and entire passage.

Page 224 Headlines and captions will vary, but should focus on the main ideas of the articles and pictures.

Page 225 1. no 2. 30% 3. 2 oz. 4. 3 5. vitamin A, vitamin C, calcium 6. Answers will vary, but the ingredients all appear to be natural.

Page 226 *Possible kitchen tools:* rolling pin, carving knife, mixing spoon, meat thermometer, spatula, can opener, pot, pan, trash can, scissors, cellophane tape, ruler *Possible workshop tools:* pliers, hammer, nails, screws, saw, wrench, screwdriver, trash can, shovel, scissors, cellophane tape, ruler

Page 227 *Missing senses:* sight, taste, touch, hearing; Wording will vary, but answers on the left should focus on smell and memory and answers on the right should focus on the mechanism of smell.

Page 228 Answers will vary.

Page 229 Ideas will vary.

Page 230 Stories will vary.

Page 231 Summaries will vary, but should tell the basic plot of the story.

Page 232 Comic strips and plot summaries will vary.

Page 233 Story selections and answers will vary.

Page 234 Answers and stories will vary.

Page 235 1. G, P 2. JI, VU 3. 555–3647 4. "fishing for compliments" is in the next to last sentence

5.

Page 236 Results will vary.

Page 237 1. c 2. a 3. c 4. c 5. b

Page 238 *Conclusions:* 1. Darin is relaxing at a beach. 2. Hettie is a spy or a detective. 3. Darin is a scientist. 4. Hettie is doing a crossword puzzle. 5. Darin is painting a picture. 6. Hettie is riding a motorcycle. 7. Darin is parachuting from a plane. 8. Hettie is conducting an orchestra. 9. Darin is in charge of a rocket launch.

Page 239 *Top pair:* description at right *Second pair:* description at right *Third pair:* description at left *Bottom pair:* description at right; pictures will vary

Page 240 Descriptions will vary.

Page 241 *Things wrong in picture:* bird flying upside down, weather vane with north, south, east, west reversed, child ice-skating on sidewalk, dog with five legs, thermometer showing 40°, child walking pet dinosaur, sale sign for 120% off, clock with numbers in reverse order, bike floating above ground, snowperson, trash can with "Please Litter" sign, man reading upside-down newspaper, one-way sign pointing in two directions, volcano spouting bubbles, pig driving car, "News" sign with

backwards *s*, door on second floor of building, frog in top hat walking along street

Page 242 Answers and results will vary.

Page 243 1. F, measured 2. O 3. F, checked a reference 4. F, counted 5. O 6. F, measured 7. F, checked a reference 8. F, counted 9. O 10. F, measured 11. F, counted 12. F, checked a reference 13. O 14. F, measured

Page 244 Facts and opinions will vary.

Page 245 1. C 2. A 3. B 4. C 5. A

Page 246 Stories will vary.

Page 247 1. P 2. E 3. I 4. E; answers will vary

Page 248 Notes and letters or ads will vary.

Page 249 1. upper right corner 2. XXX 3. at the very top of the page 4. The Daily Paper 5. City Celebrates 150th Anniversary in Style 6. Teresa Jenks 7. *Circled:* Riverside Park Before Visitors Arrived for Anniversary Celebration

Page 250 Answers and articles will vary.

Page 251 Answers will vary.

Page 252 *Sides of corner:* 3 and 4 spaces *Side opposite corner:* 5 spaces

Page 253 Answers will vary.

Page 254 Answers and results will vary.

Page 255 *Top entry:* toothbrush *Second entry:* elevator *Third entry:* cellophane tape *Bottom entry:* typewriter

Page 256 Answers and oral histories will vary.

Page 257 *Left column:* R, F *Middle column:* F, R *Right column:* R, F; stories will vary

Page 258 Stories will vary.

Page 259 1. FETCH! 2. five (four people plus toy hamster) 3. in Dwayne's backyard 4. a thin black thread held by a stagehand 5. answers will vary

Page 260 Notes and radio plays will vary.

Page 261 1. the elephant's trunk 2. the elephant, with its great strength, has flattened it 3. and 4. answers will vary; words will vary

Page 262 Poems will vary.

Page 263 why cats have whiskers that are the width of their bodies; titles and pictures will vary

Page 264 Tall tales and pictures will vary.